AFRICAN WOMEN IMMIGRANTS IN THE UNITED STATES

AFRICAN WOMEN IMMIGRANTS IN THE UNITED STATES

CROSSING TRANSNATIONAL BORDERS

John A. Arthur

First published in 2009 by PALGRAVE MACMILLAN® in the United States—a division of St. Martin's Press LLC, 175 Fifth Avenue, New York, NY 10010.

Where this book is distributed in the UK, Europe, and the rest of the world, this is by Palgrave Macmillan, a division of Macmillan Publishers Limited, registered in England, company number 785998, of Houndmills, Basingstoke, Hampshire RG21 6XS.

Palgrave Macmillan is the global academic imprint of the above companies and has companies and representatives throughout the world.

Palgrave® and Macmillan® are registered trademarks in the United States, the United Kingdom, Europe and other countries.

ISBN: 978-0-230-61778-0

Library of Congress Cataloging-in-Publication Data

Arthur, John A., 1958-
    African women immigrants in the United States : crossing
    transnational borders / by John A. Arthur.
        p. cm.
    Includes bibliographical references and index.
    ISBN 978-0-230-61778-0
        1. West Africans—United States—Social conditions. 2. Women
        immigrants—United States—Social conditions. 3. Africa, West—
        Emigration and immigration. I. Title.

    E184.A24.A73 2009
    305.896'6073—dc22   2009004018

A catalogue record of the book is available from the British Library.

Design by Scribe Inc.

First edition: September 2009

10 9 8 7 6 5 4 3 2 1

Printed in the United States of America.

This book is dedicated to Madam Agnes Tagoe, affectionately called Nii Ami. Your enduring sage and refrain *"adjo"* and *"efee noko"* are timeless and very soothing to the ears of all your children, grandchildren, and great-grandchildren. These simple words are gems of truth. They continue to brighten and illuminate our collective paths and journeys as we strive to live by your precepts, humility, and enduring strength. In your often-soft voice, you taught, uplifted, and touched so many lives. For all the adversities and challenges you endured, you were still able to preserve your capacity to show gratitude. We stand in awe of your selflessness. Thank you.

Contents

PREFACE

According to United Nations (UN) data, in 2005, women migrants represented half of the world's migrant population. This means that nearly 100 million women regularly move across international boundaries (Morrison, Schiff, and Sjoblom 2008, 2). African women form a significant portion of this transnational movement. Migration theorists have assumed that women's migration is largely determined by the migratory decisions usually made by men who migrate to the major global labor and economic centers. Women's migration is explained through the lens of their male counterparts, implying that women are not autonomous and independent actors when it comes to migration. The need for migration scholars to incorporate gender sensitivities in migration studies is warranted.

This book is about the transnational migration of West African women to the United States. The aim of the book is to center the migration of West African women in the global migration of skilled and unskilled labor to the advanced nations. West African women now migrate at almost the same rate as their male counterparts. Unearthing the unique processes by which West African migrant women come to shape, forge, and create self-sustaining social, cultural, and economic capacities to enhance their empowerment and status are sociologically interesting and invigorating.

Impacted and shaped by continued globalization, economic incorporation, technology, easy access to transportation, information flows from core to periphery countries, and the demand for cheap sources of skilled and unskilled labor, West African women are responding to the global demand for skilled and unskilled female workers by leaving home and carving occupational and employment niches for themselves and their families. Often driven and pushed to leave home due to ethnic strife, civil wars, poverty, chronic and mass unemployment, structural adjustments of economies, decline in food production, patriarchal oppression, ecological destruction, growth in informal economy, and the segmentation of labor in the West, numerous young West African women have come to see international migration as a way of ensuring their own economic survival as well as that of their families. Some of the women go to the United States in search of work, while others pursue cultural goals (attend school and upgrade their credentials) to enhance the odds of finding higher paying jobs upon completion of their educational training. Still others enter the country with the sole purpose of reuniting with a spouse or extended family members who have already settled in the United States. For others, migration is involuntary or forced as a result of wars and conflicts. For all the women whose transnational migratory journeys are chronicled in this book, international migration is constructed as a strategy and agency to achieve autonomy while contesting the boundaries of gendered structural institutions used by African men to suppress and subjugate women's aspirations.

Whether they are in the country legally or illegally, the African women described in this book are united by a common goal: to recreate multiple forms of their gendered Black and international identities in a foreign land, and to assert their economic and social autonomy through work, mobility, collective empowerment, the assumption of new roles, and working toward incorporation into the new and emerging forms of transnational citizenship. The portrait of the West African immigrant woman that is presented in this book is one of resilience, strong work ethic, a firm conviction in altruism, and collectivized action to meet and confront obstacles posed by their marginalized and alienated statuses in the United States. Added to this is a strong commitment to family relationships and the understanding that the experiences garnered in the process of international migration have placed them in a unique position to assist and contribute to community building and national reconstruction in their respective countries in Africa.

For many of the immigrant women, the concepts of citizenship, nationalism, family, community, and identity are often constructed in fluid ways to allow for the redefinitions and reconfigurations of their statuses and roles as circumstances may warrant. This adaptive mechanism ensures that the immigrant women will be able to respond to normative and cultural changes and challenges regarding their identities, transnational foci, femininity, and roles as immigrants. Fluid definitions of transnational identity afford the women opportunities to reconstruct new identities and contextualize the spatial and place dimensions within which images associated with their gendered identities are played out.

Projecting a predominantly African-centered identity, but certainly not bound by its cultural and normative renditions, these immigrant women are extending the boundaries of race, ethnicity, class, and gender relationships as they shape, and are in turn shaped, by their interactions with minority populations in the United States. In leaving West Africa and migrating abroad, the women gain economic power, some control, and a presence at the table of familial decision making over the appropriation of family resources in spite of their absence from home. Some of the women use this power to deconstruct the existing unequal gender structures at home through advocacy, resource utilization, and directives concerning the need to equalize the social relationships between men and women.

I have benefited immensely from several friends and colleagues in writing this book. I owe a debt of gratitude to Geraldine Gomes Hughes for reading and bringing her superb editing skills and insights to earlier drafts of this manuscript. I could not have completed this book without her assistance. Special thanks also to Brandy Hoffman for her insightful editorial craftsmanship. I am equally grateful to Dr. Linda Krug and Dr. Vince Magnuson for their continued financial support in aid of my research. I am indebted to the respondents who took time from their busy schedules to participate in the interviews and numerous focus groups sessions. Without your assistance, I could not have written this book. Special thanks to the staff at the Minnesota Population Center at the University of Minnesota for making available the IPUMS data. To all of you, thank you very much.

Dr. John A. Arthur, Professor
Former Chair, Department of Sociology and Anthropology
Former Director, University of Minnesota Study in England Program
Minnesota, U.S.

CHAPTER 1

INTRODUCTION AND ORGANIZATION

This book is about the migration of West African women to the United States. It recognizes the importance of previous theoretical paradigms (such as the push-pull model of migration and the world systems perspective), but also goes beyond these approaches by incorporating aspects of nationality, culture, normative systems, and the institutional processes that immigrants forge to anchor their immigrant experiences and lived realities in the host society. The aim is to portray the social, economic, and cultural processes by which the women create and give meanings and contents to their diaspora experiences in the United States.

The book highlights the full range of the migrant women's transnational experiences and seeks to provide a lens through which to view the multifaceted dimensions of their cultural communities, particularly how they express and define identity, cope with the transnational changes in their lives brought upon by international migration, and the specific circumstances defining the intersections of gender, class, race, and economic relationships that the women form to link them not only to their native homelands but also to the new country and lives that they continue to form in the United States.

In giving a voice to the experiences of the West African immigrant women, this study explores the creative forms and the mechanisms of adaptation, integration, and incorporation that are fostered by the women to ensure their survival in America. The study offers a window through which to view the gendered transnational relationships that the West African immigrant women establish in this country. Overall, the book is cast within the nexus of the intersections of class, race, gender, and ethnicity and how these shared and negotiated experiences inform the voices and experiences of the West African immigrant women who have undertaken the journey to the United States.

As a subpopulation group, not much is known about the migratory behavior of African women. Often invisible due to being overshadowed by their male counterparts and immigrants from Latin America and Asia, African women form a growing portion of the migration of Africans to the United States, ranging from a low of 25 percent to a high of 40 percent. Like their male counterparts, these women migrants travel to the United States to pursue economic and cultural goals. Responding to better economic conditions in the West and pushed out by deteriorating economic and political conditions in Africa, these women become part of the growing transnational migration and movement of both skilled and unskilled labor to the advanced countries.

In focusing on the social, cultural, political, and economic issues that have influenced the migration of the women, the narratives in this book bring contextual considerations to the specific cultural forces underlying the different processes shaping the migratory behaviors of the women. More significantly, the study informs and provides insights into the emerging new forms of migration by a group about which not much is known. At the same time, it provides a new lens through which to view the impact of gendered relations in migration studies and gives content to the broad conceptual issues (theoretical and empirical) in terms of how to understand women in the global context of international migration.

Ultimately, the aim of the book is to show that the West African women whose immigrant lives are chronicled here are not (individually or collectively) passive and mere appendages of their male migratory counterparts. Rather, these migrant women are active and independent players in the new migration who are responding to the same global geopolitical, economic, and social forces at the core of the movement and transfer of human capital and labor from the developing to the developed regions of the world. They are initiators and implementers of their migratory journeys. Their immigrant journeys and voices cannot be solely understood on the basis of the economic imperatives that have propelled and motivated them to travel to the United States. Their immigrant stories rest on the notion that complex noneconomic social and cultural forces (ethnicity, nationalism, gender, religion, marriage, family, kin group networks, civic mindedness, and community volunteerism) all converge to form a kaleidoscope and portraits of women from diverse backgrounds who are united by a common denominator: the desire to forge incorporation into global systems via the channel of international migration.

The study demonstrates that work, family networks, gendered identities, ethnic affinities, and children are given prominence and central focus in constructing notions and ideologies that define women's roles in the unfolding supranational economic and geopolitical systems. As they stress these aspects of their lives, the women also contest the rise in globally structured gendered inequalities by speaking in collective tones to mobilize and agitate for justice, fairness, and improved standards of living for the millions of migrant women workers who have come to dominate the low-paying, underground, and informal transnational economies.

A key feature of the women's immigrant portrait is how they straddle multiple cultures as they create a mélange of identities not only in the United States but also in Africa and other parts of the world. These women utilize inter- and intraethnic immigrant associations and transnational networks to bridge the cultural divide that some of them continually experience in the United States. These networks foster solidarity among the immigrant women and other secondary groups and are usually relied upon as a conduit for gaining access to multiple realms of the American experience. The reinforcement of ties of solidarity thus becomes a social capital that allows the women an agency to attain individual and collective economic and cultural goals. In forming and anchoring their African immigrant diasporic identities, these women work tirelessly to disaggregate notions of ethnicity and race by redefining what it means to be Black and foreign in an American society that is increasingly becoming more and more fractured along the lines of ethnicity, race, class, and gender. These women reject the social labels associated with their alien, marginalized, and subordinate status by seeking to deconstruct their ethnicity, gender, and class attributes to stress social differences with mainstream American society. At the same time, they use the opportunities offered by international migration to reconfigure and translate their differences with American culture into meaningful opportunities to accentuate African-centered identities. This reconfiguration, as Barot, Bradley, and Fenton (1999) affirmed, is a cultural tool often used by marginalized groups to reposition their stigmatized identifications and cultures to counterbalance the power of superordinate groups.

When African women migrate to the United States, they confine their geographic settlement patterns to the southeastern, mid-Atlantic, and northeastern corridors of the country, including the Texas, northern Illinois, and Indiana corridors. Historically, like their male counterparts, the immigrant women choose to settle in towns and cities with a large presence of African American, Latino, and immigrant populations. These cities include New York, Washington, D.C., Philadelphia, Atlanta, Chicago, Boston, and Houston. Recently, however, census data show that these immigrants are charting new directions in terms of their settlement patterns. Their settlement patterns are no longer confined to the eastern seaboard. Census data for 1990 and 2000 show a pattern of secondary migration among African and other recent immigrants to the lower Midwest and western parts of the country in search of better economic and cultural opportunities, quality schools, affordable housing, relatively low costs of living, open spaces, and low crime rates.

The westward movement of immigrants coincided with shifts in the general population from the northeastern states to the Midwest, Southwest, and West Coast of the United States. The secondary migration of Africans to the center and the Western frontiers of the country is thus a mirror reflection of the national trend. The migration to new destinations and frontiers has presented new racial and ethnic experiences as well economic opportunities for the immigrants. New media for the expression and creation of immigrant identities are fostered. Fresh interpretations and contexts are given to the multilayered contents of gender and the nuances that underpin the formation of migratory journeys and identities in a foreign land. In this regard, one expects that the opportunity to create and recreate their communities away from the eastern seaboard provides a new vista and a cultural lens to examine how gender and international migration intersects to depict a unique portrait and genre of West African migration to the United States. Above all, West African immigrant women make economic and cultural contributions to American society. They work in every sector of the U.S. economy, and their Black African cultural identities, family life, and social participation and engagement all contribute in significant ways to enrich American society.

RESEARCH DESIGN AND METHODOLOGIES

The unit of analysis in this research is a group of 150 women from West Africa who have settled in four Midwestern cities: Minneapolis-St. Paul, Omaha, St. Louis, and Des Moines. The primary source of data for this book came from survey and telephone interviews conducted between 2004 and 2007. Due to the dearth of previous scholarship specifically focusing on African immigrant women, the survey and telephone interviews were structured and approached with one goal in mind: to collect baseline primary data covering the migratory experiences of immigrant women living in the United States.

The most challenging aspect of the data collection was identification of the participants. Using snowball, purposive, and nonrandom techniques for identifying the subjects, I visited communities where West African female immigrants live and work. Networks of individuals and groups representing various immigrant national and ethnic groups that I had encountered in prior focus-group research on African immigrants paved the way toward developing a registry of immigrant women representing different countries in West Africa. While the nonrandom and snowball approaches to identifying participants for inclusion in the study did not yield a representative sample, every effort was made to ensure that immigrant women from diverse backgrounds were invited to participate in the study. In several instances, immigrant women who were clustered in specific occupations were all invited to participate in the study even where all of them were of the same national origin. This was certainly the case with migrant farm women, who tend to cluster along occupational and national-origin lines.

Data were also obtained from secondary archival sources such as the U.S. census, particularly the micro data on households. Known as the Integrated Public Use Microdata Series (IPUMS), this vital public records archive generated from the census provides information about income, educational level attained, labor force participation, type of household (single or multiple family dwelling), and other social and demographic characteristics of the population. The IPUMS is a useful data source because it sheds some understanding into microlevel traits for several units of analyses. The IPUMS data also sheds light on secondary and internal migration.

Data were obtained from various immigrant associations representing various countries in the West African region. Officials from various immigrant associations that represent immigrants from West Africa were contacted solely for the purpose of recommending prospective participants for the study. Letters were sent to about 350 prospective participants, inviting them to participate in the study. Because the study focused on four research sites located in different states, in order to reduce costs, a decision was made to limit the number of subjects. One hundred and fifty women consented to participate in the study. Prospective respondents were informed about the goals of the study. Ultimately, the decision to participate or not was entirely the discretion of each respondent. The purpose of the interviews was to collect quantitative and qualitative data from immigrant women from nine countries in West Africa. These countries are Senegal, Guinea, Togo,

Mali, and the Ivory Coast (comprising Francophone West Africa), and Gambia, Sierra Leone, Liberia, and Ghana (forming Anglophone West Africa).

The standard research mode among sociologists studying migration is to use a variety of quantitative and qualitative data sources to depict the forms, patterns, and the lived experiences of immigrants. This book follows this line of tradition and relies upon multiple data sources to document the migratory experiences of West African immigrant women currently living in the United States. Though the data gathered from the survey interviews and from the U.S. census provided insights about how these women construct and bring meanings to their gendered identities in the United States, it was the ethnographic approach that yielded better insights into the subjective and objective worlds of the women immigrants. The purpose of the study was to use the ethnographic approach to identify individuals to participate in a focus-group session. The focus-group sessions enriched the contexts defining the transnational migratory experiences of each of the immigrant women, particularly considering that it was during these sessions that the immigrants opened up and freely chatted about issues germane to their lived realities at home in West Africa and in the United States. The focus-group sessions generated thematic issues that were specific to the experiences of the migrant women. These included issues such as family formation, finding employment, navigating immigration requirements, adjusting to life in the United States, and the negotiation of racial, ethnic, class, and gender identities. The focus-group sessions gave voice to the women's migratory journeys to the United States and at the same time formed the basis of the narratives that are found throughout this book. From these narratives, specific themes and nuances defining the immigrant women's experiences are outlined and explained.

The narratives brought to life the gendered complexities about how migration is shaping the lives of women who, for the most part, remain marginalized in American society. It provided a lens through which to view the micro and macro factors that have come to define what it means to be foreign-born, Black, female, an immigrant, and living in the United States. The ethnographic approach gave contexts to the full range of the women's individual and collective experiences. More importantly, it enabled me to position the identities of the immigrant women within the broader transnational contacts and lifestyles that are forged by these women. At the same time, the use of the qualitative approach provided insights into how the immigrants straddle between multiple transnational systems and multiple cultures to engage in the ongoing affairs in the host society while taking active roles and participation in the affairs at home in West Africa. When some of the women spoke eloquently about the lives of other immigrant relatives from their home countries living outside of the United States, they directed my research focus to the growing social movement of an active and globally minded cadre of African women who are implementing strategies to confront the often negative stereotypes that have come to dominate and shape how the rest of the world views Black Africa: a land of missed opportunities, failed promises, and what could have been. The new identities that they are forging in transnational and local spaces are poignant because they show the diverse ways and forms of creating modalities of international integration different from the ones that they are accustomed to. These immigrant women are therefore pioneers, forging newer identities in faraway destinations while at the same time agitating for newer ways to represent Black African women on the global scene. To protect the identities and confidentiality of the study participants, all the names that are used in this book are pseudonyms.

THEMATIC OUTLINE

The chapters in this book find common ground in articulating the experiences of West African immigrant women who travel to the United States. Situated within the broad context of transnational migration, the focus on the West African woman is intended to incorporate and bring an interdisciplinary, gendered perspective to African migrations to the West. A systematic and comprehensive sociological understanding of a gendered approach to African migration is critical because such a perspective recognizes and gives voice to the complex array of economic and noneconomic decisions that define the interplay of gender networks and global labor markets in voluntary and involuntary, or forced, migrations.

In each of the chapters, efforts are made to identify the multilayered and interrelatedness of the key forms of West African migration to the West. What emerges in each chapter, therefore, is a mélange of transnational gendered identities that are based upon the intersections of cultural and economic imperatives, the goal of which is to create and sustain a foothold in the global market of shifting labor. In a nutshell, the narratives in each chapter point to migration as an economic empowering strategy to redefine traditional normative expectations and at the same time renegotiate a fresh sense of panethnic, gender, and class identities that span across specific geographic locals.

Chapter 2 centers gender in African translocal and internal migration. It examines the varied discourses and narratives that provide the contextual background underlying the women's motivations to migrate. The chapter also explores the multiple realities and experiences influencing women's migration. Though economic factors (poverty, low standards of living) and cultural factors (patriarchal dominance, gendered restrictions of property ownership) are the root causes of their migration, structured global imperatives (demand for cheap and abundant supply of women workers) are equally critical components in defining the migration of West African women. The focus on internal migration in the subregion is important because its outcomes are inextricably linked to international migration of West Africans to destinations beyond Africa.

Chapter 3 describes specific factors that spur the migration of African women to the United States. The chapter positions migration within the broader socioeconomic, cultural, and political forces behind the motivation to engage in international migration. The migratory experiences of some of the immigrant women are used to illustrate and describe the often-arduous processes involved in crossing transnational borders. In stressing the individual and specific contexts of the women's experiences, the chapter is able to depict the sociological and nonsociological factors that converge to highlight and explain the migration of African women to the United States.

Chapter 4 recounts the experiences of some of the immigrant women who have experienced involuntary or forced migration. The focus of the chapter is centered on how these women re-create newer lives, the realities and experiences that shape the women's contestation and expression of transnational gendered identities, and the motivations that drive their aspirations for a better life in the United States. The problems that the women encounter as they explore different forms of gendered identities and the strategies they employ in facing these challenges are highlighted.

Migration studies continue to give attention and focus to how immigrants construct migratory networks and structures designed to enable them to adjust and cope with the uncertainties of their new environment. Chapter 5 investigates an important aspect of the transnational migration experiences of West African immigrant women. It focuses on the immigrant women's transnational networks, the processes involved in creating bonds and affinities for collective empowerment, and on ensuring group solidarity. It is within these networks that a shared sense of community is fostered and resources are marshaled to deal with problems that emanate from living in a different cultural and normative system. The chapter demonstrates that it is through these shared networks that resources are mobilized and capitalized to confront and ameliorate the problems the immigrant women encounter not only in the United States but also at home in Africa.

The purpose of Chapter 6 is to investigate multiple dimensions of the women's economic activities, occupational structures, forms and types of work, and labor force participation. Emphasis is placed on the migrant farmworkers, agricultural workers, and the structural components that define the growing feminization of migrant farm labor across the United States. The chapter also examines the relationships between West African immigrant live-in and live-out domestic workers (caregivers, maids, nannies, and housekeepers) and their predominantly white, suburban, educated, and more affluent female employers. Focus is given to the intersections of gender, class, race, and ethnicity as well as the hierarchies of power and the political economy that shapes how the immigrant maids define and express gendered identities and cope with marginality within the nexus of the unequal status that they share with their employers.

Chapter 7 examines fertility behavior and decision making among the immigrant women. It seeks to investigate how immigrant women thread African traditional norms of fertility by attempting to give it meaning within their new settings in the United States. The chapter stresses the determinants of high and low fertility among the immigrant women and the rationalizations given to account for fertility decisions.

Chapter 8 focuses on the policy implications of African women and international migration to the United States in particular and the West in general. An attempt is made to develop new paradigms and postulates to anchor the study of African women in the new transnational migration. The chapter delineates what role, if any, the public and private sectors can play in developing and implementing protocols for managing the cross-border movements of African women to destinations outside the region. African migrations are cast within broader geopolitical and economic considerations affecting the short- and long-term migratory behavior of African women.

CHAPTER 2

CENTERING GENDER IN AFRICAN REGIONAL MIGRATION

West African women have always been on the move, often crossing national and international barriers for commercial purposes; to pursue economic activities to maximize their earnings and raise their living standards; to educate themselves; and often to reunite with extended family members or spouses living far away from home. The primary motivation for internal migration is economic, or unmet, needs. Decades following the postindependence era, many of the countries in the region have failed to bring about meaningful and sustained economic and political progress. Parts of the continent are mired in perpetual economic stagnation. There are not many areas or regions boasting of robust economic prosperity and stable governance structures and regimes.

The postindependence economic scenarios of the countries in the region have called into question the interplay between economic and political independence. The provision of the basic needs of their citizens is heighten by frequent food shortages, poor housing, disease, crumbling infrastructures, and a generalized sense that things have gone awry across the continent. Self-rule was expected to usher in a sense of autonomy in every facet of human endeavors. Rather, as Ayitey (1992) argued, the result is a betrayal of the dreams and aspirations of Africans.[1] For some of the countries, the attainment of self-rule has worsened the economic outlook, leading some to suggest the need for regional supranational integration and cooperation to mobilize every available resource to ensure economic and industrial takeoff.[2]

For hundreds of thousands of West Africans, migration has become a promising alternative for people to improve upon their lives. The purpose of migration is to maximize the human and economic capital prospects of those who are able to migrate. In the quest to search for better standards of living, every part of the world is seen as a possible destination point. No location is ruled out. This reflects the dire economic circumstances facing everyone in the region. The yearning desire of young and old alike is to become incorporated into the global macroeconomical systems via international migration. This includes the migration of young secondary-school-leavers, particularly those from the agriculturally depressed rural communities where industrial and manufacturing activities have stymied and where wage-based jobs in both the private and public sectors are hard to come by. The push among West Africans to seek economic gains away from their towns and villages is so intense that this process may be described as one of the major sources of social change in Africa today. Population mobility has become one of the fascinating aspects of social and economic life in the region. Whether it is migration from a small, rural village to a medium-sized town or to an urban metropolis, many West Africans have come to realize that internal or international migration is perhaps the only way they can leverage and bring added value to their economic or cultural potential. This dynamic demographic process is still unraveling as streams and waves of West Africans migrate to form squatter settlements in and around the major urban centers of the region. Migrant transit routes have developed along the western corridor of the continent. Senegal, Gambia, and Cape Verde are on routes followed to reach Spain or Portugal, the Mediterranean, and, subsequently, the European Union. Some of the migrant routes pass through the central interior of the continent, through Mali and into North Africa, and eventually to the Mediterranean countries and Europe (Arthur 2008). For others, the journey takes them from West Africa to the interior regions forming the Congo Basin and, subsequently, to the southern parts of the continent. This is truly remarkable considering that migrants may travel by lorry, bus, or, as stated, sometimes on foot.

For most of the nations in this region, rich though they may be in natural resources, migration (internal, interregional, and international) has become a cultural phenomenon heavily relied upon by many as a means of mitigating extreme poverty and chronic economic hardships. Migration has created its own subculture, norms, and fad. To West Africa's young, migration is the way to connect to the broader geopolitical and economic forces brought upon by global dispersion of capital and investments. It is also a way to tap into the reservoir of foreign exchange earnings, which migrants earn overseas and remit home. To the old, the hope is that a dependent or a relative will get the opportunity to travel abroad by joining the caravan of West African travelers who have cast their eyes far away from West Africa to find jobs so that they, too (the elderly), can attain some degree of economic security and well-being.

In an environment that is characterized by scarcity and economic deprivation, particularly in rural areas where the bulk of the population resides, the opportunity to receive a remittance from relatives who have migrated abroad is considered a blessing. It makes a difference in terms of whether children will be fed, clothed, educated, and school fees paid. For the elderly, remittances, no matter how small, will determine whether they will have access to health care, the medications they need, a place to stay, and yes, food to eat. In nearly all of the countries forming West Africa, there are no social safety nets to provide support for those who are in dire need and cannot be taken care of by extended families. Ordinarily, the family will step in and ensure that those in its ranks who cannot fend for themselves economically will be taken care of. This cultural altruism is beneficial because it enables the family to organize its resources to take care of the young and elderly in the absence of state-sponsored social security systems. Relying on successful family members to take care of extended family members has its drawbacks. It puts immense financial pressure and burden on the family members who are successful. They have to bear the burden of providing economic assistance to all. This is a huge responsibility. Ultimately, some of the providers, male or female, come to the realization that going abroad to work is the best way to meet the economic challenges of having to provide for a large number of immediate and distant relations. The chance to go abroad and work is designed, in part, to ameliorate the economic burdens confronting the vast majority of extended families in West Africa.

Internal and international migrations are integral aspects of the cultures of African societies. Now, as in the past, the migration of Africans to the West or to cities within Africa is largely influenced by the deterioration of the economic and political conditions of the continent. The inability of most Africans to meet their daily economic needs, extreme poverty, the high rates of unemployment and underemployment, coupled with the erosion of political institutions, combine to create a social environment of economic hellishness and political insecurity. The latter condition is exemplified by the loss of civility and rule of law and the replacement of legal-rational political authority with the institutionalization of political violence as a means of conflict management. For those Africans who have the skills, the economic resources, and a network of contacts outside of Africa, the preferred solution is to seek greener pastures elsewhere, preferably in the West. Africans migrate in search of economic advancement, status, and mobility relative to what they are accustomed to at home. And like other immigrants who travel to the United States and the West in general, the desire to improve economically plays a crucial role in how African immigrants forge their inclusion in various institutional spheres of their host societies.

According to Chant (1992), the migratory movements of women in developing countries suggests that, by and large, males migrate in larger numbers than females, undertake their migration independently, and have better access to employment opportunities than their female counterparts. While women develop and nurture stronger networks facilitating migration, they are nonetheless disadvantaged when males migrate, often resulting in decreased incomes and dwindled food production. Though the literature on African migration to the West suggests that the stream of migrants is predominantly male, African women continue to bridge the gender gap in international migration. Increased access to information flows and exchanges between immigrant-sending and immigrant-receiving destinations, increased schooling for girls, and the growth in women-specific jobs in the industrialized countries are among a few of the reasons for the rise in cross-border migrations of women. According to INS statistics for 1998, this gender gap is diminishing, with 52 percent of African migrants to the United States being male and 48 percent female. Little is known about the motivations of African women who migrate to the West. A growing number of studies on African migration have sought to delineate the factors that spur African migration to the West in general.[3]

Generally, the motivations for migration reflect a gender-neutral approach, which basically sees no significant differences in the motivations behind male and female migration. Such an aggregated approach obfuscates the individual and collective mechanisms within which female migration can be framed. The links between the intersections of household systems, gender, and class with internal and international migration patterns have yet to be delineated. Power-gendered relationships within Africa's predominantly rural-based agricultural economy promoted and entrenched norms that favor a patriarchal approach to any analysis of the interplay between migration, gender, economic organization, and political capital. Women's lack of access to economic production resources (land and capital) inhibits and affects when, where, how, and if they will have opportunities to engage in cross-border migration, let alone intraregional migration.

Men and women have differential access to resources and opportunities for economic, cultural, and political empowerments. The result is that the central role and place of women in the migratory process is not clearly delineated. A common pattern noted by scholars is that when Africans move, it is the men who initially engage in the move. Micro and macro forces shaping the international migration of Africans see women as passive actors who follow the migrant paths of their husbands or male acquaintances at a subsequent time. The migratory dreams of African women are formed and mediated through the lens of male migration. This model of African migration casts women in the role of persons who need the assistance of their male counterparts in facilitating their migration.

Historically, systems of gendered stratification and sex roles enforced the eminence of men over women in African migration. The penetration of capitalist systems of economic and cultural production further entrenched the male-dominant system, relegating women to subsidiary production roles. This form of economic violence against women heightened the economic and cultural disadvantages of women. For most women, migration is the only alternative for leveling the playing field and uplifting their economic status. Women who have capital will often migrate to the urban and business centers to establish retail kiosks and stalls to sell imported or locally produced merchandise. For other women, education provides an outlet for improving women's standards of living and gaining access and entry into the formal and informal sectors of the economies of Africa.

Education, Gender, and Migration

The colonial and postcolonial systems of education continue to foster a climate where women's roles become marginalized from full participation and access to economic and political decision making. Where there are no structural or institutional barriers limiting their full incorporation into the affairs of African societies, social norms and customs may thwart the career aspirations of young girls. Secondary school and university curricula steer men into fields such as science and engineering, which, for the developing countries, are seen as male territories.

Today, significant changes have occurred in the cultural perceptions and ethos regarding the education of women. Prominent among the cultural factors that continue to spur the migration of African women to the West is the proliferation of primary and secondary school educational institutions. In the past, gender stereotypes about the role of women in African society kept the bulk of women in subservient relationships. In these relationships, many women were denied access to primary and elementary education, especially those in rural Africa. Cultural norms steered these women into homemaking roles, agriculture, taking care of children and elderly relatives, and the hawking of petty consumer goods. The cultural ethos showed a preference for sons, and this hampered the full participation and inclusion of girls in the educational process. Boys were the beneficiaries of family resources, particularly when it comes to education. The expectation was that boys would carry the family name and legacy, inherit the family property, and manage the family business. Their education was therefore considered premium. Girls were often cast in the role of reproducers or future mothers and were groomed for marriage usually after the onset of puberty. The socialization and training that girls received was tailored to domestic roles. Young girls often accompanied their mothers to the farm, where they engaged in labor-intensive work tilling the land and planting subsistence and cash crops. During the harvesting season, these same women were tapped to work on the harvesting and preparing the produce for sale. On market days, which may take place once or twice a week, these girls accompanied their parents to the agricultural marketing and distribution centers to sell their produce or wares.[4]

When boys complete elementary school, they may again be encouraged and given the financial support to pursue secondary education, sometimes hundreds of miles away from home. For boys who successfully complete senior secondary school, opportunities abound for attending teacher training colleges, polytechnic schools, or the university. The opportunities open to males to pursue secondary and tertiary education, unhindered by discrimination and sex stereotypes, ultimately position them to become favorable candidates for international migration. For those specializing in engineering, computer science, mathematics, and business administration, the prospects of pursuing graduate or postgraduate education in a foreign university are very high. Overall, the educational credentials of males position them for an array of economic and cultural opportunities in the West. In addition, boys are able to plug into the networks of contacts vital for undertaking the journey to the West. Through these networks, they are able to ascertain postgraduate educational and economic opportunities abroad, identify which countries in the West will best suit their economic and cultural interests, become acquainted with the visa application process, and learn about existing circuits of assistance that they can tap into once they are abroad. The education they receive is viewed as a passport to leave the country in search of a better economic status and better opportunities. This is particularly the case for college or university graduates who are often faced with unemployment or underemployment.

For many of Africa's women, opportunities to compete shoulder to shoulder with their male counterparts in all aspects of education did not become a reality until the advent of mass primary and secondary school education. Following the attainment of political independence, several countries (Ghana, Kenya, Tanzania, Ivory Coast, and Nigeria) embarked on an ambitious program of primary and secondary school education for their citizens. The goal was to produce a literate population that would provide an abundant supply of skilled and semi-skilled workers for both the public and private sectors. Following political independence, massive public education programs were seen as a way of training a cadre of Africans who would then fill important jobs.

The period after colonization was a great period of transition and national reconstruction in Africa. The old political order (foreign domination and colonization) was ending. A new era was about to be ushered in to bring about economic and political emancipation and give meaning to the long-held notion that Africans are capable of self-governance and self-determination. Educational initiatives and public campaigns were initiated at all levels of society to encourage parents to take advantage of the free systems of public education. Countries like Ghana, Tanzania, Zambia, and Egypt expanded their primary and secondary school systems, often at the expense of their tertiary educational systems.

Secondary, vocational-technical, and polytechnic education proliferated throughout Africa during the 1960s and 1970s. The opening up of secondary and tertiary institutions brought more women into the educational system. These institutions trained African women to become nurses, public health practitioners, teachers, civil servants, journalists, doctors, engineers, and lawyers. Initially, the labor markets of the majority of the African countries were able to absorb the graduates produced by these institutions. This was due in part to an expansion in public sector employment, particularly in the civil service, manufacturing, and industrial sectors.

By the beginning of the 1980s, the progress that African nations had made in secondary and postsecondary education began to fizzle. Unemployment and underemployment among graduates became a major social issue. There was a call for government to restrict the growth in secondary and tertiary education as funding from the central government for the existing public institutions of higher learning began to dwindle. Pressure to develop arterial roads, provide health care, provide pipe-borne water, expand electricity to rural areas, and to cope with rising population growth meant that the national treasuries of a vast majority of the countries were no longer able to provide education for every African. From the perspective of taxpayers, government funding of primary and secondary education ought to continue, but a significant decrease in public funding for tertiary and postsecondary education was needed because of the serious problems posed by unemployment and underemployment among the educated. Additionally, the fiscal crisis facing African countries worsened as international commodity prices for their raw materials began to drop. Drought and mismanagement due to the failure to pay farmers for their produce worsened the fiscal situation of many countries. Coupled with these problems were the growing problems of political and economic corruption, foreign indebtedness, civil unrest, and the ascendancy of militarism and ethnic-tribal factionalisms. While gender stereotypes and disparate systems of stratification continue to favor and influence the eminence of men in international migration across Africa, women are gradually breaking the cultural strictures associated with gender discrimination by initiating and implementing their own migration independent of their male counterparts.

For women who have secondary or postsecondary educational credentials, migration offers the best opportunity to achieve social mobility. Patriarchal norms may thwart the efforts of many of these women from gaining job promotions and earning high wages. Remnants of discriminatory practices favoring men over women continue to persist. For most educated women, the returns from their education positioned them to earn higher wages in the developed countries than they will receive if they stay in West Africa. Educated women encounter a glass-ceiling culture in both public and private sectors of employment. They are also less likely than their male counterparts to be successful in finding employment that matches their skills and credentials. For educated women who are single and do not have children, the prospect of migration intensifies once they come into contact with other women who have engaged in international migration. For women who have children, opportunities to engage in international migration are not ruled out. Arrangements are often made for the children to stay with extended relatives if the husband cannot shoulder the day-to-day responsibilities of caring for them. It is unusual for husbands to raise children alone. Even in cases of divorce, separation, or death of a parent, children may be sent away to stay with maternal or paternal relatives. Having child care responsibilities and obligations will not prevent many West African women from migrating abroad to work. Husbands may be compelled to consider the long-term economic benefits of spousal migration in the interest of the entire family. Husbands may receive remittances, thereby lessening their financial burdens at home. In the long term, chances of sponsorship for the husband and children to go to the United States may overshadow the husband's unwillingness to cooperate in raising the children who are left in his care. This finding contrasts other studies about women's migration that have reported that the presence of children may hinder women's chances of migration to the United States (Segura and Zavella 2007, 6).

Dismantling Old Traditions and Creating New Aspirations

Many West African women are driven to migrate in order to flee from the patriarchal and patrilineal dominations of their lives by fathers, uncles, brothers, and husbands. All too often, migration for this purpose is to reestablish a new life away from the social controls and, at times, away from the violence and abusive mistreatments some of them endure. Vulnerable to sexual and physical abuse and lacking any form of institutional protective measures and intervention by state or government agencies, leaving home is undeniably an effective strategy to curtail *de jure* and *de facto* gendered discrimination toward women. Driven away from their rural abodes as a result of dwindling agricultural lands and discriminatory land tenure rules that favor men over women, a growing number of West African women are compelled to leave home to forge new identities and ways of living that are totally different from the traditional lore and norms that they are accustomed to. International migration may be shaking the foundations of the patriarchal system of authority and social control. The status and fortunes of elderly patriarchs as well as young men have become dependent on the resources remitted home by family members who have undertaken the journey to a foreign land to work. There is a new realization by the extended family unit that the human and labor resources of women can be tapped and harnessed for the purposes of international migration.

Families concede that it is in the economic interest of the family unit as an entity of economic production to allow women to migrate so that the family's total assets can be increased and the standard of living of its members improved by the remittances that women migrants send home. Excluding or limiting the involvement of women in the migratory process came to be viewed as illogical and inimical to the future economic prosperity of the family or clan. The rigidly defined boundaries of gender roles, which served the interests of the patrilineal structures, had to be relaxed to permit young and capable women to migrate along with their male counterparts. West African women are responding in droves to this new era that presents an opportunity to renegotiate a new form of gendered relations, particularly one that will serve their interests as well as the economic interests of extended kin relatives.

Historically, West African women's migrations have taken them to the centers of commerce and industry in both the Anglophone and Francophone states in the subregion where they engage in retail and wholesale trading, often buying Western and indigenous consumer goods for sale at marketing and distribution centers across the region. Often relying on micro credits provided by extended family members to start their trading businesses, West African women are competent, economically savvy, and well organized in their trading operations. Living in societies in which women control the bulk of the sale and marketing of food and essential consumer commodities, the entrepreneurial acumen of West African women in carving economic niches is legendary. Marketing centers—such as Makola and Kejetia in Ghana's two largest cities, Accra and Kumasi—are often filled with throngs of women trading and selling foodstuffs, household items, livestock, clothing, and building supplies. In markets in Lagos, Dakar, Freetown, Monrovia, and across the region in general, throngs of youths can be seen carrying goods on their heads from one part of the market to another. Sometimes they wheel their merchandise on improvised flat-bed carts to the market centers. On market days, these market centers are filled with life. Noisy and colorful, these open-air markets attract buyers and sellers from near and far. Women trade their wares alongside their male counterparts. Agricultural produce from the rural areas bring huge profits to women traders, including those who specialized in the buying and selling of Dutch wax prints and silk materials.

With the money they make, some of the women are able to build a home where they stay with their children, sometimes without a male partner. Male partners and husbands may prefer taking up residence in their paternal family home, often leaving the wife to raise the children and, at times, pay for the children's school fees. Over time, some of these women not only become the economic mainstay of their family, they also come to acquire a sense of financial autonomy and independence, thereby closing the gap of inequality between men and women in predominantly traditional societies where male power is entrenched. In pursuing economic empowerment through trading, the women who migrate to the urban centers are able to educate their children. In a growing number of cases, profits from selling and trading enable women to send children to a private preparatory boarding school where many civil servants and middle-class workers often send their children. If their children perform well in school and are able to complete secondary school, family sponsorship to travel abroad and attend school, reunite with family members, or look for work is high. If it occurs, this sponsorship will be an investment in the long-term economic prosperity and well-being of the family. Going abroad is an adaptive mechanism to confront and deal with extended-family poverty and economic deprivation.

Female entrepreneurship has emerged as the principal mechanism of economic integration for most West African women, particularly those who do not possess formal education. Even when they possess primary and elementary school credentials, some women prefer to find work in the informal sector rather than find work in the private sector or civil service where wages are very low. Population growth and overurbanization have created the need for consumer markets in and around burgeoning capital city centers. Young women continue to migrate from the rural areas to these centers to start their own trading ventures. Once in the urban centers, they form the networks that will ultimately link them to the global economy and, in due course, trigger their migration to international labor and business markets. When they travel throughout the region forming what is now known as the Economic Community of West African States (ECOWAS), these women bring central place to women's experiences in the emerging new economies of the region. Women's visibility in intra- and interstate economic and business trading enhances the prospects of establishing commercial linkages and exchanges between producers and retailers or wholesalers. The knowledge gained from these transactions and interlocking trading channels may open new vistas of economic opportunities to the women as well. The net effect of these structural changes is that they have made it possible for West African women to develop new systems of economic production outside of the traditional household economy. Trading affords West African women opportunities to participate in regional and international border crossings to buy commodities for resale. At times, entire households or families may mobilize and harness household and inter-family resources to start family owned businesses. As they continue to move into low and high capital-intensive ventures, brought upon by increased commerce in the region, the women are able to garner the social capital they need to agitate for better economic representation in regional, state, and international decision making affecting every aspect of production and manufacturing.

In the past, many West African women confined their migration and trading activities to the West African region, often to the epicenters of agricultural production such as the cocoa producing centers of the Ivory Coast, Togo, and Ghana. While here, some of the women may set up restaurants or *chop bars* to sell food to the thousands of migrant male cocoa farmworkers who come from all over the region. The epicenters of mining activities have also attracted cadres of women who migrate to these towns either to join a spouse, start a trading venture, or manage a kiosk. Other women may set up trading posts, often selling consumer items such as batteries, clothing, confectionaries, cigarettes, and sundry goods. The capital needed to set up these commercial kiosk ventures in the centers of economic activity is minimal. With a sum of US$150, a migrant woman from the rural areas of Togo, Liberia, Ghana, and Sierra Leone who migrates to Lomé, Accra, Monrovia, or Freetown can set up a kiosk to sell local or imported merchandise. Scrap metal, a few wooden boards, or a handful of tree trunks are all that is needed to put these trading kiosks together. More expensive and fanciful kiosks may cost in excess of US$300 if built with a cemented floor, electricity, or a solid roof to withstand the vagaries of the tropical weather. Trading is the business of choice. The "buy-and-sell" economy enhances the income-earning potential of women, particularly in the absence of regulated price controls. These women traders understand the laws of supply and demand. Sometimes, they will use well proven methods, such as refusal to sell and hoarding their wares, to create artificial shortages of consumer goods that are much needed by the urban populace. By manipulating availability and prices, women traders are able to reap huge profits.

The deterioration of their economies shortly after gaining independence also altered the direction and destinations for prospective female migrants. A boom in industrial development and manufacturing in the Southern African region, spearheaded by South Africa, Botswana, and Mozambique, provided further opportunities for women to migrate. While some of the women migrate to join relatives and family members, scores of them migrate on their own to look for jobs in teaching, business, and trading. Those who are fortunate are able to find employment in the gold mines in South Africa. While there, these women engage in several cross-border migrations within the region, searching for economic and industrial production centers where they can maximize their income.

Porous and unattended border posts and corrupt border guards make it easier for migrants to travel within the region as they seek better economic opportunities. For English-speaking West African women with secondary and postsecondary credentials, economic opportunities became available in both the formal and informal sectors of Southern Africa's economy. For women who have not attended secondary school and who have poor vocational skills, living and working in Southern Africa may pose serious challenges and hardships, including recruitment into prostitution rings to work in the sexual tourism businesses located in and around mining centers. The end of the apartheid period witnessed the flow of massive Western and foreign capital investments into South Africa, which once again, made the country the preferred choice of migrant destination for many West Africans. For the many West African women who embark upon the trip to South Africa, migration is seen as a temporary fix for economic woes rather than a long and planned journey to seek permanent relocation (Dodson 2000). This is in contrast to their male counterparts who prefer long-term migratory sojourns in South Africa, with the ultimate aim of saving enough money to head to the West, preferably to Great Britain or the United States. Today, women from the West African region continue to join the ranks of other Africans heading to Southern Africa in general, seeking better economic and cultural opportunities away from their home countries (McDonald 2000; Adepoju 1995, 2000).[5]

For many West African women, a major component of migration is the transition from rural to urban areas, the goal of which is to find wage employment in the urban sector, to pursue secondary and postsecondary education, or to reunite with relatives who have already undertaken the journey to the urban centers. As countries on the continent expanded upon industrial and manufacturing production, a need for cheap labor in the urban areas was created. This also started to push rural folks to migrate. The colonial business model, whereby industries and government services and administrative infrastructure were located in the capital cities or regional centers, set in motion internal and transnational population mobility in Africa. The postcolonial cities of Africa continue to attract many young men and women from the rural areas who are eager to seek better economic and cultural opportunities for themselves. As indicated, the decline in agricultural productivity, rising conflicts over land ownership rights, deforestation, vagaries of the weather, lack of farm extension services, poor marketing, and the lack of feeder roads to connect food-growing to food-consuming areas are just some of the factors affecting rural farming communities across West Africa. Migration to the cities provided young men and women with opportunities to work and contribute to the economic well-being of their extended families.

The flow of labor out of Africa's rural areas intensified as the continent's cash crop and mining economies expanded after colonization. In Southern Africa, for example, the expansion of copper, nickel, gold, and diamond mining brought hundreds of thousands from rural hamlets in Africa to seek wage-based employment in South Africa and Botswana. In West Africa, oil production in southern Nigeria brought workers from Ghana, Liberia, Benin, and Niger. So did the production of cocoa in Ghana, Cameroon, Togo, and the Ivory Coast. Workers from as far as Mali, Niger, Burkina Faso, and Niger migrate to Ghana to work in the cocoa industry. As shown, the establishment of the economic union of West Africa has also spurred the movement of skilled and unskilled migrant laborers to the economic and industrial production centers in the Ivory Coast, Ghana, and Nigeria. The protocol of free trade and the unrestricted movement of people, goods, and services are also transforming the nature of economic and industrial organization in the subregion of West Africa. As international barriers disintegrate, the geographic domain of employment is shifting to the attractive labor markets in the region.

The expansion of capitalist economic production systems in the developing countries have served as one of the mechanisms whereby African women have become incorporated into the global economy. In the past, institutionalized forms of gender inequality meant that the status of African women was largely dependent upon the socioeconomic position of the husband. Despite the fact that the system of economic and political power continues to favor African males over women, the continued penetration of the capitalist mode of production and the gradual breakdown of gender-based stereotypes have enabled African women to assert their influence in family decision making regarding regional and international migration. In many areas of Africa where male migration continues to oscillate between one labor employment center and another, the women who remain behind to take care of and manage the family's finances through the remittances sent home by spouses have gained considerable leverage in shaping the future migratory behavior of the family unit.

In households where migration is the norm, women often give equal chances to both male and female siblings to undertake the migration journey to join maternal or paternal relations. Decisions about migration are made to maximize the economic standing of, first, the woman's immediate family, and second, the extended family. Not willing to limit the economic opportunities of their female children, many women who head households where the husband has migrated often sponsor female daughters to embark on the trip to the urban areas. Waves of male out-migration in countries such as Botswana, South Africa, Zimbabwe, Liberia, Ghana, and Uganda (to mention a few) to mining and business centers created a power vacuum in the social, economic, and political organization of rural communities. Women have risen to fill the void, often managing extended family units and making decisions regarding the next in line to migrate or to join paternal relations in urban and industrial production centers, including mining centers. Male out-migration has strengthened the status of women, giving them greater independence and autonomy to forge egalitarian relationships and identities with their male counterparts. This newfound sense of mutually shared family goals regarding migration serves to strengthen the family unit and help create a new power base for women through the networks African women form as they seek to become part of the new transglobal economy of migration. The ability to manage remittances and determine how the remitted money is used means that women are increasingly becoming equal partners with a hand in family decision making. Ultimately, this power is leveraged to allow the entire family to reunite with male migrants.

Women have always played a pivotal role in national and transnational migration. In Latin America and Africa, women migrants often travel from the rural to urban centers to seek education, form marketing cooperatives, find employment as civil servants, work as domestics, or to establish trading posts in close proximity to mining, agricultural, and manufacturing arteries. New economic and cultural realities in Africa—the gradual breakdown of sex roles; the growth in the number of young girls who complete middle and secondary schools; the harnessing of extended family resources to promote the economic standing of families; increased consumerism and the penetration of Chinese and Asian-made goods into African markets; and the improvements in air transportation between the West African region and the Middle East—have transformed and spurred accessibility to trading or marketing and production centers all across the region.

Additionally, the postcolonial system of economic and cultural production in British and French West Africa put in place a capitalist system that concentrated core economic and cultural activities in particular geographic regions and centers. These centers then became the epicenters of the colonial system. African cities like Lagos (Nigeria), Dakar (Senegal), Accra (Ghana), Freetown (Sierra Leone), Bamako (Mali), Nairobi (Kenya), and Kampala (Uganda) all developed as centers for business, commerce, education, and culture. Migration from rural to urban Africa was viewed as a way to participate in the new economic and cultural production brought upon by colonization and capitalist penetration. The imposition of poll taxes levied on the local population by the colonial powers created an added economic burden on many Africans. This burden is how to make enough wage income to offset the taxes levied by the colonial regimes. Taxation was a new phenomenon to the rural and urban populations. Considering that the bulk of the economies of African countries were based on informal production, as opposed to the more formalized sectors of the economy, the pressure to find the money to pay for the new taxes imposed severe economic hardships on all, particularly the rural dwellers who depended on the land for subsistence farming and who bartered goods and services. The taxes led to migration to towns and cities where wage employment in the informal sectors could be obtained. For middle- and secondary-school-leavers, this also triggered migration to the urban centers as these places boasted of better economic opportunities than their rural counterparts. The exigencies of engaging in the informal economic sectors meant that for most African women, going to the urban centers of commerce was considered to be economically prudent and logical. While there, women also enhance their prospects of participating in the formal sectors of the economy as well acquire new skills or update old skills to make them more employable.[6]

Due to their migrations to international labor market and cultural destinations across the world, women in general are forging new identities and redefining gender relations in their new locales. The growing number of women in the new migration has shattered age-old beliefs that as a group, women constitute a passive voice in migration and the decision-making processes associated with the intent to emigrate. An outcome of this apparent invisibility is the notion that women embark on migration to reunite with family members or join male husbands who have preceded them earlier in the journey. Migration is often approached from a male perspective. This perspective is structured on the assumption that women's migratory behavior is peripheral and unimportant, though studies continue to show that women now outnumber their male counterparts to the immigrant destinations of the United States, Canada, Australia, and other migrant receiving countries in Europe, particularly Britain, Netherlands, Spain, and Italy. More recently, much of the transnational migrations within and outside of the developing countries involve women. Evidence from Africa, Latin America, and Asia certainly supports the growing "feminization of migration" concept.[7] As women continue to engage in international migration, it is expected that West African women will continue to play an active role in transnational migrations, joining the caravan of women searching for global economic opportunities. Considering that they are the last group of women to look to the West for better economic opportunities, the thousands of West African immigrant women who engage in migration may be viewed as social actors who are shaping and defining their own terms of economic, social, and cultural engagements in a world that is often characterized by gender, class, tribal, and religious hierarchies based upon inequality and institutionalized forms of exclusion. And though African women are slightly outnumbered by their male counterparts when it comes to migration to the United States and the West in general, significant shifts have now occurred in the gender composition of African migrations to the United States. Like other immigrants from Latin America, the Caribbean, and Asia streaming into the United States, West Africans now equate travel to the West as a necessary mechanism to improve upon their standard of living in light of dwindling hopes that their governments are going to implement economic and social development plans to ease their ever-worsening abject poverty and deprivations. Distinct expectations are formed by the immigrants even before they enter the United States. These expectations are anchored in the economic realities at home, pushing them to leave, and the relatively better economic conditions in the United States and the West, pulling them to come and pursue their quest for better standards of living.

CHAPTER 3

PASSAGE FROM THE SAVANNAH
GRASSLANDS OF AFRICA TO AMERICA

I just wanted to come to America to earn an income and help alleviate the poverty we face at home in my family. I was not discouraged by the border guards, neither was I fearful of arrest. One must always take a chance. I am here now. And I am working two jobs. I could work three jobs if I want to. Some of my friends from Africa do. Most of them do not have valid papers, yet they are here as well. Life here is very hard. But at least there are plenty of jobs in the Twin Cities.

—Saadiaa, a Liberian immigrant

Life was very hard in Africa. Our leaders have failed to meet the basic needs of our people. We are experiencing a brain drain to the West because we cannot support ourselves anymore. We need a bold and fresh start. We severed colonial ties from Europe over fifty years ago. More than five decades later, we have nothing to show to the rest of the world, except poverty and miseries.

—Hawa, a Gambian immigrant

With these opening statements, Saadiaa and Hawa capture the essence and presence of the growing West African women immigrant communities across the United States. A common theme in the stories of West African migratory journeys is economic strife, the driving force compelling their migration to the United States. The personal discourses and immigrant journeys of each of the West African women who are profiled here speak to one central issue and theme: that individually and collectively, the women bring a diverse portfolio of tapestries to the United States. In each of their immigrant accounts, these women express a collective desire to renew themselves and work toward the fulfillment of predetermined economic goals. Their voices and intonations reveal an unshaken belief in the American dream and the promises, real or perceived, that it offers. The reasons and motivations behind their journeys to the United States are as diverse as the various forms, ways, and mechanisms that they employ to reach the shores of the United States. Whether they come to America via conventional migration or engage in sequential, chain migration or come as displaced refugees fleeing from war torn and failed states, a prevailing view among the immigrant women is that they will achieve a way of life that is relatively better than what they were accustomed to in West Africa. The risks they assume are purposive and instrumental, often designed to forge new transnational and global identities with the members of the host society and beyond. At the same time, their migratory journeys are punctuated by their intense yearnings to tackle some of the pressing economic problems they face.[1]

DESCRIPTION OF WEST AFRICAN IMMIGRANT WOMEN IN THE U.S. CENSUS

Based on U.S. census data for 1990, 2000, and for the intercensus years of 2001 through 2006, general descriptions of West African immigrant women in the United States can be ascertained. The following are some of the demographic characteristics or profiles of West African immigrant women residing in the country. The top-tier immigrant-sending countries are Nigeria (43 percent), Ghana (21.2 percent), Liberia (16.4 percent), and Sierra Leone (7.5 percent). Immigrant women tend to settle in the immigrant-rich states forming the Middle and South Atlantic regions of the country, with the highest number of settlements found in the South Atlantic states, including Virginia, Maryland, North and South Carolina, Georgia, and the Washington, D.C., area. Outside of this region, the east north central and west south central regions of the country recorded the next highest population of West African immigrant women living in the United States.

The top major metropolitan areas of West African immigrant residence are New York (including northeastern New Jersey), Washington, D.C. (including northern Virginia and Maryland), Baltimore, Atlanta, Houston, Chicago, Philadelphia, Dallas-Ft. Worth, Boston, and Los Angeles. Nearly 4 percent (3.4 percent) of West African immigrants own their homes free and clear; another 45.3 percent pay a mortgage, and one-half (50.0 percent) rent. In terms of marital status, 41.8 percent are married with a spouse present; 6.6 percent are married with a spouse absent; 35.0 percent are never married or single; and 16.7 percent are separated, widowed, or divorced. Regarding citizenship and naturalization status, the majority (64.3 percent) are not citizens of the United States. Naturalized citizens comprise 31.8 percent of the group. Approximately 4 percent (3.9 percent) were born abroad of American parents. The principal languages spoken at home are English (28.9 percent) and French and Creole (10.8 percent). Only 1 percent indicated that they do not speak English, compared with another 5 percent who speak English but not well. Sixty-three percent speak English very well or well, while nearly 29 percent (28.9 percent) speak only English.

The immigrant women's educational attainment levels are noteworthy. Twenty-eight percent have four or more years of college education, while 27.2 percent have one to three years of college. This means that more than one-half have some college or postsecondary education. Relative to other minority immigrant groups, particularly Hispanic and Asian Americans, African women immigrants reported higher educational credentials. These credentials were obtained in Africa as well as in the United States. According to the United States census, this accomplishment exceeded the educational attainment profiles of European immigrants, including native-born white Americans.

Slightly more than one-half (54.2 percent) of the women are currently working full-time, while about one-quarter (26.0 percent) are not in the labor force. Three percent have a job but are currently not working. Six percent of the women are unemployed. Regarding the number of years the immigrant women have been in the United States, the data reveal that 61 percent have been in the country between one and ten years; another 24 percent have been living in the United States between eleven and twenty years; and only 15 percent have been living in the country for twenty-one or more years. Class-of-work information about the immigrant women reveals that only 4 percent of the women are self-employed. Nearly 48 percent of them are employed in the private sector, while 9 percent work in the nonprofit sector. Twelve percent of the women work for the federal, state, or local governments. A third of the women did not look for work while another third reported looking for work. And nearly 70 percent of them worked the year before the censuses were taken. Internal migration data show that the majority of the women (62.4 percent) stayed in the same area of residence the year before the census occurred. Only 12.3 percent lived in a different house or location during the census years, while 4 percent lived abroad.

The age breakdown shows that 5 percent of the women were under ten years old; 12.4 percent were between ten and twenty-nine years old; 18 percent were twenty to twenty-nine years old; 27.4 percent were between thirty to thirty-nine years old; 23 percent were forty to forty-nine years old; 9 percent were fifty to fifty-nine years old; and 11 percent were aged sixty and above.

POSITIONING WEST AFRICAN WOMEN'S MIGRATION TO THE UNITED STATES

West African immigrant women who come to the United States form part of the growing trend of continental African migration to the West in general. Like other new immigrants streaming into the country from Asia, Latin America, and the Caribbean, economic reasons motivate the migration of West Africans to the United States. West Africa is one of the poorest regions in the world. Per capita incomes and gross domestic products are among the lowest in the world. The average West African earns less than $800 per year.

The countries of the West African region emerged from the aftermath of European colonization during the 1950s and 1960s with renewed ambition and hope that the end of foreign colonization would usher in a new era—an era of self-determination and autonomy. After all, the white colonialists had been replaced by a new cadre of Black West African leaders, mostly educated in the West. The expectation was that these new postindependence leaders would be positioned to define a new African agenda unique to the region's experiences. Slogans like "Africa for the Africans" dominated the social and cultural landscape. For the teeming masses of the region's poor, a new hope had dawned. Their new leaders claimed they had the panacea to ease the economic plight of the people.

However, nearly a little more than half a century after the independence movement started, the region has yet to show any measurable and sustained progress in terms of raising the economic and social lives of the people. By all accounts, the fulfillment of the economic needs of the people are lagging behind and failing to materialize. A few of the countries, notably Senegal, Ivory Coast, Ghana, Uganda, Botswana, and Nigeria, have all made moderate improvements in raising the standards of living of their people. But on the whole, the region is characterized by economic despair, stillborn democracies, weak manufacturing and industrial bases, and poor to nonexistent infrastructures coupled with simmering political and civil instabilities and unrests.

Migrating to America is seen as a way of escaping deteriorating economic conditions and the breakdown of political and civil institutions. Human capital models in migration offer useful theoretical insights into

West African women's migration to the United States. The motivations of West African women to leave home are shaped by their expected earnings, chances of securing employment (irrespective of the wages), the potential costs of undertaking the journey, and the presence of family networks at the intended destination. Included in these migratory determinants are factors such as the age of the prospective migrant, educational credentials, the number of years of schooling prior to migration, willingness to assume risk, household attributes, gender relationships, presence or absence of younger children, and income constraints (Kanaiaupuni 2000; Mora and Taylor 2006).

Irrespective of the factors spurring their migration, America offers the prospects for achieving stalled economic goals, finding employment, saving money, and improving the overall standards of living. As Malkin (2004) points out, "People migrate internationally in an effort to get ahead, to provide a better life for themselves, their children, or their family members left at home." Adepoju (2002) noted that poverty has become both widespread and intense and that the proportion of West Africa's population living in abject poverty continues to increase. As shown in the previous chapter, rural to urban migration has intensified as landless farm laborers, deprived of the means to improve their living conditions, are pressured to abandon work and life in the rural areas and emigrate in search of wage labor in the urban areas (Adepoju 2002, 4). Even when they travel to the United States as students on nonimmigrant visas to pursue postsecondary education or to reunite with family members, the dominant motivation for their migration is the chance for better economic and cultural opportunities. The journey to America is characterized as a life-saving strategy designed to improve upon and maximize the living standards of the prospective immigrants.

Gordon (1998, 79) identified five broad causal factors behind African immigration to the United States. These are globalization and integration of the world economy, economic and political development failures in Africa, immigration and refugee policies in Europe and the United States, Anglophone backgrounds, and finally, historic ties of sending countries to the United States.[2] Gordon's (1998) analyses delved into the structural explanations of African migrations to the United States. Her findings showed that are detailed descriptions of how globally structured inequalities and systems of international stratifications stifled African economies causing social unrests and discontent among the urban and poor rural masses. For decades following the postindependence era, the continued manifestations of globally induced economic stagnation aggravated the ethnic, tribal, and religious tensions often resulting in protracted civil unrests and social uncertainties. Coupled with this is the imbalance and wide gap between the richer and poorer countries. In particular, she noted how income disparities among the developed and developing countries created favorable conditions and the motivations among the citizens of the poorer countries to migrate to the richer countries in search of better economic opportunities. Walter Rodney's (1982, vii) assertion that "the decision to migrate to another country often reflects the failure of development at home" is salient in the context of African migration to the United States.

For many of West Africa's youth, there is one principal goal in life. It is to find a way, legal or not, to make it to the United States or to the West in general. The same can be said for adults, whether they are gainfully employed at home or not. In planning to migrate, every prospective immigrant perceives that life's chances will be relatively better in the West than they are at home. The prospect of encountering challenges, including that of safely reaching the destination, finding a place to stay, and having to find a job, is often minimized or downplayed. A majority of those who have preceded the prospective migrants send glowing testimonies about life in the United States. Information channels are filled with accounts and stories about those who have recently made the journey.

Accounts of how recent immigrants have been successful in finding employment, a place to stay, and even having some money left to buy consumer goods like cars and televisions are usually relayed back to West Africa. Information about jobs that pay (on average, $7 or more an hour), are disseminated to every sector of urban and rural society in West Africa. When prospective migrants at home hear that their friends and relatives who recently arrived abroad are working two jobs, this information is used to further justify the imperative to migrate. This imperative is further strengthened by the fact that many of those immigrants who make it to the United States without valid papers have not been involuntarily repatriated or deported. For some of the undocumented, it is not impossible to live and work in the country for decades without being found and deported.

While there are obvious challenges and obstacles facing nondocumented immigrants who work in the underground economy (poor conditions of employment, sometimes labor exploitation, including threats of deportation or arrest), these obstacles have yet to deter prospective travelers from coming to the United States. To most West Africans, this can only mean one thing: that life in America is good. Problems and challenges may be encountered. However, these problems, if and when they occur, are surmountable. The prospective immigrant's rationalization is that there is an immigrant cultural underworld that has developed its own set of coping strategies to support burgeoning undocumented workers in the United States. For masses of unemployed rural and urban youths, including secondary and postsecondary school graduates, the risks of immigration pale in comparison to the short- and long-term benefits of going to America. To show that the grass is much greener in the United States than in West Africa, some of the recent arrivers, upon finding work, remit home immediately. Even a small remittance is fodder to invigorate the efforts of those who are aspiring to leave.

For these immigrant women and their families in the United States and in Africa, the experience of international migration is framed in such a way to incorporate the household and extended family as an economic production unit. Decisions concerning internal and international migrations are rationalized and set within the nexus of the extended family unit. In that regard, the household is recognized as a unit of consumption whose economic capital must be efficiently maximized or optimized.[3] The benefits of international migration are shared by the households. This form of economic altruism is pervasive in Black African migration. Migration is a cooperative enterprise designed to maximize the family's social and economic status. This configuration corresponds to Stark's (1991) and Sjaastad's (1962) modeling of the cost-benefits of migration for families. For West African women immigrants, the perceived benefits of international migration are critical components in predicting the short- and long-term future economic well-being of households.

The desperation and pressure to migrate dominate the numerous Internet cafes and chat rooms that have sprung up in small and large cities across West Africa. Here, information about the immigrant-receiving countries is disseminated. The drive to leave West Africa is further aggravated by the home visits of those who have been successful in implementing the journey to the United States. These returnees, who come for short or long visits, usually flash the material symbols and goods they have obtained in the West. They usually save several months' wages before making the trip home, and when they exchange or convert their money to the local currency, returnees usually have loads of money even though the purchasing power of the local currencies is limited. Hyperinflationary cycles have eroded the value of the currencies of the various countries in the region. And though it takes a lot in their local currencies to purchase luxury goods and items, inflation at home in West Africa is not an issue if one has access to foreign currencies such as the American dollar or the British pound. With the money they exchange upon their visits, many of these returnees purchase goods and items that the locals can only dream of obtaining. This heightens the perceived sense of unfulfilled or unmet needs among those who stay behind and do not migrate. The desire to have access to foreign exchange incites continued out-migration. Immigrants and would-be immigrants perceive that in America and the West in general, one is able to afford the barest necessities of life by performing minimum wage, unskilled jobs. With their wages, many immigrants manage to save money to build a home in Africa, set up a business, or set aside money for a comfortable retirement. For those who do not migrate, it is practically impossible to achieve this same feat. Consciously or unconsciously, people are made to feel that the only way they can achieve economic mobility is via international migration.

The proliferation of mass communication media outlets, where the material goods of the West are frequently disseminated, serves as catalyst for migration. Television and satellites have facilitated the process of exchanging information over wide distances. The relatively high standards of living in the West are directly beamed into the homes of poor West Africans through televisions and other media channels. Information about crime, violence, racism, and discrimination, including anti-immigration sentiments, are also channeled into the homes of many West Africans. Many West Africans believe that the economic realities in the United States and the need for American businesses to remain globally competitive create a pro-immigration sentiment in the business and corporate communities. Anti-immigrant sentiments from the American public to curb legal and illegal immigration do not cause would-be immigrants from shelving their motivations to migrate. Prospective immigrants rationalize that American businesses want access to a cheap and abundant labor supply in the farming, meat processing and packaging, construction, nursing home and elderly care, and hospitality management sectors. They further rationalize that scores of undocumented aliens are able to find unemployment in these sectors in the larger metropolitan and suburban communities where their services are in high demand relative to the number of Americans who are willing to work in these sectors. The majority of prospective immigrants from West Africa and elsewhere are driven to head to the United States to fill this void. As pointed out, information about these jobs is relayed back home to prospective immigrants in West Africa through the myriad of immigrant networks that have been established between the United States and Africa. The net effect is that the prospects of living and working in the

United States are brought home to many of West Africa's rural and urban poor, including school graduates.

The urge among potential immigrants is to become part of the global consumer society. Staying at home in West Africa will not avail one to the consumer goods or the luxuries of America or the West. In the mindset of West Africans who envisage the trip, this new global economy reduces the distance between America and West Africa. Again, as media and communication channels proliferate to distant areas of the continent, prospective immigrants discover networks of sponsors who charge exorbitant fees to process their travel documents to enable them to come to the United States. Possible modes of traveling to the point(s) of destination are also shared. For a majority of the prospective immigrants, the mode of traveling takes a conventional form, that is, through legal cross-border checkpoints or barriers. However, for a growing number of West Africans, unconventional forms of travel have become the norm.

For some West Africans like Mimi, an Ivorian fishmonger, the journey to America, the "promised land," was circuitous, starting from her native Ivory Coast, then through Mali, and subsequently to Algeria. It took her seven months to cross the Sahara Desert. In some of the village towns along the route, she heard stories about migrants dying from dehydration, swollenness, diarrhea, and hunger. She spoke about enduring cold nights and scorching daytime heat as they traversed the desert. Sand storms whipped their faces. The vehicle they were driving broke down. Some in her party fell ill and could not continue with the journey. Those who fell ill and had money were able to plead with the "middlemen" to assist them to get to the nearest hospital, which was sometimes more than a day's journey.

Despite these struggles, Mimi was not going to retreat and return home because she did not want to be seen as a failure. After offering more than $3,000 in bribes to migrant "middlemen," including fishermen in Algeria, she was able to reach Italy. Two weeks later, she left Italy and arrived in Spain, where she stayed and worked with a fishing company for a year. Here, she met several Africans who had made it across the Sahara Desert and were waiting to save enough money to move on to other parts of Western Europe or to the United States. In the case of Mimi, her ambition was to travel to the United States because she had heard accounts of good-paying agricultural jobs, including those in the poultry, meat processing and packaging, and landscaping industries. Upon saving enough money, she managed to purchase an airline ticket to Mexico

City, where, upon arrival, she immediately headed to the United States and Mexican border, paid $900, and was taken over the border into Texas.

This circuitous journey finally ended in Minnesota when Mimi arrived in Minneapolis and Saint Paul to share a house with friends and relatives who had been living in the state for twelve years. In her new migratory environment, she can form new aspirations toward a brighter future. The sheer determination and motivation on the part of Mimi to embark upon the journey to the United States is significant because it pinpoints the severity of the economic desperation that is so prevalent in the West African region. According to Mimi, her entire family was very supportive of her risky ordeal to settle in the United States via unconventional forms of traveling. "I could feel my grandmother's spirit at every inch of the way. When I got tired and felt like giving up, my mind always went back to those relatives of mine at home who were praying that I make it. They know that if I make it to the U.S., the family's economic fortunes will change. This journey was an experience that was shared by many," she said. For this West African immigrant woman, the economic and cultural opportunities awaiting her in the United States cannot be matched by the meager opportunities she left behind at home.

Mimi's stepwise migratory experiences that eventually brought her to the United States were echoed by Saadiaa, an immigrant from Liberia. When I interviewed Saadiaa, she had settled in a two-bedroom apartment in a quiet suburb of Saint Paul. Like Mimi, Saadiaa's journey was filled with risks that she was willing to undertake to reach her economic goals in the United States. She crossed the border from Mexico to enter the country illegally. Though the initial weeks proved very difficult because she did not have any work authorization papers, her relatives were able to find her an employer who did not verify employment eligibility. By her account, the opportunity to get this job was a fulfillment and culmination of her cherished desire to come and live and work in the United States. According to Saadiaa, the benefits of risking her life to reach the United States far surpassed any rewards that she would have derived by staying home. She asserted,

> I just wanted to come to America to earn an income and help alleviate the poverty we face at home in my family. I was not discouraged by the border guards, neither was I fearful of arrest. One must always take a chance. I am here now. And I am working two jobs. I could work three jobs if I want to. Some of my friends from Africa do. Most of them do not have valid papers, yet they are here as well. Life here is very hard.

But at least there are plenty of jobs in the Twin Cities metro area that many Minnesotans are not eager to perform. As immigrants, we do all types of work.

According to Saadiaa, economic impetus drives hundreds, if not thousands, of African youth to leave their home in search of better opportunities in the West. Many of her peers left West Africa at the same time that she did, some heading toward Libya, others toward Tunisia, with another group of five men and two women from her hometown heading toward Mauritania, the Canary Islands, and Egypt. A team of four women in their late twenties had left West Africa via Tunisia and Egypt, expecting to make it to Europe. All four women currently have relatives who live and work in Minnesota. These relatives assured them of jobs in the poultry and meat packaging business upon their arrival. According to Saadiaa, these women ultimately intend to settle in the United States. Before they all left home, they sold all their personal belongings, including televisions, cattle, jewelry, and cultural artifacts that had existed in their respective families for over half a century. The money they received was supplemented with money that they borrowed from extended family relations.

For those who are willing to embark upon the journey to the West, every effort is made to expedite their travels by providing them with what one respondent referred to as "road money." This is money used to pay bribes to border guards as they traverse Africa; to pay fishermen to ferry them across the Mediterranean; to pay desert villagers for shelter and, at times, food; or to pay the caravan operators who ply the Sahara, connecting it to North Africa and the Mediterranean. Families often pool their resources to assist their kin in undertaking the trip to America and the West. For those who contribute money toward the trip, the payoff could be rewarding. Such an investment is intended to boost the family's overall economic status in the long term. Some West African families may even select some of their members for sponsorship to the West, particularly those members who have acquired or possess a skill that is in high demand in the United States. This may include those with credentials in nursing, medicine, paramedical and allied health, engineering, computer science, and related high technology skills. The payoff is that upon arrival at their respectful destinations, these family members usually send for other family members and regularly remit money to assist relatives back home.

Through the remittances, some family members receive enough money for daily subsistence living, particularly if they are elderly and do not work. Even when they do work, many West African families cannot make ends meet. Having a relative remit home regularly is a proven way to boost family income and ensure the economic survival of the family. In the absence of public assistance and national welfare payments, families and individuals have to depend on the economic altruism of relatives abroad. As shown, this dependency fuels continued international migration in a bid to expand and increase the family's share of capital and tangible resources. Over a period of time, the quantity or number of relatives abroad who remit is far more significant than the quality of the migratory experiences that the migrants form or experience abroad.[4] The principal motivation is not to amass a lot of wealth. What drives this movement to America is simply the need to make enough money to support oneself, live a basic life, and send the rest of the money home. The prospect of earning relatively higher wages in the United States relative to what is earned at home in West Africa is behind the formation of the rationalizations for migration. The basic truism is that the more family members join the caravan of international migration to the West, the better the economic standing of the migrants' immediate and extended families.

Charisse's situation is illustrative of the systemic relationship that exists between extended family units and global migration, particularly the economic overdependency of family members on their migrant relatives living abroad. An immigrant woman from Liberia, Charisse, completed secondary-technical school in Monrovia, training as a teacher. By Liberian standards, she was middle class, living in a small two-bedroom government-furnished flat. Two nieces lived with her to assist in household chores. In return, Charisse paid for their tuition to attend a private school on the outskirts of Monrovia. At the end of every month, relatives from far and near would come to see Charisse for financial assistance. And though she did not have enough resources to assist everyone, both immediate and extended relatives kept flocking to her residence. Most often, she did not have to give the relatives much money—a few dollars was sufficient to put smiles on their faces. But they would come back every few days for more help. Unable to cope with the stream of relatives coming in and out of her house any longer, Charisse approached a friend in the United States who had sent her a letter of invitation to come for a visit. Though she had only a visitor's visa, she was able to find work through well-established Liberian émigrés already settled in the United States. She overstayed her visitor's visa, working two jobs and, by her own estimate, remitted over one-half of the money she earned to relatives back home.

To ease the financial plight of her relatives at home, Charisse's plan was to find a well-established Liberian immigrant to assist in sponsoring five of her immediate and extended relatives to come to the United States. She paid various sums of money to travel facilitators who were able to get two of her relatives to Mexico. Here, they worked odd jobs for nine months, saved their money, and paid smugglers who brought them across the border to Arizona. According to Charisse, it was imperative for her to sponsor these relatives because their presence in the United States would make it possible for them to combine their resources and assist more members of their family. She explained,

> I needed to have some of my relatives here in America so that together, we can all contribute to the economic renaissance of our family members at home. I could not do it alone. I was hurting very badly economically. Everyone was relying on me for support to pay for children's school fees, the costs of funerals, provide money for daily living, pay for health and medical costs of elderly relatives and in some cases pay for the rent of relatives I have yet to meet face-to-face. The cultural pressure to provide financial support for relatives is very intense including relatives you do not know or have not seen before. Once they hear that you are abroad, they contact you and start telling you about their problems. Their assumption is that life in America is much better than it is in West Africa; that Africans who come to America mostly do very well and therefore have to share their assets with folks at home. This can be financially draining.

Assisting immediate and extended relatives with their economic needs is burdensome. But as Charisse opined, "This assistance is an investment in the future economic well-being and prosperity of the entire family. It is a collective spirit rather than the individualistic spirit which pertains in the West. I always receive letters from relatives and friends in West Africa. They tell me never to forget them and always remember to send money home, no matter how small. Without the remittances, some will go without food.

Abject poverty and lack of employment prospects for young adults continue to push people out, including Charisse's relatives. With three of her immediate relations now living and working in the United States, the burden of shouldering the economic needs of relatives at home had been eased but not completely eliminated. It is Charisse's ambition to assist two other relatives who have recently completed nursing education in Liberia to come to the United States and work. She anticipates that with the growing public anti-immigration fervor in the United States, visa standards will remain tight and the borders vigilantly monitored. Charisse's option is to initially get the two relatives to enter Canada or Britain as skilled workers because of their medical backgrounds. Once in Britain or Canada, getting them over to the United States will not be as difficult as getting them out of Africa directly to the United States.

Culturally, the expectation that Africans who are successful in the West should support their less fortunate siblings and extended family members is so entrenched that it can exert pressure on young men and women to leave home to go abroad. As explained, in the absence of social welfare benefits for people in West Africa, family members who have become relatively successful become the economic safety nets for young and old alike. Sometimes, large extended families depend on the money sent home by a single contributor. Even when successful members of the family do not migrate, but stay at home and are able to find well-paid employment in the public or private sector, scores of extended family members regularly visit them at home and in their offices to obtain money for daily subsistence living. At times, this may involve traveling long distances and staying with the relative for a long time. For example, young boys and girls sometimes travel from the villages to the urban areas to stay with these relatives. While there, they may attend school. Ultimately, this altruism has the potential to stifle local investments as too many people become dependent on a handful of individuals. Overdependence on a few family members has the potential to promote corruption—economic or political—such as when successful family members become overly pressured to find a lasting solution to family poverty by hiring unqualified relatives or favoring coethnic groups for employment or promotion. Usually, not much money is left to save after taking care of the economic needs of extended kith and kin.

STRUCTURAL PROBLEMS FORMING
THE DECISION TO LEAVE

The continued depression of rural economic activities is central to the understanding of why throngs of rural dwellers flock to the cities and urban centers of economic activity. Relative to the urban areas, life is hardest for rural folks in West Africa. The prevailing levels of economic activity and infrastructural support are often woefully inadequate to sustain and retain the population of the rural areas. Lacking their fair share of economic and industrial development projects, the rural areas are not in any position to compete with the urban centers. Added to this is the problem of governmental bias in the allocation of funds for development projects in favor of the urban centers. Though agriculture is the lifeblood of these areas, lack of capital investments in the form of mechanized farming and high-yield crop seedlings coupled with the lack of irrigation systems have further aggravated the problems of the rural communities. Crop failures, drought, declining producer prices, administrative encumbrances, and political patronage and corruption are but a few of the problems thwarting the effective and sustained development of rural economies in the region.

Structural adjustment policies embarked upon by several of the countries in West Africa—as a precondition for World Bank and International Monetary Fund (IMF) economic assistance—have forced governments to lay off hundreds of thousands of civil and public sector employees. Under IMF's austerity measures, subsidies for water, electricity, petrol, and public transportation are often targeted for gradual elimination. This has brought economic hardships to many in both rural and urban areas. With less government economic support, people turn to multiple-income generating activities, some through home-based self-employment. Such policies compel people to create other opportunities to offset the removal of government subsidies. For many, the only option is to engage in international migration (Staudt 1999). Under such difficult economic conditions, having access to foreign currencies offers access to both local- and foreign-made consumer goods. For many who do not have such access, going abroad to seek better economic opportunities remains the most viable option.

In mapping out the forces and circumstances spurring the migration of West African women to the United States, a common but often overlooked structural issue is the frequent economic spiraling and downturn in cocoa production in the hinterlands of West Africa and the role women play in the planting, harvesting, and marketing of cocoa beans. Ghana, the Ivory Coast, and Togo are all major producers of cocoa. Enormously lucrative as a primary commodity that brings foreign exchange to these countries (Ghana, Togo, and the Ivory Coast), the production of this cash crop drew young men and women from the rural areas to the cocoa belt. At times, entire families migrated to these centers to work as migrant farmers. Some of these families transformed their economic status by coming to own cocoa farms, bringing vast hectares of land under cultivation. Ownership of the land and the added value brought about by cocoa cultivation profited several of these families headed by both patrilineal and matrilineal kin. Though land tenure rights have made it difficult for most women to own cocoa farming lands outright, some women in the region have been successful in passing the land and the cocoa production economy on to their heirs, particularly in the southern tier cocoa-producing areas.

For women in the northern areas where Hausa and Muslim religious practices are found, land issues remain tenuous for many women. Hausa women do not inherit land except as trustees for their sons. Hausa men believe that women's inheritance of land is unnecessary, as they (women) are catered for by their husbands or male guardians who do not farm (Wanyeki 2003, 11). In matrilineal and patrilineal descent areas of West Africa, the land area brought under the production of cocoa by women is very small. This is due to the fact that land rights are often restricted to usufruct which allowed men to obtain more control over the land. Even where land ownership rights are structured along the lines of community property or kinship land, ownership rights still required women to pay rent for land utilization, including providing a share of the crop yield to male land overseers. With what they are able to produce on the land (particularly the production of cocoa, beans, groundnuts, and maize), some women are able to generate sufficient economic resources to met their day-to-day expenditures. Others are able to save enough to fund the education of their children, including sponsoring some of them for urban migration, and later, international migration. This sponsorship initially takes the form of providing primary and secondary education for girls, and later, for those who are successful in passing nationally standardized tests, better opportunities often come in the form of family defined avenues for pursuing higher education abroad.

The lack of comprehensive institutional structures to ensure that the poor are taken care of by their respective governments is a major push factor informing the necessity of engaging in regional, international, or some other form of migration. The focus of these countries is currently on solving more pressing infrastructural problems, like building roads, schools, and hospitals, or laying the foundation for economic and industrial expansion in both the public and private sectors to promote the hiring of school graduates. Other pressing needs may include spending valuable resources to contain civil strife and political instability in the hope that this will create the necessary conditions to attract foreign and indigenous capital investments, potentially sparking an economic renaissance. The challenges are daunting and the available resources meager for several of these countries as the sources of foreign aid continue to dwindle. Even with foreign aid, the preconditions that donors often attach to these loans may lead to the removal of subsidies that the poor have become dependent upon, causing job loss or mass redeployments and the sale and divestiture of government shares in vital state-owned enterprises.

The historical spread and distribution of economic and industrial activities has also created uneven levels of development across West Africa as well as Africa as a whole. European colonialists concentrated on the development of the national and regional capital districts almost to the exclusion of economic developments in other parts of these countries. The infrastructural systems needed for ensuring economic, cultural, and political developments started and ended in these large cities. The railways, road transportation networks, port facilities, educational institutions, government offices, hospitals, and the centers of art and culture were all located in the cities. Rural areas were completely ignored, though their resources were highly prized. Rural centers of food, agricultural raw materials, and mineral production were linked with feeder roads to enable the safe transportation of goods to the coast for shipment to the West. The niche that the rural areas have had since colonial times until now has yet to change. Despite their contribution to overall national and regional development, these areas lack adequate roads, hospitals, industries, and wage-sustaining manufacturing establishments. Postindependence governments followed the colonial model by their continued neglect and lip service to develop rural Africa. The disparities in the distribution of economic development projects between rural and urban areas are a determinant of rural to city migration. The urban areas typically have better infrastructures relative to their rural counterparts. Sustaining economic life in rural places is difficult. Economic development is stymied by lack of investment in the rural sector. The tendency is for rural dwellers to depend on the urban economy to supply their basic needs, including consumer goods. Thousands of rural folks are pushed out as a result of the impoverishment faced by many in the rural areas. For those who are compelled to leave because of economic reasons, migration to an urban center, or possibly to the West, is the preferred option.

Rural and Urban Youth Unemployment and Migration

Desirous of having some of the amenities enjoyed by urban areas, rural dwellers continue their flock to urban centers in search of jobs. With this persistent migration of the youth, the elderly have been left behind in the rural areas. Agriculture and food production, the lifeblood of some of West Africa's rural areas, have stymied. Additionally, there are structural constraints brought about by increasing population growth as infant mortality rates dwindle in West Africa. The pressure of unchecked population growth on the quality of life and on economic resources is immense. The persistence of high fertility rates means that family size continues to be relatively higher in West Africa than in other developing regions such as Malaysia or Brazil.

Among college-educated and middle-class West African urbanites, fertility rates have dropped and the average number of children per household is four compared to almost seven per rural or agrarian family. The economic cost of providing quality education and health care for these children and their families is staggering. The resulting high levels of rural poverty feed the caravan of international migration. The absence of a robust program for rural economic and industrial development has resulted in a cultural ethos among West Africans that to gain social mobility, one must look beyond the rural environment to fulfill one's aspirations. The development of self-sustaining, medium-sized towns and cities with mixed but robust economies interlaced with available utilities (electricity, hospitals, quality housing, roads, schools, water), would assist in the retention of West Africa's rural population.[5]

Over 60 percent of West Africa's population is under thirty years old. With the bulk of West Africa's population residing in the rural areas (65 percent), it has become very difficult for the governments to provide employment for rural youth who complete elementary or secondary school. As most of the youth are reluctant to embrace farming as a career, many are forced to look to urban centers for employment. A direct result of this rural-urban drift is overurbanization and the rise of shantytowns or slums (*zongos*) surrounding major cities like Lagos, Accra, Abidjan, Freetown, Banjul, and Monrovia. Youths who are fortunate find employment in the government sector, but many have to fend for themselves, performing odd jobs. If they have no source of support, their only recourse is to join the throng of youth who hawk their wares on the busy streets of capitals like Freetown, Dakar, Accra, Lagos, and Lomé, to name just a few. Every inch of public space and pavement is a potential spot for hawking consumer wares.

Hawa's case is illustrative of the pressures faced by rural youths to find new economic niches away from home. When Hawa completed middle school in rural Gambia, she wanted to continue her education at the secondary-school level and possibly enter the university. Her parents, both peasant rice farmers, had to work extra hard to pay for her school clothes, tuition, and fees. With seven other siblings to provide for, Hawa's family faced mounting economic problems. All the siblings helped on the rice paddy that Hawa's parents owned. After the harvest, the girls in the family bagged the rice in small polythene bags, put them on a wooden tray, and walked through the local markets carrying their ware and calling for buyers. Recognizing that the cultivation and sale of rice was not easing the family's economic plight, Hawa decided to go to Bathurst. Here, she could sell consumer goods and earn more money. Her parents were reluctant to let her go but the family's economic situation was becoming dire. When Hawa arrived in Bathurst, she joined several other youth who had been recruited by wholesalers and retailers to carry and sell consumer goods in the streets of Bathurst. At the end of the day's work, these urban youth were paid a token wage, not even enough to afford a nutritious supper.

The majority of Hawa's friends had left the agricultural areas of the country to make a living in the city. According to Hawa, several of them sent back a large portion of what they earned to their parents in the villages. At times, the wholesalers and retailers did not pay them for days, and for some of the youth, this led to begging for alms and panhandling. Exploited, abused, and undernourished, some of the youth would use cardboard and corrugated panels to construct a place to sleep at night. According to Hawa, "Life was very hard in West Africa. Our leaders have failed to meet the basic needs of our people. We are experiencing a brain drain to the West because we cannot support ourselves anymore. We need a bold and fresh start. We severed colonial ties from Europe over 50 years ago when most of the countries of West Africa attained political independence. More than five decades after independence, we have nothing to show to the rest of the world, except poverty and miseries."

Hawa's friend, Fatima, also completed middle school and was working as a street vendor in Bathurst. When Hawa learned that Fatima was going to join a group of four women who intended to travel to Cape Verde, she decided this was the opportune moment to leave Gambia. Traveling in a boat from Gambia to Cape Verde, the four women arrived safely and were able to find work after two weeks. Hawa and Fatima lived among a small enclave of Gambian immigrants. According to Hawa and Fatima, the prevailing ambition among Gambian transplants in Cape Verde was to work and eventually make the passage to the United States. Some had been successful, and Hawa and Fatima anticipated that it would soon be their turn. After thirteen months in Cape Verde, working odd jobs and living in a cramped room with six others without any modern amenities, Hawa and Fatima earned enough money to show proof of financial support at a U.S. consulate, a necessary requirement to secure a visitor's visa to enter the United States. Assisted by friends, the two settled in Minneapolis and found work with a janitorial company. The women used informal networks set up by prior African immigrants to locate jobs or be placed for employment by agents who, for a fee, will often overlook whether immigrants are certified to work or not. Hawa noted that the networks and job placement agents would typically match women with specific jobs based upon their skills. For most of the women, Hawa suggested, the labor recruiters often found them jobs as domestic helpers or cooks or in cleaning jobs and elderly care. Looking back at their experiences, both Hawa and Fatima believe that the lack of entry-level employment opportunities for rural and urban youth in West Africa is a primary reason for migration. Channeling the energies of West African urban and rural youth, and school-leavers in general, into gainful industrial and manufacturing jobs or in skills retraining is imperative if youth migration is to be curbed.

In a bid to tap the economic potential of every family member to ameliorate the problem of poverty, West Africa's children are often-times exploited for their economic value. Meanwhile, their education and well-being are sacrificed. Children are viewed as assets in the fight against poverty, and as soon as they reach, in a growing number of cases, age eight, they are put to work in the urban centers, particularly in the bustling commercial and business centers, where they sell a wide range of consumer products. Some serve as head porters, carrying loads of commercial goods from one part of the city to another in the tropical sun. For those children who are fortunate, their day at the market centers may begin only after they have come home from school. But despite mandatory laws requiring children under eighteen years old to attend school, many parents view their education as a waste of hard-earned family resources. The money that these child laborers make forms a significant portion of their family's total income. For a growing number of these children, the end of the day's work may be followed by roaming the streets and congregating under market stalls or kiosks that also serve as places of sleep. These children are not likely to make it to universities or other tertiary institutions of learning in West Africa. Some of them will finish primary or elementary school with yet another few going on to finish secondary or grammar school. Sooner rather than later they will join the burgeoning ranks of prospective international migrants seeking greener pastures in the United States or other Western countries. Life in the urban centers hardens these children who, upon becoming young adults, will become prime candidates for, first, interregional migration in West Africa, and second, international migration to the West in search of better economic opportunities.

Persisting youth unemployment and underemployment in the region are major catalysts for international migration. The inability of both the public and private sectors to create more jobs will continue to exacerbate the outlook for gainful employment. Unable to make ends meet and confined to a life of abject poverty and deprivation, many of the region's youth look outside West Africa for meeting their economic goals. Unless sustained and concerted efforts are implemented for the entire region and, by extension, the entire continent of Africa, these youth will continue to form the core of "foot immigrants" who will use every form of transportation possible to reach the shores of Europe and, ultimately, the United States. Graduates from all levels of education will continue to swell the ranks of the unemployed and underemployed. For college and university graduates, the possibility of finding gainful employment is of major concern. These graduates are not able to contribute their full quota to national development due to the problem of unemployment and underemployment. They are therefore likely to join the ranks of those who will seek better economic opportunities far away from Africa. This further exacerbates an already precarious brain drain, which is now a major obstacle to economic growth and development.

Immigration Policies and Preparations for Leaving

Immigration policies in the countries of migrant destinations are as important as the motivations or the rationales that prospective migrants frame to inform their decision to leave. According to Morrison, Schiff, and Sjoblom (2008, 20), immigration laws and policies in the country of migrant-intended destination is an important component of a person's migration decision. Among prospective immigrants in West Africa, there is intense interest in every aspect of U.S. immigration policy. The process entails learning about specific laws, when they were passed, the goals of the laws, impacts of the laws on current and future immigrants, and how to navigate the boundaries of the law to the benefit of the immigrant. Part of this learning process may entail finding out about the financial and legal resources that will be needed to obviate the law. The goal is simply to be well-informed about the expectations associated with their migration and at the same time explore and create opportunities to stay a couple of steps ahead of U.S. immigration policies and officials. Young people openly chat about these policies in the cabarets, cafes, barbershops, and, indeed, in most social gatherings. During these conversations, ways and means to obviate any barriers that prospective migrants will encounter if they make it to the United States are discussed. Information about the latest immigration laws and its implications for prospective migrants are frequently discussed by family members. Networks that will facilitate employment upon arrival are sought as well.

For the thousands of skilled and unskilled West Africans who desire to migrate to the United States, restrictive immigration policies have not thwarted their motivations or plans to enter the United States. When West Africans congregate in small and large social circles to chat about traveling abroad, they often focus on what they have to do to migrate to the West, but they rarely express concern over the tightening of immigration policies in America and other Western countries. The perception is that once they arrive, they can find an economic niche somewhere, with or without valid working-authorization documents.

Finding ways around complex immigration laws upon arrival in the United States is an art, if not a science. The West Africans know about the underground and informal labor market where there is a high demand for cheap labor. They are also aware of the amnesty and guest-worker provisions sometimes made by the advanced countries to ensure a steady supply of skilled and unskilled labor. Moreover, they observe that many of those who travel to the United States overstay and do not voluntarily come back unless they commit a felony crime and are apprehended, therefore becoming subject to deportation proceedings. In other words, West Africans perceive that they can successfully migrate to the United States, legally or otherwise. The prospective migrant's favorable perception of what they stand to gain in America (economically or culturally) certainly makes the risk-taking worthwhile. For the prospective migrant, this risk-taking is not only worthwhile but also a rational calculus premised on the perception that earlier or past migrants were able to find ways to avoid immigration authorities.

The reasons why West African women migrate to the United States are varied. The most frequently cited reasons for migration, in order of frequency, include reunification with family members who are already in the United States (35 percent); the pursuit of postsecondary or postgraduate education (22 percent); seeking refugee status due to wars, civil strife, and political instability (18 percent); finding employment (15 percent); taking advantage of the immigration diversity lottery system (8 percent), and other reasons (2 percent).

Many West African immigrant women are beneficiaries of the 1986 Immigration Reform and Control Act (IRCA), which was passed by the U.S. Congress and signed into law by President Ronald Reagan. This legislation sought to curtail and control illegal immigration (Cerrutti and Massey 2004); legalize the status of undocumented immigrants; and penalize employers who knowingly hire undocumented workers. Thousands of immigrants, including some of the West African women in the country at that time, became beneficiaries of IRCA (Cornelius 1990). For many West Africans with relatives in the United States, IRCA afforded many of them the chance to join and reunite with siblings. It is frequently the norm that well-established immigrants who have become naturalized citizens or hold permanent residency status will sponsor relatives to come to the United States. The process is tedious and painstakingly long for those women who come to join relatives who hold a permanent resident status and who are not yet naturalized. On the average, it took some of these women seven years before they were granted a visa by a U.S. consular office to enter the country. For those women who joined a spouse, the waiting period for a visa was about five years. The waiting period is further aggravated by the difficulties involved in navigating the bureaucratic thicket of applying for and securing a valid passport in Africa prior to embarking upon the journey.

For those women who were qualified to petition the U.S. government for a visa following the passage of IRCA, most described the predeparture process as challenging and daunting. Some of them (65 percent) mentioned having to pay bribes to expedite official processing of travel documents in West Africa. Some had to travel long distances away from their homes to obtain the passport forms and to check on the status of the application once it was submitted to the passport office. Some of the women relied on the assistance of passport brokers who, for a prenegotiated sum of money, would handle all the paperwork, including checking the status of the application. National and regional passport offices in West Africa are usually located in the capital cities and regional administrative and business centers. For those women who lived far away from these centers, the process involved in preparing to apply for a passport, visa, or health and medical certification could be laborious and daunting. Some of the women indicated that they had to travel to these centers and stay for a week or two at a time while processing their travel documents. Despite the administrative problems that a majority of the women encountered as they made preparations to come to the United States, these problems pale in comparison to the distress experienced by the refugee women in the study. For these women, the process of arriving in the United States was involuntary. Considering that they had to flee for safety from the ravages of war or civil disturbances, many of them did not have the luxury to plan their migratory journeys. This theme is examined in the next chapter.

The data show that for some of the immigrant women (particularly those who were not direct beneficiaries of IRCA), the journey to the United States was sometimes circuitous and emotionally and physically strenuous. Some of the women engaged in chain or stepwise migration, leaving for a temporary sojourn in another ECOWAS-member country, such as Nigeria, Senegal, Ghana, or the Ivory Coast. This was the first leg of a long trip to the West. After finding employment and working for awhile to save money, the second leg of the trip took some of the women to destinations such as Egypt, Sudan, Libya, South Korea, the Philippines, China, Taiwan, Malaysia, and Eastern Europe. Once they arrived at the second stage of their migration, they may find work, save money, and qualify for a visitor's visa to any of the Western countries, particularly the United Kingdom, Canada, or the United States. Pushed out from their respective countries as a result of dire economic and political morass, some of these women risked their lives by paying various sums of money to traffickers who took them from one locale to another.

Akosua's migratory passage from Ghana first took her to Nigeria during the early 1980s. Like the hundreds of thousands of Ghanaians who flocked to Nigeria during this time, her goal was to find work in the booming economy of oil-rich Nigeria. Ghanaians left their country to chase the Nigerian *naira*, which, during the 1970s and early 1980s, was a stronger currency than the American dollar and almost at parity with the British sterling. Ghanaians from all walks of life headed to Nigeria in what was known as the *agege* phenomenon.[6]

In Nigeria, Akosua became a consumer trader, selling Dutch wax prints and lace materials. By her account, she was earning more money in Nigeria than she did in Ghana, where she had been laid off from her civil service job. Unfortunately for Akosua, the Nigerian government passed a law that all Ghanaians had to leave the country. There was an economic and political uproar. Some saw the expulsion as a knee-jerk retaliatory reaction from the Nigerian government, scapegoating foreigners for the country's social and economic ills. The expulsion order was seen as a retaliatory measure designed to pay Ghana back for an earlier expulsion of Nigerians and other aliens under that country's Aliens Compliance Order during the tenure of Prime Minister Dr. Kofi Abrefa Busia.

Traveling on foot in many instances, with their personal belongings on their heads, thousands of Ghanaians headed out of Nigeria toward the Ghanaian border. Many were robbed along the way. Ako-sua was one of the Ghanaians forced to flee from Nigeria. Rather than return to Ghana, where economic and political conditions were dire, she headed to Cameroon, where she lived and worked for six months. Later, she applied and was granted a visitor's visa to France, where she stayed for a year. Before her French visa expired, she applied for a visitor's permit to enter Canada for six weeks as a tourist. Her visa application was approved because she was able to demonstrate to the Canadian consulate that she had enough money to support herself while in Canada. Days before the visa was to expire, she managed to renew it for another six weeks. Meanwhile, she was making prepara-tory plans to enter the United States through the Pacific Northwest border. Knowing that her visa was not going to be renewed further, and aided by a friend, she was able to illegally cross the border into the United States.

Akosua's migratory experience took her through three countries before arriving in the United States. In her words, the mass expulsion from Nigeria was a blessing: "It gave me the chance to implement and put in place a plan to eventually get to the U.S., my long-term dream. Some of the Ghanaians who were with me when the expulsion order was announced did not go back home. They initially repatriated elsewhere before finally coming to the U.S. Ghana's situation was very bad then (economically and politically). Only those who had not saved enough or were not gainfully employed carried their worldly possessions on their heads and headed home to Ghana."

Akosua's sister, who also joined the Ghanaian exodus to Nigeria, went home to Ghana after the Nigerian government's expulsion of illegal aliens. Unlike Akosua, she had not been able to save enough money before the forced repatriation. When she got to Ghana, things were tough. For nearly a year, she was without any gainful employment. With her secondary-school-leaving certificate, she could not even find an office job. Her reasons for leaving Ghana were framed by the cyclical downturn in the country's economy, coupled with the erosion of civil order. As she remarked, referencing the 1970s and 1980s:

These were dark periods in Ghana's history. Everywhere in the country, there was an economic collapse. The economic pinch was felt by all, including those in the armed forces and the police. Inflation was hyper. The economy stagnated. Corruption was rampant. The mili-tary were ruthless. Smuggling and foreign currency trafficking were common. The market women charged exorbitantly for everything. And people feared the military. The economic and political conditions in Ghana pushed me out again. I thought at that time it was best to struggle and make it in Nigeria where one was assured of getting something rather than stay in Ghana where things were deteriorating. I bet on Nigeria then, and I never regretted doing so.

Crossing into Nigeria a second time was another fresh start for Akosua's sister. She followed in her sister's previous line of work, selling Dutch wax prints. She started saving almost all her income. Two years after arriving back in Nigeria, she had saved enough to leave Africa. Her choice of destination was the former East Germany because visas were not required for entry at that time. "I arrived in Berlin not knowing anyone. This was in the middle of winter. Fortunately, I had some money on me. I met a few Africans, and they all proved helpful in assisting me find a job," according to Akosua's sister. While there, she worked for two more years and saved enough money to obtain a visitor's visa to Holland, where she discovered a thriving Ghanaian community. It was this experience that made her come to realize the large number of Ghanaians who had left the country. In Holland, she felt almost like she was living in Ghana. The Ghanaians she encountered were all living very well by African standards. They straddle between European and African cultures, living out their economic dreams, albeit faraway from home in Africa, and manifesting blended cultural and ethnic identities representing their migratory experiences. They had African foods at the African stores and markets. Jobs were plentiful as long as one was willing to do odd jobs. Some with shortwave radios were able to tune in to news from home. Ghanaian musicians and cultural troupes often visited to perform for the immigrants. There were daily flights from Amsterdam to Accra. New arrivals brought news from home. They all followed, with keen interest, the downward economic and political spiraling of Ghana. One of the Ghanaians was able to provide her a contact in the United States who sent her an invitation letter, which she took to the U.S. consular office in order to apply for a visitor's visa. Upon being granted the visa, she headed straight to twin cities of Minneapolis and Saint Paul to reunite with relatives who had fled Ghana nearly a decade before the economic situation got worse.

Currently an undocumented worker, Akosua's sister holds two jobs and is quietly living her American dream with her two children. Like other immigrants who do not have valid working papers, she is relying on the magnanimity of family members who have allowed her to use their immigration documents to secure employment. She now feels somewhat safe because she knows that her two children are both American citizens. This, to her, is "insurance for the short term until

Congress enacts legislation to legalize the status of illegal immigrants with American-born children." She is patiently waiting for that day.

Upon arrival at their final destination, a majority of West African immigrant women find employment in the service sector, particularly in the hospitality, meat packaging, construction, and janitorial sectors. In Minnesota, some of the women have found gainful employment in the poultry processing plants in the southwestern and southern parts of the state. For those with professional skills, particularly in nursing and paramedical or allied health, the prospects of finding employment are bright due to the high demand for health care workers. Before arriving in the United States, a majority of the women had formed distinct goals and strategies as to how they would engage the employment sector. For those whose educational credentials fell below what is required to land them a good job, the first step is usually to enroll at a community or technical college to hone their skills. Areas of study are carefully selected to ensure that there would be employment upon graduation. Continuing education is the preferred mechanism for achieving social mobility and enhancing the prospects of earning higher wages.

Technology-based employment is also gaining popularity among West African immigrant women. This area of work has not traditionally been a source of employment for African women immigrants in the United States due to the fact that only a small number of them are willing to pursue this line of professional work. Most of the women employed in the technology sector have a technical education background, training they acquired since entering the United States. The key to their gradual but successful entry into the technology sector was spurred by the popularity of community and technical schools over universities among new immigrants in the United States. Recent immigrants have embraced two-year community and technical schools because of their lower fees and tuition, smaller class sizes, hands-on and experiential learning modules, and the wide range of professional courses that they offer. Moreover, most of these courses lead directly to gainful employment. The pay per hour among this group of women averages $14 and comes with health care benefits and employer-defined retirement benefits.

Jemina and Rose, both immigrants from Liberia, have been successful in finding work in the technology sector. Both women were able to secure a job upon completion of a certificate program in network computing and computer technology. For the two West African women, employment was assured by their community college's career center even before they graduated. Initially, the two women expressed apprehension about entering a male-dominated sector of employment, but the skills they acquired boosted their confidence that they could work shoulder to shoulder with their male counterparts without any threats or intimidation. According to Jemina, being a woman is not an important issue as far as working in the technology sector. "All the women who work with me have the same credentials as their male counterparts and we do not tell them what to do, neither do they boss us around insisting that we learn from them. There is mutual recognition and respect and it goes without saying that we women are capable of doing the same job as men," Jemina said. For her part, Rose indicated that immigrant women working in the technology sector often must prove to fellow workers that they are capable of doing the work. "It is not about affirmative action. It is about who can perform the job very well. I do believe it is about education and the skills I have acquired. My gender did not play a big role in my hiring," she said.

Abigail, an immigrant from Sierra Leone, also found work in the technology sector. She completed a program of study in computer technology and was successfully placed in an unpaid internship with a major computer networking and software development company based in Minneapolis and Saint Paul. Upon the completion of the internship, the company offered her full-time employment with benefits. With the job offer, and an employer that was willing to support her application for permanent residence status, Abigail was able to fulfill a long-term economic goal: to seek the kind of employment that would enable her to accumulate funds toward the sponsorship of her relatives in Sierra Leone to come to the United States.

For Jemina, Rose, and Abigail, entry into the technology sector was facilitated not only by their educational training but also by liberal immigration laws favoring foreign-born workers who have acquired training in computer and technology related skills. In 2000, Congress passed legislation increasing the annual visas (H-1B visas) allotted to foreign-born high-tech workers from an original cap of 20,000 visas to 195,000. The petition to increase the cap was led by computer technology companies in California. Congress granted the increases. However, the government expected the increase to 195,000 to be temporary, proposing that after 2000, H-1B visas will reverse to the original number of 20,000. However, this did not materialize. The technology companies kept the pressure on Congress to maintain the higher threshold of visas for skilled immigrants. This resulted in hundreds of thousands of H-1B visas being issued beyond the limit. The pressure from the technology industries for more visas died down only after the technology sector bubble of the 1990s.

By all accounts, Jemina, Rose, and Abigail were fortunate. A heavy burden was lifted once valid work permits were secured. With this comes empowerment, protection in the work place, and the opportunity to live one's American dream. This ensures a pathway to eventual naturalization. Should any of these West African immigrant women face job loss, they stand to collect unemployment benefits, possibly including social welfare assistance for their children. For those women without any valid working documents, working underground can be traumatizing. The need to maintain steady employment and earn an income to support themselves and their children puts immense pressure on some of the women to endure mistreatment and unfair labor practices by their employers or supervisors.

When some of the women who worked with Abila (an immigrant from the Gambia living in Minneapolis) approached her about forming a labor union to agitate for more pay, better working conditions, and increased benefits, she was skeptical and afraid that this might affect her relationship with the supervisor and eventually lead to the loss of her job. She was determined not to have anything to do with the organizers of the union even though she supported their agenda and covertly attended some of their meetings. To Abila, an hourly wage rate of $12 was more than she ever dreamed of earning. Though living in the United States, she would convert her hourly pay to her home currency, which enabled her to observe that she was earning far more than most of her Gambian counterparts at home where the average daily wage was less than a dollar. Despite the fact that the costs and standard of living are much higher in the United States than in the Gambia, Abila rationalized that the opportunity to earn almost a hundred times what most Gambians make in a day is an opportunity she ought to protect because it allows her to support fifteen close and extended relatives at home.

Abila eventually explained her reluctance to support the union to her coworkers, a third of whom were from Africa. She rationalized that

there are thousands of Africans in this city who will want a job that pays $12 an hour even if there are no retirement or health care benefits. And being a single mother means that I cannot afford to have any periods of protracted unemployment. I feel very bad for my African sisters here who are forcing the issue of unionization. How can you agitate for unionization when you do not have legal status in this country? Most of them do not have a safety net should they be fired. Sometimes, those of us who are immigrants have to endure and tolerate wage and benefits inequities or even poor working conditions. Some of us have worked in conditions back home that are far worse than what pertains here in America.

In defining the trajectories of their immigrant lives in the United States, many West African women embrace the notion that continued and long-term participation in the labor force is far more crucial to them than the relationships they form and establish with male partners. The overarching reason is that in the long term, the fulfillment of economic goals provides a safety net, a cushion from the uncertainties of marital or conjugal relationships.

As they engage in the labor force to improve upon their economic standing in the United States, some West African women have come to accept that there is a price they have to pay for concentrating their energies outside the home environment, including sacrificing time spent with their children or other family members. But as one of the women indicated, "for most American women who are single and raising their children, work outside the home is an imperative if one is to have enough money to pay for childcare, accommodations, food, and other expenses. In this, we are all united with a common goal."

To find employment, the immigrant women rely on social networks they form upon arrival with others from their ethnic, tribal, alumni, or national associations. Included in the networks are religious organizations and print media that cater to different immigrant groups based on national origins. Networking facilitates access to the employment niches that other immigrant women have already established in various employment and labor centers across the country. Information about prospective employers who do not check work permits is disseminated through these informal networks. More established immigrant workers often recommend recently arrived immigrants to their employers. The same networks are used to recommend new immigrants to American families seeking domestic maids or nannies for their children. The use of these informal networks encourages new immigrants toward occupational integration into the host society. The result is that in certain sectors of employment, there appears to be a clustering of West African immigrant women. Such clusters of coethnics from the same country, tribal, clan, ethnic, or geographic region can be found working in the poultry, hospitality, nursing home, and assisted-living establishments in Minnesota and the Midwest.

In Aba's case, having relatives and friends already working in the hospitality industry proved very helpful. Shortly upon arriving in Minneapolis, her sister and some friends introduced her to the management of a major hotel chain located near Edina, a suburb of Minneapolis-St. Paul. She was hired the same day and assigned to an apprenticeship status under the tutelage of her friends. Following her probationary period, her net pay increased from $250 per week to $370 per week based on eight hours of work per day. She took on an additional job that paid $120 per week, mainly working at night and on weekends. To maximize her cost of living, she stayed with another immigrant woman from West Africa in a three-bedroom apartment in close proximity to her places of work. By sharing the rent and all utilities, the women were able to save substantial money, which they either send home or save. The existence of a growing and established community of West Africans in the Twin Cities metropolitan area of Minnesota facilitates the job search process for many of the women immigrants. Even when they have acquired legal status, some of the immigrants prefer using informal networks to locate jobs in their communities. It is these same informal networks that most West Africans rely on to find employment back home. Leeriness of using formal employment agencies to find jobs is symptomatic of the mistrust and the insecurity that many new immigrants feel when they have to deal with formal social service agencies.

The West African immigrant women moved to the United States to fulfill an economic need. Though they utilized many forms of conventional and unconventional means of traveling to arrive at their destinations, the desire to achieve a higher standard of living relative to what they were accustomed to in Africa was the main driving force motivating them to come to the United States. Microlevel factors such as family economic status, the desire of the family to improve upon their earnings, the pressure on relatively successful family members to take care of immediate and sometimes extended family units, the ever-increasing use of children for street hawking and manual labor in the informal economy, and the problem of youth unemployment were all core determinants of the decision to emigrate. Added to these factors is the cultural notion among West Africans that economic success can hardly be attained at home and the staunch belief held among West Africans that non-movers are more disadvantaged economically and fare worse than their counterparts who risk travel to the West in search of better standards of living.

At the macro level, additional problems influence migration to the United States. These include stymied economic and industrial production, the inability of the public and private sectors to absorb the region's secondary and postsecondary school graduates, and the uneven distribution and bias in the selection and location of economic development projects favoring the urban over rural areas. Other factors might include the persistence of ethnic and tribal warfare, often resulting in the forceful uprooting of hundreds of thousands of people who become refugees inside their own national borders. The governments of some of the West African countries have come to see the mass exodus of their inhabitants to the West as a mixed blessing. The brain drain that this exodus causes is felt by the inability of the countries to staff and meet the health care needs of their citizens. These health care personnel prefer to come to the West where they are assured higher salaries with benefits and the opportunity to work with modern medical equipment. On the other hand, when they leave home, West Africans continue to maintain ties with their home communities, remitting regularly, and thereby continuing to assist in raising the overall economic standing of their immediate and extended family members. The desire to work abroad in the West and to be in a position to remit home is therefore a primary motivation behind the decision to emigrate.

The lack of a concerted and systemic national or international program to reduce the exodus of skilled and unskilled West Africans is a major concern for the governments of the region. Of equal concern is the absence of poverty-reduction programs. From an economic and public policy perspective, passivity on the part of West African governments reveals the tacit acknowledgement that international migration has become an acceptable mechanism for alleviating the economic hardships faced by their citizens. Overreliance on the West as a source of consumer goods and employment for their citizens stifles local production and manufacturing, which has the potential to create jobs and employ more school graduates. With the approval of government agencies in these countries, international labor recruiters come to West Africa to recruit cheap labor, particularly for construction projects and manual labor in the Middle East. In essence, labor exportation to foreign destinations is now considered an acceptable proposition because it links these poor countries to the global and transnational labor pipeline.

The short- and long-term shortages of workers in certain sectors of the European and North American economies (agriculture, food processing, construction, and hospitality services), coupled with the aging of their populations and the proliferation of foreign guest-worker provisions, continue to entice West African women to hedge their bets by using every available method to enter the West. Chronically unemployed and underemployed youths and adults alike in the region's capital cities capitalize on the opportunity to work in the Middle East, where they expect to earn more money than they are accustomed to earning in West Africa. For many of them who are recruited, the opportunity to work in the Middle East provides a gateway to the West, particularly to the United Kingdom, Canada, and the United States. Policies to manage the exodus of skilled and unskilled citizens must be addressed by the governments in the region. A beginning point is to cast international migration as an integral component of national development initiatives. The goal of such initiatives is to ensure the use of bilateral and multilateral assistance to ensure robust economic growth and sustainability. This would ensure full economic and industrial production capacities, which could ultimately address the problem of population retention and minimize the brain drain.

Similarly, the retraining of unskilled youth in the rural and urban sectors to engage in more productive economic activities requiring small capital is warranted. The strengthening of child and youth labor laws to curb economic exploitation by adults could reduce the increasing number of youth who run away from home only to end up being recruited as prostitutes or into sexual enslavements in the Middle East. Lured by the prospects of earning high wages by recruiters, some girls may never return home or be seen by their families because of the rigid social controls exercised over them by the recruiters. For some of the girls, the need to provide economic assistance to their parents and other siblings may also motivate them to join the ranks of other girls from West Africa who have already made the trip to the Middle East.

For those women who traveled to the United States primarily to seek employment, it remains clear that economic motivations played a major role in their journey. In an American society in which employment is seen as a barometer of life chances, mobility, advancement, status, and class formation, West African immigrant women take every step to educate themselves about labor market conditions, often exchanging information about growth areas of the economy, changes in wages and benefits, and which employers are immigrant-friendly. Like their male counterparts who come to the United States, the women come to America to escape from the myriad of economic, social, and political problems confronting their respective countries. The desire to make money in the United States is so strong that every type or form of employment is considered to be better than the work performed back home in West Africa. The appeal of America as a land of abundant opportunity resonates throughout every fabric of West African society. Both skilled and unskilled West Africans, young and old, educated and uneducated, often spend years planning how to implement the journey to the West in search of greener pastures.

CHAPTER 4

GENDER AND FORCED MIGRATION

REBUILDING SHATTERED LIVES

The soldiers were ruthless. People carried machetes and administered instant justice on the spot on their foes. No one could stop them. Everyone was terrified, notably the children. Everything fell apart.

—Mina, a Liberian immigrant

People identify you purely by your racial and ethnic attributes. And being Black has become like a burden for me. We are not accepted here like we were in Denmark. The Danes were very kind to us and went out of the way to make sure we had everything we wanted. In America, people treat you with disdain and with a condescending attitude because you are Black.

—Kendra, a Sierra Leonean immigrant

This section presents a sociological rendering and portrait of West African refugee immigrants who have fled their war torn countries to seek safety in the United States. It describes the social and political factors that converged to shatter the lives of these women and their families. Structured to give voices to the contents and realities that these women had to contend with, the analysis portrays a people who emerged from the ravages of war to reconstruct a new life for themselves. The research follows the women as they strive to become incorporated and integrated in the affairs of their host societies and to forge inclusiveness. Having experienced extreme marginality and violence, the process whereby the women begin to reshape their lives offers a sociological glimpse into the cultural mechanisms that are actively at work to redefine or bring a new social order to the lives of the displaced and uprooted women. Again, the analysis employs the use of extensive narratives to tease out the new hopes and aspirations that are formed among the women upon their arrival in the United States and how they strategize to confront new problems and challenges presented by a new environment. As these women confront the uncertainties of not knowing what will happen to them from one day to another, the women (in their collective struggles to become), speak to the resiliency of the human spirit to overcome hardships and at the same time develop a sense of altruism to place and center the needs of relatives at home who have to struggle on a daily basis to face abject and grinding poverty.

Whether through a poem, a narrative, a song, or portraits of the family members they had lost, the women are able to capture the breadth and depth of their lived experiences, giving them form and meaning. Sometimes stigmatized, shunned, or excluded from the core society on the basis of their gendered powerlessness, class struggles, their blackness, and religious fervor, these women ultimately find niches for themselves, however tenuous and weak the adaptive niches for survival are articulated or realized in the host society. What is significant is the strident, deliberative, and rationalized manner in which these refugee women resolve major issues emanating from their interlocking transnational gendered identities to define their presence and identities in the United States. The new life they have in the United States is being shaped and influenced by many forces, including the learning of new roles, interactions with selected members and institutions of the host society, and other secondary groups such as minority and immigrant groups. In addition, their presence in the United States is also helping in redefining how they view their respective places of national origins. Whether they engage in the affairs of their home societies or not, these women ultimately help shape the discourses of social and economic progress currently occurring in their homelands. Fleeing from war to come to America as refugees and working to save money to build or purchase a house in their home countries is considered a triumph of the human spirit. America, the women attested, is a part of this ultimate, shared triumph.

There is an African proverb that states, "When elephants fight, it is the grass that suffers." This sage is applicable to the problems faced by the twin countries of Sierra Leone and Liberia during last two decades. When war came to these countries, it was the already struggling poor, village folks, the children, women, and the aged who had to suffer the untold consequences of being displaced, uprooted, and forced to involuntarily migrate as refugees. These people are the "grass" figuratively stumped and trampled upon by the "elephants" (those who fanned the flames of war, the military, their cronies, the politicians, warlords, and the power hungry elites who usually end up reaping the benefits and spoils of war). The pillaging, thievery, rape, and violence that attend to these instabilities are unfathomable to those who have not witnessed its disruptive impact on the lives of ordinary folks.

Internal and external conflicts in Africa continue to ravage the already fragile economic conditions in the African region as a whole. In Sierra Leone, Liberia, Somalia, the Democratic Republic of the Congo (DRC), Rwanda, Ivory Coast, and Ethiopia (to name a few), internal and external conflicts have resulted in the mass displacement of children, women, and the elderly. As Falola and Afolabi (2007) reported, more than 75 percent of the displaced in Africa's raging interethnic conflicts have been females and children. Refugee children and the elderly are even more susceptible to sexual enslavement and physical victimizations due to their vulnerabilities. The children experience alienation, traumas, and separation from their parents and family members. These traumas and their psychological consequences have lasting impacts on them and only some are able to recover from these abuses.

Deaths and physical maiming from live land mines often injure women and children as they go about performing their household and agricultural responsibilities (Falola and Afolabi 2007, 340). The institutions of state and civil society ceased to function, jeopardizing public security, and threatening the rule of law. Unfortunately, this is the saga of too many African countries since the demise of foreign colonization. The postcolonial militarization of political culture and the legitimization of violence as a means of conflict management and resolution continue to fracture intra- and interethnic and tribal tensions. The political unrests that have engulfed parts of the continent for nearly twenty years continue to cause the displacement of tens of thousands of people fleeing from their own military, rebel forces, and, at times, even their civilian governments. In such an atmosphere, the right of the people to live in peace and determine their own destiny is always lost, shattering aspirations that left the people of Sierra Leone and Liberia, for example, with no choice but to flee to nearby countries for their own protection.

On its part, Liberia, the oldest Republic in Africa with a population of nearly 4 million, remained a peaceful country until about 1980 when it, too, like the rest of Black Africa, was plunged into political and economic morass. Dubbed as the "Land of the Free" by freed

African American and Caribbean slaves returning from the United States, this West African country became an independent country in 1847. The new country had to strive to build its institutions, governance structures, and, like Sierra Leone, incorporate, or bring, sixteen ethnic groups into nationhood. The returning free slaves often clashed violently with the indigenous Black Africans who were the original settlers of the country. They dueled over citizenship rights, political participation, and over economic hegemony. Political powers were in the hands of the True Whig Party (TWP) and its leader, American-born Joseph Jenkins, who became the country's first president. For nearly a century and a half (1847–1980), the TWP dominated the affairs of the country, barely sharing power with the indigenous Blacks. This came to an end in 1980 when a master sergeant, Samuel Doe, staged a coup, invading Liberia from neighboring Sierra Leone, seized over the reigns of government and publicly executed President William Tolbert and some of the political hierarchy of the ruling TWP.

Doe's coup did not bring lasting peace to the republic. He started a policy whereby he brought members of his ethnic group, the Krahns, into the political and economic system. This caused interethnic rancor and conflicts among the general population, including the elite ranks of the American-backed TWP. Doe cemented his power in office in the 1985 elections, which, by all accounts, were rigged with fraud and corruption. Abortive coups were staged, albeit unsuccessfully, to get rid of Doe. Despite his heavy handedness and his crackdown on dissent, Doe was able to find an ally in Washington, D.C., with the Reagan Administration. In spite of his friendship with the United States, in 1989, Doe was overthrown by Charles Taylor, who had organized a band of rebel army soldiers to fight Doe. The conflict lasted for seven years (1989–96). Hundreds of thousands of Liberians were killed and massacred, including Doe. Taylor's government, the National Patriotic Front of Liberia (NPFL) presided over one of the bloodiest civil disturbances in Africa. Insurgent groups founded the United Liberation Movement of Liberia Democracy (ULIMO), which was based in Sierra Leone. Their principal goal was to oust Taylor's government. The ULIMO and the Taylor-led NPFL fought time and time again. As the fighting intensified, masses of Liberians suffered. The capital district of Monrovia had no electricity or running water, and food prices skyrocketed. Unemployment became chronic and political corruption and pillaging of state property became the norm. Efforts aimed at establishing peace and stability became elusive.

Taylor's government failed miserably to improve upon the economic circumstances of ordinary Liberians. The incessant wars and military skirmishes had taken a toll on the international standing of the country, choking investments and bringing a halt to the delivery of social service and the improvement of the country's infrastructure. Taylor tried to draw other countries in the region into the conflict. He supported the rebel group Revolutionary United Front (RUF) in Sierra Leone, thereby wasting the hard-earned resources of Liberia. Opposition factions led by the Movement for Democracy in Liberia (MODEL) and ULIMO joined together to fight Taylor. In 2003, Taylor came under international pressure to resign, as his forces were hemmed in by the opposition. Taylor left the country and went into exile in Nigeria. His departure calmed things down and led to the arrival of a UN peacekeeping force. A transitional government was installed. On October 11, 2005, elections were held and U.S.-educated economist and former finance minister Ellen Johnson-Sirleaf won, defeating international soccer star George Weah to become the first democratically elected woman president of Africa. Peace finally came but not without cost. Hundreds of thousands of refugees were displaced and uprooted as a result of the numerous wars and civil disorders. The bulk of the displaced took refuge in Ghana. Others fanned out to other countries in West Africa. The violence persisted, resulting in the deaths of innocent civilians. The war shattered the hopes and future prospects of building institutions to foster democracy and civil governance. More importantly, it shattered the dim prospects for rebuilding the tattered economy of the country.

The current geopolitical and economic saga of Sierra Leone and Liberia can be described as missteps, failed aspirations, lost opportunities, and unfulfilled dreams. It was to Freetown (Sierra Leone) and Monrovia (Liberia), the capital of these two West African countries, that returning slaves from the Americas flocked to after the abolishment of the transatlantic slavery. The returning slaves, often referred to as the Krios, marked the start of a British settlement colony. For example, Sierra Leone became a hub for education for all of British West Africa. For most of the twentieth century, the country was peaceful even when it was getting ready to transition from colonial rule to political independence and self-rule. At the cusp of her independence from Britain in 1961, Sierra Leone was a shining oasis and a beacon of hope. Moderate improvements in infrastructural developments (roads, hospitals, and schools) had been implemented by the pre- and postindependence regimes. Fouray Bay College was set up by the British, and it emerged as a premier tertiary institution of learning and higher education in Black Africa, leading the charge in the education of high caliber graduates who subsequently found jobs in both the public and private sectors of employment.

Naturally endowed with raw materials and minerals, foreign receipts derived from exportable commodities such as diamonds, cocoa, and coffee provided the postindependent government of Sierra Leone with adequate funds to spark the country's industrial and economic development. Agriculture is the mainstay of the country's economy, forming about 52 percent of the economy, with industry at 30 percent, and the service sector at 19 percent. The major ethnic groups are the Temne (30 percent), who live in the north, Mende (30 percent), who live in the south, and the Krio (1 percent).

Despite the fact that Sierra Leone was on the path to economic and political stability following independence, the period following the departure of the British has been marked by economic malaise and political corruption. The wealth from the lucrative diamond trade enriched small urban, educated, and business elites at the expense of the mass society. The average yearly income for ordinary Sierra Leoneans was about $220. Like other countries in the subregion, poverty, illiteracy, tribalism, and political corruption dominate the cultural and social landscape of the country. Growth stifled, causing political tensions in the country. Life expectancy is about forty-one years, and the infant mortality rate is 158 deaths per every 1,000 live births. The gross domestic product for 2006 is estimated at $1,200 billion.[1] Urban unemployment was in excess of 50 percent. Graduates from the country's secondary and tertiary institutions could not cope with the lack of unemployment and massive underemployment. The civil service did not fare well either. The country was ripe for a massive conflict with the potential of causing mass internal and external displacement of its citizens.

The instability that roiled Sierra Leone started immediately after the country gained its independence in 1961. Independence ushered in a Westminster-style parliamentary system led by the country's first prime minister, Sir Milton Margai of the Sierra Leone People's Party (SLPP). Margai's rule was marked by the consolidation of political independence and the integration of diverse ethnic groups into the nation-state, including the continuation of economic policies started by the British. Following Margai's death, his brother, Sir Albert Margai, became the prime minister. In March of 1967, national elections were held and the All Peoples Congress (APC), led by Siaka Stevens, came to power. Stevens's reign was short-lived when a military coup staged by Brigadier David Lansana placed Stevens and Margai under arrest. A second military coup was staged against Lansana. This coup reinstated Siaka Stevens as prime minister, and he ruled the country until 1985. Stevens's rule was characterized by political intimidation. All political party activities were proscribed except for the APC. This amounted to the declaration of one-party rule and the subsequent quelling of political dissent.

In 1985, Major General Joseph Saidu Momoh was elected president. Only the ruling party took part in this election. Upon winning the election, Momoh immediately took steps to reinstate multiparty politics. But Momoh's rule did not bring an end to the political corruption that started following the departure of the British, when the country gained independence. In 1991, the rebel group RUF, led by Corporal Foday Sankoh, started an insurrection against the government of Momoh. Sankoh's soldiers wanted control over the diamond-mining district and attacked the villages near the border shared with Liberia. In 1992, another coup was staged by Captain Valentine Strasser, who established the National Provisional Ruling Council (NPRC), sending Momoh into exile. Like Momoh's regime, Strasser continued fighting to quell the activities of RUF, which had then made significant gains capturing and bringing parts of the country under its tutelage. Again, the source of this bitter political contestation is to control the vast diamond wealth of the nation.

The international community did not know how to respond to the mounting political crisis and the continued impact of the devastation of the war on the lives of the common folks. The strife between the RUF and the NPRC intensified and hundreds, perhaps thousands by some accounts, perished. Hopes were high to end the carnage when another election was held in 1996. Ahmad Tejan Kabbah won the election and became president. But once again, hopes of firming up political stability were dashed. A coup led by Major Johnny Paul Koroma in 1997 served to overthrow President Kabbah. Koroma's regime, the Armed Forces Revolutionary Council (AFRC), attempted to forge a government of national unity by extending an olive branch to the RUF to become part of the new government. But the spiraling of the country's political fortunes persisted. Frustrated by the chronic political impasse, Nigeria intervened, overthrowing the AFRC and reinstating Kabbah, who later signed the Lomé Peace Agreement with the RUF. The outcome of the Lomé agreement was that it called for the establishment of the UN peacekeeping forces to maintain order and shore up an already fragile political system. Guided by greed and the desire to gain total control over the country, the RUF turned its attention toward destabilizing the country once again, this time taking up arms against the UN forces policing the fragile peace. A cease-fire to resolve this new impasse was implemented in Abuja, Nigeria, in 2000, but like the one that was finalized in Lomé, this one also failed. Guinea soldiers entered Sierra Leone and fought the RUF. There were calls for disarming and reintegrating factions of the RUF into political governance. This time, the parties were able to end the conflict. Kabbah was reelected, and hope that the peace would prevail was once again renewed. Attempts were made at reconciling the various factions. Victims of the wars were identified and a scheme was set up to provide them with compensation and restitution. As part of the reconciliation, a special court was set up by the UN to try those who had committed war crimes. Indictments were issued for the arrest of Charles Taylor, then president of Liberia, for his role in the atrocities. The leaders of the RUF were also indicted for war crimes. Taylor fled to Nigeria. While in exile there, he tried to flee, but he was captured and handed over to the Sierra Leone government for prosecution for crimes committed against humanity. It was against the backdrop of stymied and stillborn democracy, violence, and political chaos that Kendra and Lois were forced to flee Sierra Leone as the civil war ravaged their country. It was also the political instabilities described above that forced two Liberian women, Mia and Wilhelmina (Mina), and their four children to flee Liberia and seek refugee in Ghana.

Fleeing with the Clothes on Your Back: Voices of Refugee Women

In both Sierra Leone and Liberia, the turbulent tensions brought life to a standstill for everyone. Those who were able to flee to neighboring countries in West Africa became refugees. Kendra and Lois saw members of their family, young and old, forcefully recruited by the rebel group RUF to fight in the civil war with the government over the control of the lucrative diamond trade. RUF fighters, led by Foday Sankoh, a former corporal, attacked villages near the Liberian border, often abducting schoolchildren, who were forced into the role of child soldiers. Lois's nephew was just twelve years old when the rebels raided his school and forcefully took him and made him a soldier. Kendra reported a similar experience. Her niece was abducted, threatened to be killed if she did not join in the fight, and told not to contact anyone in her family.

During the ensuing crisis, several international agencies were providing humanitarian assistance for the victims. When they heard that an international charitable Christian organization was offering to resettle Sierra Leonean women and children in the Ivory Coast and

Ghana, Kendra and Lois started their long journey by trekking to the Ivory Coast. The two women, accompanied by their five children, traveled at night to avoid being apprehended or killed by RUF rebels. The journey was arduous and traumatic. Those fleeing were not sure if they would ever return to their homeland. All had to leave behind everything they owned to start afresh in the Ivory Coast. Finding a safer haven there brought some relief to Kendra and Lois and their families. Kendra and Lois stayed in the Ivory Coast for ten months.

"Life in the refugee camps was hellish. Male exploiters working for non-governmental humanitarian agencies traded donated food for sex with young girls under 15 years old and also raped some of them. For those women who reported such incidences, their family will be blacklisted and food and medical supplies withheld from them," Kendra hinted. Those women and their children who did not have any documents to prove nationality and status found themselves in precarious conditions. For these families, the chances of finding sponsorship were dim. And as Lois affirmed, "The registration papers are given to the male head of the households and usually some of them who have multiple wives and children pick and choose who will travel or accompany the family when sponsorship for resettlement is found by the United Nations High Commission for Refugees (UNHCR) or other refugee resettlement agencies." For Lois and Kendra, the flight to safety was fraught with problems. At border checkpoints, their personal belongings were searched and valuables were stolen by border patrol agents, policemen, and roving bandits. When they paused to rest at night, the fleeing group would often become the target of rival tribal cliques who, at times, were shelled with mortar attacks, resulting in the death of scores of fleeing persons.

While in the Ivory Coast, a Danish charitable organization launched a plan to resettle some of the refugees in Denmark. The first leg of their flight to freedom took Kendra and Lois and their children to Denmark. This was their first contact with the West. The sponsorship to flee to the West was undertaken by some members of the Lutheran Church in Denmark. The resettlement was considered temporary until such time that the two women could find a second or third country that would admit them for permanent resettlement. Narrating her experiences in Copenhagen, Lois described, in wonderment, the cultural shock she felt at the level of economic development and the standard of living in Scandinavia: "I was truly in a foreign land. I could never imagine the high standard of living I saw all around me. I had only seen these things in magazines and on television. Now it is real. I can feel its presence. Everything is planned and very orderly. Our leaders in Africa have failed us. Maybe the saying and the belief held by some that we have been cursed is true." For the first time in their lives, the two women and their children lived in their own fully furnished apartments, fervently having to learn to operate household appliances and gadgets they had never seen before. Social services provided them with vouchers for groceries and a pass that they could use for the rail and bus. The children were enrolled in a public school within walking distance from their apartment. Occasionally, and weather permitting, they rode their bikes to school. It was a change from the six-mile walk to and from school that they had to endure in West Africa.

The postarrival and adjustment process for the two women and their children was facilitated by their proficiency in English. The two women found employment with a cheese and yogurt company on the outskirts of Copenhagen. Though the distance from home to their work site involved considerable travel, the payoff was rewarding. Over a period of six months, social services weaned the two women off public assistance rolls. The Lutheran Church, however, continued providing the women with clothes and tuition payments to learn Danish. At the Danish language center, the two women met African refugees from Somalia, Ethiopia, and the Sudan. The sense of alienation was replaced with renewed hope as they established networks and ties with other Africans in Copenhagen. For the first time, the two women recognized that they were not the only ones displaced and uprooted from the ravages of war and violence. The presence of other Black African refugees eased the apprehensions associated with the adjustment of living in Scandinavia. The refugees often got together to organize parties and birthdays. The social gatherings fostered a sense of solidarity and shared goals among the refugees, helping the group members minimize the alienation and, at times, prejudice and discrimination they encountered.

Though not a self-sustaining and complete community, the African refugee enclave provided the two women and their offspring an Afro-centric life with all its promises and shortcomings. A sense of altruism prevailed among the refugees, and the level of social solidarity and group cohesiveness that existed among the refugees was facilitated by the fact that the majority of the African refugees admitted to Denmark were provided with living arrangements where there was a strong presence of other African refugees. To the Danes as a whole, this form of settlement was tantamount to residential segregation. To the African refugees, common settlement meant collective security and group enterprise to marshal group resources to weather individual and group hardships in a foreign and alien environment.

The refugees faced tremendous obstacles and challenges in their new society. Though foremost of these problems was discrimination and prejudice, a persistent problem had to do with how to ensure that their children did not suffer the lasting impact of the ravages of war and genocide. During the interviews with the two women, a constant refrain was that though forceful repatriation from home had devastated their lives and that of their children, they nonetheless felt safer and freer in Denmark than in Sierra Leone. The Danish perception of the refugees as victims and persons who are in dire need of charitable assistance somehow did not dampen the spirits and aspiration of the women to forge a new life for themselves and their children.[2] On their part, the two women remained ambivalent about their future status. Their country was embroiled in a brutal civil war. Civic and political culture had collapsed. Children were even abducted or recruited to join the ranks of the rebels fighting to control the diamond trade. As indicated, some of these child soldiers were sometimes forcefully taken away from their parents. Being refugees in Denmark was an ambiguous and tenuous status. Fear and apprehension that family members left behind in Sierra Leone would face violence at the hands of the rebels preoccupied the women's thoughts, often traumatizing them and subjecting them to restlessness and anguish for which they had to seek psychological counseling.

But despite these problems, the two women persevered, trying to create a new life for themselves and for the future of their children. Their salaries gave the women their first taste of Western consumerism. They each bought a television, kitchen appliances, toys, and a used car after social services terminated the free transportation pass. By all accounts, they were living the Danish dream. Kendra's income provided enough for a reasonable standard of living, and she was able to remit a small portion of it to relatives back home. In addition, she started a project to assist family members and others in her hometown village by collecting used children's clothing in Denmark, which she shipped home to Sierra Leone. This was her contribution to help alleviate the extreme poverty in her country. Before long, the church where they worshipped joined in this project and started sending loads of used clothing to Sierra Leone.

The sponsorship for the two women to go to the American Midwest was initiated by a group of Lutheran churches in Minnesota and Wisconsin. The group petitioned the United States Office of Refugee Resettlement (USORR), as well as the Immigration and Customs Enforcement (ICE) to allocate visas for the two refugee women. The process was long, often fraught with administrative and bureaucratic delays. The visa arrangements for the women and their dependents to enter the United States took almost three years. As preconditions for granting visas, the women had to undergo an orientation course in terms of what to expect upon arrival, take civic lessons, pass a comprehensive medical check-up, and also take lessons in English as a Second Language (ESL). Upon arrival in Minneapolis and Saint Paul, the two women and their children were settled in the United States under the auspices of USORR. As refugees, they were entitled to receive assistance from social services, including housing, medical, and some financial support to cover transportation costs. Overall, the women described the initial phase of their resettlement positively. The church that sponsored them provided them with some financial and material support while they waited for federal assistance. Housing proved to be one of the most difficult issues that the women had to face. The women wanted to share a house together with all their children. The fear about separating family members was something that Kendra and Lois did not want to entertain because of the experiences they had as refugees. After several discussions by church authorities and social service agencies, the two women decided to live in separate residences but they made sure that they would be within walking distance from each other. This allowed the children to see each other often and interact in order to maintain their strong social bonds.

For the refugee women who are rebuilding their lives in the United States, there is ambivalence about whether or not to seek professional assistance to address the traumas of war, such as the brutal killing of close kin, sexual victimizations, violent separation from relatives, and the pains of living in exile. The women seem to gravitate between the imperative of seeking assistance to manage and cope with their problems or whether to forget about the past and continue with their new lives in the United States. It was apparent from the focus-group interviews that only a small number of the immigrant refugee women (12 percent) have taken it upon themselves, in conjunction with religious and social service agencies, to seek psychological and medical assistance. The immigrant refugee women who sought professional assistance tended to be relatively better educated (secondary school and postsecondary credentials) than their counterparts who do not seek professional assistance. Immigrants seeking assistance for counseling used both public (local, city, or county hospitals and clinics) and private agencies (church groups, and nonprofit charitable organizations). Services for which assistance was sought included depression, stress, anxiety, marriage counseling, dealing with grief and loss, and difficulties forming or maintaining relationships. As Edward (2007) argued, it is pertinent to reconceptualize the needs of refugee women by positioning the services to be provided within the broader nexus of the sociopolitical, economic, cultural, and legal context defining and influencing the lives of women refugees. In essence, transforming the lives of refugees must incorporate relevant policy formulations whose goal must be to assist displaced persons create the agencies for achieving empowerment and independence.

The impact of the forced flight and displacement had a major impact on children in particular. Several of the women reported continued problems with children who are withdrawn and suffer from extreme isolation at school, sleeplessness, and difficulties interacting with nonrefugee children and school authorities, including harboring a sense of mistrust for adult and authority figures. The traumas associated with war and violence had affected the children's outlook on life, taking a toll on their education as well. As one immigrant refugee parent indicated,

> It took me a while to understand my son's behavior. He was beaten and left to die by a child soldier in Sierra Leone. These child soldiers even kill their own relatives as part of the rituals of their initiation. My son clings to me anywhere we go. He says repeatedly sometimes not to leave him. When I am a few minutes late picking him up from school, his first words when he gets in the car is to say to me, please don't forget to come for me. He tells me this to reference his hasty flight from the violence that ruptured at home in Freetown. He was lost for three weeks and separated from close relatives. This was when he fell prey to the marauding thuggish elements (mostly child soldiers) who assaulted him and made him their servant, washing their clothes, carrying water for them, and cleaning their hole-in-the-ground latrines with his bare hands.

These children, as another refugee mother attested, "are often the faceless and most vulnerable victims of war and conflicts." Emma, another refugee, recounted the cases of young refugee girls who were sexually assaulted by rebel forces during the war and during their protracted stay in the refugee tents. According to Emma, "It was very hard for me to look on when some of the guards came and took away young girls under the pretext of questioning them to help locate their missing parents and relatives. Often, these girls came back crying and were never the same from there on in terms of how they related to adults. Most of them stayed isolated for hours on end." The brutalizing effects of the violence perpetrated on the children continue to linger in Emma's memory.

Children often suffer in silent from the victimizations of war and conflicts, unable to verbalize their victimizations and untold sufferings. Nolin (2006) asserts that often, women and children bear the brunt of physical and sexual abuse, including the problem of older men who seek out girls under eighteen years of age to sexually violate in exchange for food allotment and nonliquid aid. As another refugee woman stated, "Some of these young girls do not mention or tell their relatives what happened to them beyond the point of shedding tears and remaining reclusive. But as mothers, we know when our girls have been sexually abused. Some of the families will not seek medical assistance for the children. Everything is kept hidden as reporting sometimes attracted more abuses. And worse of all, there are some families that I know who started blaming the children for the abuses they suffered. It was a terrible state of affairs all over." For the refugee women and their children who have suffered physical torture, including sexual abuse, mental and psychological problems continue to dominate their lives. Several of the women were reluctant to openly discuss the aftermath of the violent victimizations they had experienced with social service agencies in the United States. Their problems are further compounded by their poverty status, illiteracy, lack of familiarity with American customs, and, at times, poor health. Juggling these problems simultaneously and finding solutions to them are taxing. The process of recovery can be slow as well as daunting.

A coping strategy to deal with the trauma of war is to focus attention and energy toward family, caring for children, and building coalitions with other oppressed immigrant women groups. Building coalitions with other women provides an informal outlet for talking about the wars and the violent victimizations that some of the refugee women had experienced. Sensing their social and cultural vulnerabilities in the United States, these refugee women harbor a mistrust and lack of confidence in official governance structures and agencies. These agencies are considered alien and foreign and therefore to be avoided at all cost, no matter the extent of services they offer to the refugees. The preferred approach is to deal with the trauma of war and violence by localizing it within the social and cultural network structures that the immigrant refugee women have formed. But this approach has yet to meet the full range of professional services and needs that the refugee women face daily as they strive to put the past behind them and move forward. When references are made to the horrors of war that the women had experienced, the refrain is to always cast anger and resentment toward the failures of their leaders at home to offer them protection. This anger sometimes finds expression in songs, drawings, paintings, and storytelling. Listening to the narratives from the focus-group sessions, periodic references were made to the sufferings inflicted by the war.

Emotions about the aftermath of the violence were illustrated by photographs of family members who were maimed. Some of the women referenced the songs they sang to lift their spirits during the flight to safety and the degradations they had to endure in the refugee tents. Though some of the women indicated they have shared their refugee experiences with close U.S. coworkers, most seem to believe that sharing their stories is burdensome and agonizing. For most of the refugee women, the saga of having to live in exile away from family members continues to hamper their full integration into the host society. Memories of lost relatives are relived constantly. Horrors associated with the forced flight are visited regularly. Thoughts about having to flee home hastily, coupled with the realization that some of them may never get to go back home (even for a visit) or reunite with other family members, is a burden several of the immigrant and refugee women are reluctant to bear. As one of the women further indicated, "Stories about what we have endured may be told to all our children now and those yet to be born. After all, this is now part of our history. If our children decide to do something about it and get to know what happened to us, they will have to relive the pains their parents went through. Maybe then and only then will they be able to find the meaning to what happened. For some of us, we do not want to search for any meaning in what happened to us at this point in time."

MUSLIM WOMEN REFUGEES: CREATING NEW IDENTITIES AND ASPIRATIONS

Learning new expectations about the host society was a difficult period of transition for Kendra and Lois. America offered the two women the promise of a better life, a new start, and an opportunity to reconstitute their shattered lives. For both Kendra and Lois, the transition from Sierra Leone to the United States was life-changing as well. For the first time in their adult lives, the women found themselves having to negotiate a new identity similar to the one they constructed in Scandinavia. But as Kendra pointed out, the adjustment process in Denmark was easier for them relative to their postarrival experiences in the United States. In America, Kendra retorted, "People identify you purely by your racial and ethnic attributes. And being Black has become like a burden for me. We are not accepted here like we were in

Denmark. The Danes were very kind to us and went out of the way to make sure we had everything we wanted. In America, people treat you with disdain and with a condescending attitude because you are Black. We encountered that in Denmark but not to the same degree. Here in America, people only choose to see your blackness and its negative images. People do not see beyond your race."

For Kendra and Lois and their respective families, the racialized formations that they encountered upon their arrival in America were the result of their class and ethnic status. "Class and ethnic lines are clearly demarcated here in America," Lois said. "It is sort of like being told that this is your given place, your assigned place; this is where you belong. You may be able to work your way out of that status but with some difficulties," she affirmed. Lois referenced the rigidity of the class, racial, and ethnic structures in the United States when she stated, "What goes on here is like a caste system. People see us in a fixed category with little or no chances of undoing what society predetermines for you. Race is a big issue and highly significant where we now live. There is tension. Different racial and ethnic groups in the community are fighting over different issues concerning housing, jobs, police treatment of minorities, education for our kids, and health care."

For both Kendra and Lois, finding new ways to express and position their multiple racial, ethnic, and gender identities became a challenging task. While in Denmark, the two women were able to find a collective expression to represent the multiple genres defining their identities and roles. In the United States, one of the realizations the women came to was that their Muslim identity had to be re-created or constructed to conform to the images and perceptions that Americans in general have about Muslims post-9/11. When they are in public spaces, both Kendra and Lois often dressed in the traditional Muslim attire (*hijab*, or long loose and non-see-through clothing), covering every part of the body except for face and hands. Their children also dressed the same way when they appeared in public and private places. For both women, this was a nonissue, same as it was in Denmark. The children dressed in traditional Muslim attire to go to school. The parents did the same when they went out to work, shop, or attend school. But the responses that they often encountered when they went to find work, shop, or take their children to play parks reveal another important dimension of their transnational identity. On a number of occasions, both women reported being shunned whenever they went to the parks where their children liked to play. Being dressed in their traditional Muslim attire has restricted their social distance and interactions with other segments of their community. The two women indicated experiencing insults and threats, often accompanied with shouts to "go home." Being of the Islamic faith is an infinitesimal aspect of the lives of the two women. Their religion is part of a broader manifestation of their translocalized and transnational identities. Work, family life, civic and cultural community engagements, education, and their gendered roles and relationships are interwoven into their multiple identities.

The contestation of the Islamic aspect of their identities—and the hegemony and social control of this part of their lives that others see as their sole or primary identity—brings consternation to the women. They see the elevation of the religious facet of their lives by entrenched political and social interests in the community as being inimical to the principles and ideals of a democratic culture such as the United States. In a sense, the lack of tolerance regarding how their faith is viewed forcefully categorizes them into an outsider status and role. Elevating the religious identity of the two women as the national debate over Islamic extremism intensifies is a reactionary social mechanism designed to denigrate, marginalize, and portray the two women in subordinate and less desirable roles as outsiders who have very low social capital. In this outsider role, rigid lines of structured relationships are constructed to ensure that clearly demarcated power and ethnic variations in social relationships are enforced. This relationship is based on the unequal distinctions and allocation of power or resources that Americans often make about gender, class, race, religion, and ethnic affiliations. Forming part of the "new immigration" to the United States—as contrasted with the "old immigration," principally from West Europe—the two West African women are likely to join with other recent immigrants in forming their own and unique version of assimilation and acculturation that is often premised on the preservation of their ethnic identities while pursuing selected assimilation as well as transnational refugee identities.[3]

Like other new immigrants forming the "new migration" from the poorer countries of the world to the United States, Kendra and Lois seem to have accepted their plight in the United States. Their firm belief is that in a rigidly structured class and ethnic-based society such as America, finding one's footing is in and of itself a challenge because of the entrenched politicization of race and ethnicity and the revival of anti-immigrant fervor across the country as the debate on immigration intensifies. As Lois stated, "We cannot become full citizens of the U.S. as long as we remain Black and foreign. We are here only for one thing: to work and support our families. This is our prize, our goal, and our purpose. Everything else is secondary, whether someone hurls a racial slur at me or not is of no consequences to me. I keep my eyes focused on my goal." Structured gendered relations compound Lois and Kendra's integration into the society, but as both of them indicated, the energy needed to foster integration is too tasking. Kendra and Lois share and have a lot in common with the unskilled, poorly educated, foreign-born women in America. For this group, negotiation of a place in the civic culture of America is almost impossible. They will continue to occupy a peripheral status in the United States.

Without exception, Kendra and Lois's cohort of women from Africa in this country continue to experience racial segregation, poor schools for their children, inability to navigate the social safety net due to budget cuts, and, more significantly, the growing pains associated with being unable to find jobs in their respective communities. The fact is that some of these women entered the country at a rather turbulent time economically, as unemployment rates rose and minority job losses continue to double, and, in some cases, triple, in relation to their white counterparts. Urban and minority Americans continue to feel the pinch of economic downturn more so than their suburban, middle-class, predominantly white counterparts who, despite also being affected by the economic downturn, do have safety nets such as fringe benefits, access to home equity lines of credit, and employer-sponsored retirement plans to fall back on as they remedy the weak economic tide currently facing the nation. For Kendra and Lois, the reality of their status in the United States is fringe living, certainly detached, aloof, and very conscious about their plight as refugees whose collective fortune hinges on whether or not they can have access to the resources needed to improve upon their human capital via the pursuit of postsecondary education or job training and retooling. Otherwise, the two women face a perpetual conundrum, that is, how to recreate their shattered lives in a country that they now call home but whose values they have yet to identify with. The visibility of their status as Muslim women and the pejorative association of their faith with terrorism have thwarted their full integration into the community they live in and now call home.

The pains and deprivation of being displaced refugees who have sought a haven in America pales in comparison with what they were confronted with during the crisis that caused them grief and agony in the first place in West Africa. But they thought that once here in America, they would be free from some of the indignity they had suffered at home awhile back. The two refugee women rationalized that America, with its promise, would make them whole once again, restoring to them what they had lost and what had been taken away from them by violence. They are safe in America but not safer. Kendra had two white boys throw sticks and stones at her while she played with her son at the park. The third day, she went back to the park with Lois, just the two of them, and this time an elderly white male yelled, "Filthy niggers, go home!" For the two women, this felt like a revictimization of their traumatic encounter with rebel troops who had invaded their town and captured young girls, some of whom they had raped, and the rest, sold into sexual enslavement. The boys were conscripted into the rebel army. For Kendra and Lois, the alienation and trepidation associated with their religious status finally pressured them to give up appearing in public dressed in their Muslim attire. That aspect of their multiple identities and transnational cultures that they wanted to navigate in the United States was no longer tenable. The result is that the two women had to deconstruct and render illegitimate their own religion so that they can gain back their respectability, backing away from the visible manifestations of their identity, albeit temporarily, while they seek to gain access to better and more economic and cultural opportunities in the United States.

Assimilation may never occur for Kendra and Lois. If they assimilate, the outcome is more likely to reflect assimilation of the values and beliefs of other immigrant groups that they share the same social, economic, and cultural positions with, rather than becoming assimilated into American cultural values and ethos that they barely identify with. Their race, ethnicity, religion, and gender have become central in mapping out the social contents of their identities in the United States. Kendra and Lois perceive that they have less in common with America. They sense that they are separated by a wide chasm of economic and cultural inequalities from the rest of America. Most of the people they interact with and have formed acquaintances with are people like themselves, people who are pushed out by the elevated levels of anti-immigrant fervor and loathing.

The public fear and loathing defining the presence of the two West African Black Muslim women refugees sometimes feels like "having a dagger pointed behind you," according to Lois. For both women, the changing urban scene in America, with job losses, abandoned homes, poor and ill-equipped schools, is not what they had imagined prior to their arrival in the country. The alternatives available for them to become successful are equally limited. "America has lost the will to provide for their most vulnerable," Lois interjected. "The unfortunate scenario is that tens of thousands of young Black and other minorities are being squeezed continually, forced to drop out of the system, and not to rely on it as a source of safety net from the ravages of economic

and social depression," Kendra chimed. Sometimes, the way to manage some of this conundrum is to "reach inside one's belly and compose a song, a poem, or simply to cry," said Lois. She proceeded to
take out a piece of paper to read a statement that she had written to
cope with the new realities of her refugee life in the American Midwest. Lois said, "I have been working on this statement for months.
It captures how I feel about my plight as a refugee in the U.S. My
son read it and made it into a song which he sings regularly. He is
young, but he recognizes the realities of what it means to be displaced
from home and be classified as a refugee." Lois's poem and statement
represents the collective voices of the refugee women and their pains.
What follows is a paraphrase of Lois's statement: "the storm rages, the
rebels are coming; they are trotting, chanting, panting, and sweating;
children hide under wooden beds; tonight, one of them may be taken
away into the bushes; if it is a girl, she will be raped; if it is a boy, he
will be given a machete and asked if he can kill; soon, it will be my
turn if I do not flee; the sight of their tattered uniform is eerie; who
can resist them? They have shattered our innocence and broken will
wills; America saved my life."

Lois could not hold back her emotions as she spoke. She sobbed
but continued describing her refugee experiences.[4] Despite Lois's
negative experiences with what had happened in her native country,
she nonetheless remained optimistic about the future. "Being here
today is a fresh start. My eyes are now widely opened. The war taught
me a lot. Being here is very healing. I cannot undo the past, but looking ahead, I will strive to renew myself in America," she stated.

Like the other refugee women, Lois was echoing the lived experiences of her counterparts. She praised the opportunities America
offers. At the same time, she finds it difficult to place the intense disdain she encounters partly on account of her religion, Black ancestry,
and gender. "Some people like to stoke racial fears by faulting everyone who is an immigrant or a Muslim for the problems facing this
country. And they do not even have to utter a word to publicly display
their bigotry. They hide behind code words which we all know have
racial and gender overtones. They get away with a lot of immigrant
and Muslim-bashing and no one can touch them or accuse them of
hate speech," Lois retorted.

Lois can draw upon the strong networks of family and other immigrants to situate her angst and confront the problems and difficulties
associated with her inability to find incorporation and integration into
the affairs of American society at the basic level of social organization, her community. As a Muslim, Lois feels that the system of social

control targets refugees and immigrants who are Muslims. They do not have to come from the Middle East to attract the attention of the apparatus of formal social control. Any infraction, no matter how small, is usually magnified and explained in terms of their faith. And as Lois opined, it is highly improbable that she and others like her will be able to achieve full integration even if they are desirous of doing so. The institutional pathways that other immigrants and refugees followed to become "Americans" in the past have dissipated and eroded. Or if these paths are still in place, they have become a hotly contested terrain, excruciatingly painful and too tasking to negotiate.

Not all the refugee women have found a voice to express their refugee experiences. I had expected that some of the women would not want to talk about the past. So I tried to steer clear of the subject of how rebel troops had sexually assaulted women and children. I had seen photos of the atrocities and television news accounts of the physical and psychological victimization that rebel forces had wrought on innocent people in both Liberia and Sierra Leone. Whenever I steered away from the subject, some of the women made it a point to bring me back to that subject. "I want to talk about it," one Sierra Leonean woman said. She reached inside a bag on a table nearby and brought out some pictures showing the decapitated body of her son. He was killed and his body dragged on the ground by rebel soldiers who, by this woman's account, could not have been more than fourteen years old. As the conversation proceeded, I sensed that for some of the women, the painful flight to safety was carried out on the spur of the moment to avert risking more lives. And even after they arrived at the camps, they were provided with little or no counseling support to deal with their grief and confront their fears. Making it safely to the refugee camps was considered a beginning and at the same time, from the perspective of their rescuers, was suppose to mark an end to their suffering and ordeal. But as the women hinted, another form of violence reared its ugly head at the refugee camps—the problem of sex trafficking, usually targeting young girls. Here again (as one refugee woman remarked), it was African men who masqueraded as soldiers but actually were looking to forcefully capture young girls or separate them from their family and ultimately sell them off to sex traffickers.

The refugee camps were mainly inhabited by women, elderly people, and children. Their male family members had been forcefully conscripted, killed, gone missing, or had fled and separated from the rest of their family members. The small number of men who were also in the camps had been wounded during the flight to safety or were too badly malnourished to be able to fend off the soldiers and the child traffickers. This was another danger that the women had to contend with. Traffickers hand the girls they capture over to another level of organized, well-oiled criminal syndicates who swiftly transport some of these girls through the Sahara to North Africa and the Middle East where some may end up as domestic servants or in prostitution. Some of the young girls may eventually settle in the European Union. Nothing in the world ever prepares a mother to have to face and deal with this issue. Fleeing from the soldiers and finding a safer haven in the refugee camps did not minimize the anguish that some of the women said they had experienced.

Due to ineffective screening of camp workers, some child traffickers parading as security officers and soldiers managed to target young girls as well. Photographs of a few of the girls were posted as missing in some of the camps. According to the refugee women, some of the girls were later found by the UN and later reunited with family members. However, many of the young girls are still missing, according to one refugee woman. The biggest obstacle in thwarting African child sexual trafficking is the lack of comprehensive data on the extent and prevalence of the problem. Coupled with this is the half-hearted effort of African governments to develop comprehensive multilateral protocols to arrest and punish the perpetrators. Family members of victims are unwilling to publicly discuss issues related to sexual enslavement and trafficking of their children. Even where family members become aware that their children are forcefully taken or voluntarily recruited into the underground sex trade, the remittances and financial support these young girls provide their parents may overshadow the need to bring to justice the perpetrators of this crime.

For some of the women, the pains and the wounds of war are still too fresh in their collective memories. One woman expressed the meaning of what it is to carry the identity of a displaced or refugee person. Vocalizing her sentiments, this refugee woman stated thus,

> After the hastily arranged flight to safety, I got angry at the men in our society. I still feel angry when I think about what some of them did to us. If they wanted to fight, they should fight among themselves. They should not extend the fight by targeting innocent women, children, and the frail. The soldiers were only interested in using force to obtain sex. They took away the innocence of young girls, raping them while subdued and petrified parents looked on. How can this ever be justified? Often, they (the soldiers) will be laughing as they sexually brutalized the women and girls. Nothing can contain my anger.

For this refugee woman, the violence she had experienced remains her single most important explanation about the poor state of political and civil culture in Africa today. This violence, she rationalized, is at the heart of the continued cycle of poverty and social instabilities in the region.

Violence and sexual brutalization of women and young girls never ceased as the Liberian and Sierra Leone crisis deepened. Referencing the brutalities some of them had to endure, another refugee woman stated, "Everything fell to pieces. After the rebels killed a relative of mine and threatened to take my two girls away, I had to beg them. They forced themselves on me and violated me. I never cried because in my mind, I knew I was saving my daughters from having to experience this brutality." After showing pictures of the havoc that was caused by marauding rebel fighters who ransacked their refugee camp one night while they slept, another refugee women asked, "What man in his right mind will sneak inside the camp looking for young girls to have sex with and later take them away to the bush where soldier after soldier will rape her? The sight of African men sexually brutalizing women and children was a difficult sight to behold." This refugee glanced at me and paused, waiting for a response or reaction to her statement. Once again, there was nothing in my sociological well of training that I could reference to ground this woman's solace. She continued to wait for a response as our eyes kept looking at each other. All I could do was to keep looking at her intensely. I did not feel that I was violating her space. I could tell she felt comfortable looking at me. It would have been a travesty if I had taken my eyes away from her. Maybe she would think that I did not care about her story. Finally, she said, "I wasn't expecting any answer from you." Her evocation of that statement did not bring me comfort or relief either. If it did, it was ephemeral. She had made her point with a certain air of genteelness and calming influence that has continued to linger in my memory. I examined my own situation as a Black immigrant in America and reflectively pondered the different paths we each have taken to reach America. At that moment in time, our common quest to find self-fulfillment and hope in the promises of America converged.

EXPERIENCES OF LIBERIAN REFUGEE WOMEN

For Mia and Mina, the Liberian crisis marked a watershed in the annals of the country. Despite the simmering interethnic tensions in their country over the years, no one ever thought that the conflict would result in a destabilizing civil war that cost the country a lot of its human and financial resources. The thought of Liberians becoming refugees or becoming internally displaced in their own country was unthinkable. In its heyday, Liberia's capital, Monrovia (named after American President Monroe), was a shining oasis of prosperity in the West African corridor. It attracted migrants from far and near who were looking for work in the rubber, rutile, diamond, iron ore, rice, coffee, and cocoa production sectors. Offshore fishing in the Atlantic was lucrative, creating lots of jobs for the coastal residents. As Mia acknowledged, "Liberians thought the good times the country was enjoying will continue for a long time to come. And even though there were pockets of discontentment, it was only a simmer no one imagined would escalate to such violent proportions."

The war brought a halt to Mina's sense of normalcy and personal well-being. "I had a good job with the civil service and had my own home; Taylor messed up everything, plunging the country into the abyss of despair and gloom," Mina continued. While ordinary Liberians were suffering, unsure about their subsistence, "Taylor looted the state coffers, lived extravagantly, surrounded himself with corrupt henchmen, and as if that was not enough, he wanted more of the diamond wealth in nearby Sierra Leone as well," Mina further retorted. American economic assistance created a sizable middle class of lawyers, civil servants, doctors, and businessmen and businesswomen in Liberia. However, the vast majority of Liberians lived in abject poverty in dilapidated slums and squatter colonies on the fringes of Monrovia. This group formed the underclass of Liberia, totally disconnected from the moderate gains in economic standards of living that the upper and middle echelons of Liberian society took for granted. The inhabitants of the city's slums live on less than one dollar a day. Most have to fend for themselves, working as servants and laborers. A vast majority of them suffer from chronic unemployment for protracted periods. These were some of the people who were recruited by the rebels as they waged and launched their assaults on civil society.

When the Liberian civil crisis intensified, Mia and Mina were brought to Ghana for temporary resettlement as refugees. Prior to their arrival in Ghana, Mia and Mina reported some of the atrocities that some Liberians had to endure. "Rape of children and women by soldiers and non-soldiers alike were frequent and commonplace. Some of the girls were abducted and simply taken away," Mia said. She continued, "The soldiers were ruthless. People carried machetes and administered instant justice on the spot on their foes. No one could stop them. Everyone was terrified, notably the children. Everything fell apart. It was very distressing to see how Liberians were treating their fellow citizens, as if they are not humans."

In Ghana, the two women depended on the magnanimity of the international community and the Ghanaian community at large. Mina described life at the refugee camp at Buduburam as pathetic and sometimes as treacherous as the lives they were accustomed to in Liberia. Like other refugee women, Mina had serious problems with the screening of those the UNHCR would sponsor to come to Ghana as refugees. "The UNHCR response was poorly coordinated. Rogues, criminals, and drug addicts were included in the mass mobilization of people to be allowed to move for resettlement in Ghana," Mina affirmed. Mia and Mina lived in the Buduburam refugee camp in Ghana for seven years. "The hastily arranged escape to Ghana for resettlement was life-saving for us. Ghana was calm, even though they had economic problems. Our lives were much better and it felt like being home because there wasn't much of a cultural difference between Ghanaians and Liberians. The government tried its best to assist us. The international community could have done more," Mia said. Despite the fact that they had relatives who were citizens of the United States, the processing of their visas were fraught with hurdles. Mina and Mia's relatives in the United States provided proof of economic support. Sworn affidavits were presented to the embassy that the two women and their children would not become a public charge if allowed to migrate to the United States. The bureaucratic impediments were made more strenuous for the two refugees because, in their haste to flee, they had to leave all their important documents at home, including birth certificates and what they had managed to save. "I left about $700 at home under my bed; everything was done in a rush. We left with the clothes on our backs. No one had the time to take any personal belongings with them. Some Liberians were hoping that the U.S. will grant them safe passage to enter the country as the crisis worsened. After all, we have a special relationship with the Americans," Mina said. Prior to their arrival in Ghana, rebel forces confiscated their Liberian passports. Efforts to apply for new passports in Ghana proved futile. There was a brief lull in the fighting and Mina and Mia took advantage of this to request their parents to forward their documents to Ghana. After three trials, both Mia and Mina were given a temporary visa by the U.S. consulate and were the few lucky ones who got to leave Ghana to go to the United States.

Mina and Mia arrived in New York and were met by family members. All their relatives in the United States hold advanced degrees in the arts and sciences and have done very well economically, adjusting to life in America. Their other relatives lived in the Midwest (Madison,

Wisconsin, and Minneapolis, Minnesota). The three relatives who sponsored Mina and Mia all lived in New York. The day after their arrival, the tedious process of legitimizing their stay commenced. They hired an immigration attorney to process their paperwork for refugee status. The goal was to act swiftly, "while the issue of the displaced Liberians was still current and attracting attention from media organizations," Mina had suggested. A backlog of similar cases of hundreds of thousands of other refugees further delayed the processing of their papers. Mia and Mina were informed that the waiting period to appear before a federal judge to hear their petition was almost a year. Undaunted, the two sisters found work at a restaurant close to where they were living in New York. This was risky, as apprehension by the authorities for working without valid papers could potentially affect the outcome of their asylum application. Fortunately for the two women, the waiting period was shorter than they had been led to believe. The judge granted their asylum application, paving the way for the two women and their children to acquire refugee status in the United States. They were given temporary working permits and, with this, they were able to apply for social security cards. In securing these documents, the two women were on their way to establishing and reconstructing their shattered lives in the United States.

Mina and Mia moved from New York to Minneapolis and Saint Paul, where they had relatives who operated Black African ethnic enterprises specializing in the import and export business. The family also owned a lucrative rental unit located in a predominantly Hispanic and Black African immigrant neighborhood. Mina and Mia joined with their family running the apartment complex. Despite having completed secondary school in Monrovia, the two women did not possess any postsecondary credentials. This limited the type of employment available to them and how much they were paid. With very limited funds, the two women were not able to enroll at area technical and vocational schools to pursue a trade or vocation. This situation is faced by many new African immigrants who come to the United States. For those who lack postsecondary credentials, the principal sources of employment are driving a taxi, working as parking ramp attendants, laborers (including custodial work), in construction, and some service-related jobs. With the exception of construction, most of these jobs in the metropolitan counties forming Minneapolis and St. Paul pay slightly above minimum wage ($9 per hour), without any fringe benefits. For most of the new immigrants, any form of employment is considered gainful, irrespective of the compensation. This was exactly the mind-set that Mina and Mia adopted. Through a family acquaintance, the two women were able to find employment as caregivers. The hours were very flexible, allowing both of them to take on a second job cleaning houses in the suburbs and providing babysitting services for white, middle class suburban families. The total weekly pretax income for each of the two women was $1,265. Combining their income and resources, the two women were able to rent a four-bedroom home. Six months from the start of their first jobs, the two women bought a van.

Functioning in a stratified economic and class system in the United States, the two West African refugees found that in a more formalized economy, there are certain contradictions in the gendering of work performed by immigrants and local citizens. Mia and Mina expected that having secondary education was sufficient training to enable them remain competitive in the service sector of the economy. To their surprise, they discovered that finding employment in this sector is heavily influenced by the large and surplus pool of well-educated foreign and immigrant women with postsecondary credentials who are able to find work in domestic and service capacities (jobs that they will not perform in their respective countries of immigrant origination). Due to rapid growth in the population of immigrant women in the Minneapolis and Saint Paul corridor who are competing for the vast number of domestic and service-related jobs available, many white women who used to perform some of these occupational tasks have moved up to middle and intermediate leadership roles, thus paving the way for many new immigrant women to replace them. However, these jobs often start at the apprentice or lower levels where wages are paltry and benefits are far-fetched or hard to come by. These jobs offer little protection for the labor rights of the immigrant women. The job expectations are structured to reinforce the social and economic subordination of minority and immigrant women in general. Access to institutionalized mechanisms for addressing job-related grievances and unfair labor practices are not available to the vast majority of minority immigrant women like Mia and Mina. And like the other immigrant women employed by the service sector, lodging complains and agitating for better terms of employment and working conditions for immigrant women is an anathema.

When Mia and Mina raised concerns about safety and working conditions related to their work, they were given the option to either remain silent or be terminated without cause. For Mia, Mina, and the majority of the immigrant women who work alongside them, the opportunity to have a job trumps other facets of their working environment such as employer's violation of labor standards. According to Mia, being female, Black, and foreign threatens and challenges the culturally prescribed and gendered roles and rules that these foreign migrant women are supposed to conform to or abide by. In a sense, Mia finds herself contesting and questioning the cultural and economic parameters of female labor force participation by decrying the poor working conditions, low pay, and the lack of paid employee benefits such as health care and retirement benefits. From her perspective, exploitation of working immigrant women is common due to their powerlessness and inability to mobilize for collective action to ameliorate their poor working conditions. "Most of us have become marginalized and diminished because we are foreign-born Black women," Mia affirmed. Like other immigrant and minority women employed in the service sector, Mia and Mina are earning more money than they otherwise earned in Liberia. From what they earned in Minnesota, they were able to send remittances (about $200) home every fortnight. But relative to American standards, the two consider themselves lower class and part of the growing number of America's urban and inner-city Black minority population who have to confront and deal with substandard housing and poor or inadequate social services.

For some of the West African immigrant women who have to deal with these conditions, the American dream is simmering but still attainable or within grasp. For others, the fulfillment of the dream has all but completely dissipated or disappeared. Racial and gendered categorizations continue to be poignant in the lives of these immigrant women. And as they strive to reach their economic aspirations, they realize that they also have to contest their gendered status of employment, which is characterized by low pay and unequal access to the resources they need to restructure their lives in the United States. The inescapable subtexts in the women's relationships with the host society are their Black and Islamic identities, two poignant markers in immigrant identity construction in the United States. In essence, the bulk of these immigrant and refugee women may not be able to become assimilated due to the stranger and outsider status that defines most of them as well as their low ethnic, race, and class stratification.

For Mina and Mia, assimilation may hinge on whether the members of the dominant society find their cultural practices threatening and therefore subject to legislative social control or denial of access to equal opportunity and social resources. Additionally, integration and inclusion may happen for the two women, but only in select spheres of public spaces, such as relying on public educational institutions for the education of their children and perhaps for themselves as well as they pursue further vocational and technical education to ensure job promotion and higher pay. Limited assimilation may be confined to those areas of American society in which the two women, as well as other refugees, perceive that they can share and participate in the common and everyday activities of their community, including using social agencies and institutions such as housing, library, health care, and social welfare organizations. In the main, it can be surmised that political integration is less likely to occur. So is religious participation and organization. As they distance themselves from the core of American society, the refugees may also strengthen their own cultural, social, and economic institutions to provide them with empowerment and representation in the common spheres.

Entrenched cultural practices imported from West Africa will be sustained and strengthened via familial networks that the women have formed to ensure their mutual benevolence and survival in what, to most of them, appears to be an alien and depersonalized American culture. Looking ahead, the children of the refugees will ultimately shape and determine the pace of cultural adaptation and inclusion. Preliminary evidence suggests that the children will persist in forming and expressing cultural and social ethos that are more varied and encompassing of multiple cultures and behavioral standards. By all accounts, the children might reject the binary ethnicity of two contrasting cultures, one Black and the other white. What is probable is that they might embrace a transnational identity based upon multiracial and ethnic formations that is neither pro-Black nor pro-white. In essence, a multiracial or blended second generation ethnicity may emerge. Relationships with other minority and immigrant groups, particularly Blacks, Latinos, and Asians, will become critical in modeling the diaspora communities that these women are going to forge in the United States. Additionally, their abilities to define areas of common and mutual interests with other protected groups to advocate for better economic and social programs for themselves and their children will go a long way in defining the contours of the African diaspora communities across America.

The processes whereby these refugees continue to differentiate themselves and assert their cultural and normative values are affected by the continued relegation and subjugation of their lives to a subordinated and alienated minority status. Their minority status is highlighted by their continued stigmatization as "persons in need" (PIN) and as burdens or drain on social service and welfare agency expenditures. In their day-to-day lives, these refugee women do not convey to the rest of the host society that they are dependent on the magnanimity of the welfare state. Though they are now completely independent economically and self-supporting, their initial labeling and stigmatization by social service agencies as PIN has persisted and become their permanent social marking. The result is the continued social and cultural undifferentiation and aggregation of African refugees in the West as a monolithic group whose needs are yet to be categorized according to the specific underlying circumstances unique to their experiences. The continued aggregation of African refugee groups into undifferentiated categories thwarts the institutionalization of individualistic programs to address refugee specific needs.

CARVING NICHES AS DOMESTIC MAIDS AND CAREGIVERS

As stated, the growing service sector economy in the metropolitan counties forming Minneapolis-St. Paul has become a preferred destination for many of the new immigrants from Africa, including those from Latin America and Asia..[5] The African immigrant population generally tends to be highly mobile, often moving to towns and cities across the United States where they believe economic opportunities abound or the cost of living seems reasonable and where close family members and relatives live nearby. Secondary or tertiary migrations are an enduring feature of the migratory profiles of Africans in the United States. A group of West African refugee women who initially settled in Minnesota have begun moving to St. Louis, Missouri. In a way, their secondary migrations have not taken these women far away from their original place of settlement in Minnesota. Relocating to Missouri still keeps some of the refugee women in the Midwest. For some of these refugee women, Missouri has become another frontier in their quest for full economic participation and better standards of living.

Paid domestic work is a growing source of employment for West African immigrant refugee women. This growth is fueled in part by changes in the economy of the United States, necessitating the need for both parents to work outside the home to increase the family's total income. With the ever-increasing rate of female labor force participation, a void is created in the caregiving of children during hours of work. Day care centers have responded to meet the high demand of children who are in need of supervision and care while their parents work. In addition, the dispersion of families brought upon by migration and suburbanization has affected the geographic propinquity of families. This means that relatives are hardly available to assist in providing care to children. To enhance their financial standing, more and more grandparents are working outside the home and are not always available to assist in providing care for their grandchildren. For dual income, middle class professional families across the United States, there is a strong preference to have someone at home to assist in such diverse chores like getting the children ready for school, washing, cooking, cleaning, and picking up the children from school or having someone at home for the children to come home to after school.

Although a growing number of husbands and male partners now assist with routine household responsibilities, their total amount of time spent providing care for children and performing household chores pales in comparison to the amount of time women spend doing household work. Even with egalitarian and shared responsibilities of household work, women continue to bear the brunt of the work even when they work full-time jobs. The time available for parents and guardians to care for their children continues to diminish. For a growing number of parents with adequate means, hiring someone to assist in taking care of their household and their children is considered an appropriate use of resources.

Historically in the American South, Black women were to the first to carve an employment niche in domestic work, often serving in multiple roles as nanny-housekeeper-maid to predominantly white suburban families all over the country. During the Great Migration of Blacks from the South to the North, women were typically able to find jobs in White suburban communities working as nannies, maids, and caregivers. Historically denied employment opportunities in the formal sector, Black American women often relied on domestic work to make a living. This line of work gave some of the women the opportunity to contribute to, or supplement, total household income. Secondly, for female-headed households, this form of work was the main source of livelihood for Black women and their children. The women often brought home food and clothing given to them by their proprietors, thereby enabling them to trim the cost of single-handedly providing for their dependents or wards.

Many West African refugee and immigrant women have also found employment working as domestic maids. Several of the immigrant women in this line of work have a cultural advantage in finding domestic work. First, these immigrant women are very fluent in English, have excellent communication skills, and possess secondary-school credentials earned in West Africa. Second, doing domestic work is second nature to the vast majority of the immigrant women. In their households back home, many of them had to cook and prepare meals for the family, clean the house, wash and iron clothes, and look after the children. Older siblings were expected to assist in the supervision and socialization of the younger children. Most of the women performed these tasks on a daily basis and there was no distinction made between a school day and a weekend. In the rural areas of West Africa, young girls walk miles to the water stands to fetch and carry water home every morning before going to school. They also have to sweep the compound, cook breakfast, and, at times, go and sell bread early in the morning before coming home to get ready for school. Upon returning home from school, girls are expected to continue performing household work. In a typical West African household, this can last from early evening until late at night. The next day, the same tasks are repeated. It is a busy schedule that is labor-intensive. A third advantage shared by most of the immigrant women is that they grew up in homes where multiple families coresided and shared household and domestic responsibilities. This brings an added skill—it fostered cooperation, a sense of altruism, and an ability to manage household resources. For young women of school-going age as well, these chores and the responsibilities that accompany them have become important as more and more of their parents find work outside of the home. This may be formal work such as civil service work, teaching, or working as a secretary, or informal work such as trading at the market centers or operating a *chop bar*, canteen, or restaurant. The void created by the absence of parents is usually filled by adolescents, who are seamlessly incorporated into the informal production of goods and services. An increasing number of single West African women now emigrate on their own, joining the ranks of the African immigrant population in the United States independent of the sponsorship of extended-family members. For some of these single women, particularly those with legal status, doing maid work, housekeeping, or nanny work is another way to achieve economic security. For those who do not have children of their own or a spouse, the preference is to be a live-in nanny, maid, or housekeeper. This way, the women do not have to worry too much about meeting incidental expenses related to the financial upkeep of their own households.

For the West African refugee and immigrant women who perform various forms of domestic work in the mainly affluent suburban communities surrounding St. Louis, this type of work is considered very desirable and, in some cases, lucrative as well. The income reported by the women in this line of work is $1,500 per month for those who reside with the employer, and $1,800 for those women who live on their own. Those with experience and education can earn more than $1,800 per month. For those women who reside with the employer, food and a furnished room are provided, including the use of the family's car for running errands like grocery shopping, taking the children to school, and, at times, driving the children to other extracurricular activities such as soccer and music lessons.

The majority of the refugee women working as domestic maids consider their compensation adequate. According to Grace, a live-in nanny-housekeeper from Liberia, her monthly earnings of $1,500 are far more than what she was making when working at Wal-Mart and a day care center. Grace carefully recounted,

> Having a job gives you some peace of mind, especially if you work for a family that gives you some flexibility in how things should be done and organized in the household. During the day, I have the house all to myself, cooking, washing and ironing, cleaning all the rooms, including the bathrooms. Around 3 p.m., I will go and get the kids from school, bring them home, feed them, and take them out again to their after-school activities, usually soccer, music lessons, and ballet. We follow a daily routine of chores. As long as these chores are done, I have some free time to myself. My employers do not get home until after 6:30 p.m. Without some flexibility in terms of the attention to details that comes with the role of a care giver involving children, there is the possibility of tension and conflicts with the employer.

This employment has brought a semblance of normality to Grace's life. Looking back, she never anticipated that she would be in a position to work in America let alone earn over $1,000 a month.

Despite her general contentment with her employment, Grace has encountered problems. For Grace, a major source of consternation is the exploitation that she experiences from one or two families who are friends with her employers. These families will often ask her to collect their children from school and drop them off at an afterschool program or sometimes keep them until they get home from work. For Grace, this may involve multiple trips, and she does not get paid by these two families because they are considered close friends of her employer. She brought this to the attention of her employers and they promised to look into the matter. In Grace's relationship with these two families, she has formed a strong sense of the economic and class exploitations that she faces and is ambivalent in her mind about how to find a solution to this problem. Without any hesitation, she stated, "After complaining about the extra work from these two families without pay, my employers agreed to discuss the issue with the families. They never did. I felt exploited. They hardly say much to me even when I pick up their children and bring them home. But I do not complain because they are good friends with my employers."

For another immigrant, the work of being a nanny, housekeeper, and maid came through an employment agency. After being vetted and successfully undergoing criminal background and previous work reference checks, Esi Ama, from Liberia, was hired by a suburban St. Louis family to be a live-in maid-housekeeper and nanny. This middle-class family consists of two parents, both attorneys, and three children under the age of nine years. Before Esi Ama started work, the terms of her employment, including the tasks to be performed and the compensation, were stipulated in writing. The formalized and written rules defining her job were a welcome relief for Esi Ama. If she has any concerns about the conditions of employment, she is required to forward all complaints to the agency. The agency saw it as their responsibility to explain labor laws to the families to avoid lawsuits and indentured servitudes. In previous work, Esi Ama was made to do extra work on weekends and during the weekdays, and her hours were sometimes extended to very late at night, most often until about 10 p.m., but she was only paid for work done from 6 a.m. to 5:30 p.m. When she complained about this, the employer terminated her and threatened to report her to the immigration authorities even though she has legal residence. Though the remuneration was agreed upon prior to the start of the job, Esi Ama did not receive the full amount per the contract of employment: "I was promised $350 a week, but when I cashed my check, I noticed it was short by almost $75. When I asked why, I was told that there is a marginal cost for food and housing, even though this was not pre-arranged," Esi Ama indicated.

The perspective of some of the immigrant women is that their employers have little or no understanding of labor laws and the legal liabilities they are subject to when they breach employment laws. For several of the women who perform domestic work, there is a preference for a strict interpretation of the guidelines of employment that they have to follow. Correspondingly, they expect their employers to do the same by following formal employment practices even though the nature of the work is such that it is carried out in an informal setting, that is, a family household. A clear delineation of the employment guidelines for both employee and employer is therefore pertinent. According to Leena, a refugee woman from Liberia employed as a domestic housekeeper by a suburban St. Louis doctor, "The employers prefer to operate with rather loose a guideline since that gives them the flexibility to fire and terminate employment at whim. But for the maids, we want everything in writing because that offers us protection and security from abuses and exploitation by unscrupulous employers." For Leena, this is her third job working as a maid-nanny-housekeeper. She was terminated twice for taking time off to care for a sick child and an ailing mother. Termination of her employment happened on a day she was not scheduled to work. Narrating her point of view, Leena stated, "The employer called on Saturday morning on my off day and said I was needed urgently in the house because they are taking a weekend family trip and they wanted her to watch over the children. When I said I couldn't come because my child was ill and that I had to take my mom to the city clinic, they terminated me right away and said not to show up for work on Monday. When I showed up on Monday to collect my paycheck, the wife wanted me to stay, but the husband wanted me gone for good," she said, while sobbing.

The case of Dora is another example of the entrenched exploitation that some of the West African refugees encounter. Dora's immigration status complicated her working relationship with her employer. Dora came to the United States from Sierra Leone as a refugee seeking asylum. Her trip to the United States had taken her through Australia, Britain, and Canada before eventually making it to America. Dora had extended-family relatives who had lived in the United States as immigrants for almost twenty years. An immigrant woman from Guyana brought to Dora's attention that a middle-class white family at her church was looking for a live-in nanny and domestic housekeeper. Without any experience, Dora applied and got the job. Her responsibilities included housecleaning, cooking, taking care of the family's three children, and performing other duties determined by the employers. Her initial pay was $300 for a seven-day workweek. Dora's goal was to save enough money and eventually repatriate home. The fact that she did not possess valid work authorization papers was not an issue with her employer at the time of employment. Dora was surprised the employer did not check her status. Now in her seventh year of working as a domestic without valid papers, Dora's life is filled with apprehension and fear. Her concern is that a slight error on her part or failure to meet the expectations of the employers will lead to job termination and possibly being reported to immigration authorities. With the fear of possible deportation always looming in her mind, Dora finds herself not questioning unfair treatment by the children, first and foremost, and also by the couple that employed her. In addition, she has to endure a subordinate role on account of her race, ethnicity, class, and immigration status. The social and economic inequality between Dora as a Black immigrant and her white middle-class employers is a microcosm of a much larger caregiving relationship that relatively affluent, white, suburban middle-class families have formed with urban and poor minority women all across the United States.

For Dora, the realities of this inequality based on race, ethnicity, class and gender are played out before her very own eyes at her place of employment. Economically, she is seen by the employer family as a domestic servant whose social capital and prestige is low relative to whites. Culturally, her racialized status and identity as a Black female does not endear her to many American whites. The intersections of the economic and cultural statuses of Dora converge to define and situate her within the growing international domestication of women's labor, particularly women of color. The contestation of her overall status as a domestic person is jeopardized by the fact that she lacks a support system and information about how best to challenge the unequal relationship she has with her employers. Dora explained,

> Certainly, the family I work for are privileged, but most often they treat those of us who work for them as dirt; no respect whatsoever is shown to us even by their children. The cultural images that they have about Black people in general are sickening. They do not respect anybody from Africa. They see me merely in terms of a maid; that's all. Even the children look down upon you. It is very hard to be treated like this and at the end of the work day go home to my own kids and try to raise them to respect everyone irrespective of who they are or the color of their skin.

Elderly care provides another dimension of work for some West African immigrant and refugee women. This aspect of caregiving is regulated by state and federal regulations. Private contractors and subcontractors will often hire immigrants with valid work authorization papers and place them as domestic workers in predominantly white, middle-class suburban homes. Mavis is also a refugee from Liberia. She was placed by an agency to perform domestic live-in work with an elderly Jewish couple in their 80s. Her responsibilities included cooking, washing, shopping for groceries, cleaning, and other responsibilities determined by the couple. For Mavis, this job provided an opportunity to achieve social mobility. Her compensation was nearly $1,000 per month. She did not have to worry about food, clothing, transportation, and housing. She drove the family's 1998 Toyota Corolla, which she was allowed to use even when she traveled to Minnesota to visit with her extended relatives once every year. During the peak of winter every year, the family traveled to Florida, where they owned a townhome. Mavis often accompanied them, though sometimes she stays behind. "This work was sent from heaven. I hardly spend any of my pay. I do remit to relatives at home every fortnight. I am particularly grateful for the chance to live and work in the U.S. I get free clothes which I ship to West Africa where the need is greatest. I have managed to buy land at home in Monrovia. And recently, I started building a four bedroom house with a boy's quarters," Mavis admitted.

For Mavis, an important aspect in the remaking of her once war-shattered life as a refugee is to continue working, save enough money, and eventually sponsor her parents to join her in the United States. "Life is still hard at home in Liberia. The war has ended but people are still living with the scars. Perhaps the wounds of war can never be healed. Most of the young men and women are leaving the country in droves, even to go to places where historically Liberians have stayed away from (Asia and the Middle East). I don't blame them as rebuilding the country is a monumental task," she said. To better prepare herself for the future, Mavis is pursuing a course of study at a St. Louis college to get a licensed practitioner diploma in nursing. Ultimately, her goal is to become a nurse. But as she pursues these dreams, she also realizes that she must put her family life on hold. "Most of the single refugees I know are postponing having children. I think the crisis did something to us. It makes us doubt and wonder why one should bring a child into this world when you consider what has happened at home," Mavis said, revealing her anger and disappointment in her tone. And like other refugee women, living in America has brought her some degree of personal safety and economic security. But there is consternation, she said, "that the good times in America is about to end or is slowing due to the society's anti-immigrant feelings and the threat posed to immigrants by hate groups." While her blackness is sometimes an issue with some of the people who come to visit her employer family, she does not allow that to bother her. She mentioned that some of the whites who come to visit often treat her condescendingly, but she has remained indomitable, keeping her eyes focused on her priorities and goals. "Some of the guests never control their children," she said. "They make a mess all over the house and then call me to come and clean after them. They never acknowledge me or show their gratitude each time I clean after them. To them, I am trash, poor, Black, African, a foreigner with no rights they care to respect." Mavis consoles herself in the belief that many of her country folks will find a way to get to America if they know they have a job that pays $1,000, with free accommodations and transportation, waiting for them. After all, she reasoned, "the average Liberian earns and lives on less than a dollar a day. And some of them are still living in refugee camps all over West Africa for almost two decades now." This feeling is echoed by a unanimity of the refugees specifically, and also by the West African immigrants in general. No matter the racial, ethnic, and class problems they face as a result of their subordinate status, the economic and cultural advantages that they derive living in America far outweigh the myriad of issues that they have to contend with at home had they not migrated.

In the end, the common belief is that these refugees are also living their American dreams, and that there are many people all over Black Africa who are yearning for the opportunity to come to the United States, legally or illegally. That is why economically driven and frustrated youths from Africa continue to risk life and limb trekking across the Sahara on foot—to make a beachhead in the Mediterranean, marking the first leg of a long and treacherous migratory journey to the European Union and, ultimately, to America. International migration has become the dominant form of economic adaptation to the harsh realities of the African economic and political sagas. The economic plight of many is dire. Leaving to find better economic opportunities is the accepted norm in order to ameliorate chronic hardships. Meanwhile, those who have been fortunate to migrate to the United States are quietly pursuing their economic dreams without allowing the country's racial polarization to affect their goals even when they become the targets of racism and discrimination. Most have accepted the status of second-and third-class citizens, and even when they contest their subordinate status, the essence is not to become embroiled in sustained conflicts with the members of the host society since that may call attention and bring them some visibility. Most do not mind living on the margins of society and being excluded from the core society as long as they are able to pursue economic goals. Most of the refugee women prefer to be left alone to pursue work, further their education, raise their children, save some money, and, ultimately, repatriate home. As one of the refugee women confidently stated, "Calling attention to oneself or to others is not a way to deal with their subordinate status when the rules of society are always stacked against you. You need to deflect attention so that in case you are here illegally, you will not become the center of attention with neighbors, the police, or anyone with the authority to report you to the immigration authorities. You must stay invisible the best way you can. Sort of like being in exile, watching every step you take and mindful of those with power to change your life chances." What this means for some of the women is self-imposed, purposive marginalization and alienation designed to minimize the prospects of conflict with anyone with the power and resources to have you sent home for good. And to confirm this belief or perception, one immigrant woman reiterated, "some of us have lived and worked in the underground economy without any legal identity for decades and we intend to continue living in the same way."

For refugee women with children of their own, performing domestic work presents a major problem. Finding enough time to spend with and raise their children is problematic. Often, for these women, balancing and meeting the needs of their own children and having to take care of other people's children involves working for more than eight hours every day and then going home to be with their children or male partner or husband. For those who are married, the men usually step in to fill the void of their frequent absences. These men usually perform the bulk of the household chores, including cooking, feeding the children, and washing clothes as well as assisting children with their schoolwork. Migration has altered the gender roles of these men as they have become more egalitarian in their relationship with their partners. Back home in West Africa, these men may never be that involved in the lives of their children or in assisting with household chores as these roles are gendered, with the women performing the bulk of the chores. Child care and household work is feminized. And even when wives work outside the home, they are still the primary reproducers of culture, often providing the care and nurturing of young and old alike, cooking, washing, cleaning, and tending to the family's farm.

Where there is no male partner residing at home, some of the West African immigrant women often rely on friends in their social network to look after their children while they are working. Usually, for the women who assist, monetary payments may not be given for the services rendered. Instead, for those who benefit from the services of other women, a common practice is cooking and the sharing of children's clothing. A lot of bartering goes on among the women. This is one of the reasons why they prefer to live in close proximity to other African immigrant or refugee women that they know. Some of them may even contribute their spare time to assisting those among them who have to work or have children at home. One woman revealed, "We are always in and out of each other's place of residence. We always know when someone is at home; and they know that no matter what time it is, there is always plenty of food for all to share and a place to sleep at night if parents are working, taking classes, or attending to other chores. We always know when someone has a need. People step in and assist without even thinking about it."

This collective altruism among the women minimizes the economic cost of running their respective homes. It also fosters a sense of bonding and philanthropy among the women. For the children, an added advantage is that they always have a wide circle of friends to play with and they assist each other with their schoolwork. At times, the parents organize the children and drop them off at area parks, allowing the women to also spend time with each other. Time spent with other immigrant women and children also affords parents the opportunity to anchor the lives of their children in proven traditional West African values and thereby shape the future identities of their children. More importantly, it gives the parents the opportunity to exchange information about future employment and develop strategies for holding on to their current jobs and for dealing with recalcitrant employer families.

West African refugee and immigrant women are resilient. They are highly motivated and assiduous, desirous of alleviating the poverty that confronts them and finding ways of improving upon their economic conditions. Before coming to the United States, many of them had to endure hardships and challenges (both political and economic) that are daunting and a test of human will. Wars, violence, extreme poverty, political turmoil, unmet needs, shattered lives, and unfulfilled aspirations dominated the lives of many of the women. But once they are able to leave West Africa, most of them experienced a rebirth, a reinvigorated life, and a new vision or lens through which to define and find meaningful solutions to the myriad of problems that confront them. When these refugee women encounter obstacles and feel like they are "down in the dumps," these women hardly retreat from the despair that surrounds them. They act relentlessly to find their way "out of the dumps." Armed with a clear and articulated vision of what they expect from life and their hopes for the future, many of these women implement a variety of strategies to rebuild and reconstruct their shattered lives in new, foreign, and distant lands away from home and family members. Like other minority Americans, these refugee women find themselves in the trenches, facing and living with deindustrialization, strangulation by poor housing, protracted periods of unemployment, poverty, continued dehumanization and denigration of blackness, and segregation. But these problems are often temporary and pale in comparison with what they have experienced and what some of their relatives continue to live through at home in West Africa. As one of the refugee women affirmed, "We are always learning to cope and deal with problems everyday. That is what we have to do to survive. When you learn to survive in a refugee camp, you can survive anywhere."

The narratives from the West African refugees suggest three con-clusions. First, a majority of the women have found ways to manage and adapt to the economic expectations and uncertainties in their lives via an active participation in the labor force. Work has become an important cog in the multiple identities that these women have estab-lished with the host society. In this regard, it is correct to surmise that their adaptation process has been facilitated by their high rate of labor force participation. Relative to their economic positions at home in West Africa prior to their arrival in America, it cannot be denied that the women have experienced social mobility as measured by income, literacy, quality of housing, and by cultural commodities such as own-ing a car, a place to live, and reasonable standards of living that are the envy of many in Africa. Central to their ethos regarding full employ-ment is the cultural expectation that they have imported from Africa that work and family life are the fulcrum around which self and com-munal improvements become fostered and actualized.

Equally persuasive is the cultural belief held by the refugee women that individual well-being is contingent upon familial well-being. In this regard, a cooperative approach based on economic and cultural altruism is equally promoted to tap and mobilize familial resources and capital for collective enterprise and achievement. But at the same time, the forces of globalization and the increased demand for female labor in the service production sector of the U.S. economy means that many of the women are experiencing problems that are attributable to the lack of oversight and governmental regulations regarding trans-national women and the service sector. Gendered inequalities and the commoditization of women's work is creating favorable environments where some employers continue to violate labor and employment practices when dealing with mainly foreign women who lack a strong power base to begin with, let alone the institutions to agitate for effec-tive representation with management and employers in general. In addition, the reintegration and resettlement of refugees who have been legally admitted to stay in the United States can at best be char-acterized as a piecemeal approach with the lack of interagency coordi-nation. The result is that interagency services designed to achieve the full integration of refugees in the economic and cultural domains have had little impact on the lives of the affected persons. Coupled with this is the lack of a unified national policy on refugee resettlement. Federal and state initiatives designed to settle refugees oftentimes do not converge and at times even appear to be contradictory.

Second, for the vast majority of the West African refugee women, efforts toward integration have been thwarted by the persistent racialization of people of Black African ancestry and descent in the United States. Central to this is the inability of the refugee women to find self-actualization in American society. The cultural paradox confronting them is that, on the one hand, they see the openness of American society and its culture of individual responsibility and the right to define one's one identity based on lived experiences. However, this freedom and right is somehow limited to, and confined by, the intersections of gender, class, ethnic, and racial identities. Worst of all, though their jobs and social position places them at the lowest hierarchy of social stratification—thereby making it difficult, if not impossible, for the refugee women to negotiate and construct their own sense of identity—the women also find they have to confront and deal with the sustained assault on their religious identity as well. On the one hand, the refugee women see an America with its promises and bountiful opportunities where people are fair, strive to affirm others, and are engaged in finding solutions to problems when times are hard and trying. On the other hand, these women see an America that is fractured by gender, class, race, and ethnicity. In this fracture is a fault line that is teetering on the brink of intense conflicts and divisiveness. Having to deal with the subtleties of discrimination and racism seem to suggest to some of the refugee women that the violence they experienced will not necessarily abate even though they now live in the United States.[6]

Third, encountering the voices of refugee women who have been displaced from their respective homelands reveals the fractious and volatile nature of African social systems. These women registered their intense disdain for the politicians, soldiers, and warlords who use tribalism and ethnic divisions to fan hate and thereby promote their egotistical interests. Refugee after refugee lamented about the state of Black African politics today and decried the hegemonic hold on power by a mostly patriarchal-controlled system in which women have little or no input despite the rising number of women graduates and postgraduates working in both the private and public sectors of West Africa.

CHAPTER 5

GENDER AND TRANSNATIONAL
BLACK IMMIGRANT IDENTITIES

*A little bit from each family member living and working abroad
goes a long way in changing the economic conditions of relatives
living at home.*

—Theresa, a Senegalese immigrant

*This is not the identity we want to present to the world as Black
folks. I agree that hip-hop is a cultural form designed to depict
the struggles in the community. But it objectifies women as sexual
commodities. This is how children learn at an early age to disrespect
women. Later, this same disrespect is extrapolated to include other
authority figures.*

—Georgina, a Liberian immigrant

As in the past, different groups of Africans from different countries
forming the continent are still lumped together into the general category of Black Africans. Though the women immigrants discussed
in this book come from countries with similar economic and political circumstances, this form of unitary group identity obfuscates the
huge differences and internal diversity commonly found among Black
Africans—differences in languages, cultures, normative systems, and
social structures. The West African subregion is no different. As indicated, the heritage of the region has been shaped by indigenous Black
African cultures, Arabian cultures, and European colonization. This
heritage confers on the region a rich tapestry of cultures oftentimes
romanticized as well as celebrated by all. This heritage and legacy
endears the region to the rest of the world as a gateway and *mecca* of

cultural hybridity. Sometimes forgotten by the rest of the world due to its seemingly intractable social, economic, and political problems, the region is home to a diverse wealth of natural resources that have yet to be tapped for improvement in the quality of life of its peoples. The depiction of the region on the world scene is one of human misery, despair, and unforgiving poverty. Occasionally, it is also seen as an oasis of hope—that sooner rather than later the peoples of the region will realize their dreams and promises for a better life. While they anticipate this possibility, a majority of the citizens are looking outside the region to fulfill their economic aspirations, dreams, and hopes.

For West Africans who are successful in coming to the United States, the representations and manifestations of gender, class, racial, and ethnic identities are often cast in a transnational focus. This focus recognizes that identities are multifaceted and often transcend geography, space, locality, and nationalities. A transnational paradigm has an intuitive appeal in explaining the elaborate networks that immigrants form to connect and link them to local as well as cross-national resources. The perspective allows for ways to understand how immigrants marshal resources and strategies to maximize their opportunities in both the immigrant sending and receiving countries. These networks exert an influence on immigrant economic outcomes, including labor and employment opportunities. Referencing Grosfoguel and Cordero-Guzman (1998), Conway, Bailey, and Ellis (2001) reported that the establishment of these transnational networks contributes to the understanding of the material and cultural relationships that are fostered by these groups. Within the context of the African diaspora, examples of these networks are those that group and form along tribal, clan, family, and kinship membership, religious identification groupings, cultural alliances, educational and political affiliations, secret societies, benevolent, mutual aid associations, and national as well as supranational institutions whose memberships are drawn from the intra- and inter-nation states in Africa.

For West African immigrant women, the transnational realities that have come to inform their immigrant journeys are yet to be fully comprehended. For example, the processes entailing the transnational and collective mobilization of economic resources from multiple points around the world has yet to be fully studied. Equally missing is how, as a group, West African women immigrants in Europe and North America engage in multiple secondary or chain migrations with one principle objective in mind—to rationalize and locate the optimum town or city where they stand the best chance of tapping their fullest human capital potential. For West African immigrant women in particular, transnational spaces provide powerful contexts for under-standing how these networks, once created, become sites where gendered, class, racial, and ethnic relationships are manifested and contested. A gendered lens is critical if we are to understand how and why African women have come to dominate the transnational net-work spaces that immigrants from Africa who are domiciled in Europe and North America create.

The formation of identities among West African immigrant women, once they encounter each other in the United States, is largely influ-enced by their status as a racial and ethnic minority. Cordero-Guzman, Smith, and Grosfoguel (2001) pointed out that new immigrant groups entering the country have to confront and cope with structural racial-ization the outcome of which define economic, cultural, and social incorporation into the host society. The construction and contesta-tion of the form(s) of racial and ethnic identities that are portrayed by the immigrant women are typically influenced by the women's sub-jective and objective responses and perceptions about the systematic and enduring legacies of discrimination against Blacks and persons of color in the United States. From the women's perspective, therefore, the racialized identities and low status of Blacks are important con-siderations in how the immigrant women form their notions about equality, fairness, and inclusiveness into American society. For the African immigrants entering the United States, the racial and ethnic experiences of America's native-born Blacks is an essential reference point for the construction and expression of their immigrant identi-ties. The history of discrimination and its persistence in the American psyche therefore assumes a collective or group meaning for the immi-grant women in explaining how they view and express racial and ethnic identity. Their cues about race and ethnic relationships in the United States are structured and defined against the backdrop of the historical legacies of discrimination and racism against minority groups in the United States. In defining their identities, the collective experiences of Blacks and their resistance of oppression become the reference points and lenses through which a sense of racialized group marginality and alienation are formed by immigrant Blacks. Despite the existence of cultural differences, a unifying factor among the immigrants is their unflinching support and identification with the experiences of native-born Blacks. For these non-Western immigrant women trying to map their own ethnic, racial, and gender trajectories in Western societies, it becomes obvious that there is not a common template that they can follow or adopt to ground their identities. As they seek to create the infrastructures to enable them become more visible in American society, the West African immigrant women have come to recognize that systematic efforts will be made by superordinate groups and the critics of immigration to define them as a problem-people living on the fringes of society. Their presence may even evoke, as Gates and West (1996, 85) opined, "uneasiness and discomfort even among whites of goodwill." As Black women in America, the immigrants recognize that their essence and presence in America will be contested as they seek to become more visible. This contestation, as Lenoir and Kidane noted, is attributable to the growth in the Black African immigrant population in major cities across the country. African immigrants, Lenoir and Kidane pointed out, are often discriminated against and scapegoated for the economic ills of the country.

For many of the immigrant women, total assimilation into white society has yet to occur, though some are beginning to vigorously pursue ethnic integration and identification with native-born Black Americans. This is the case irrespective of how long the women have been living in the United States. The boundaries of their own ethnic communities are persistently blurred due to interactions with immigrants from the Caribbean and South America. In this new alliance of panethnicity that brings together migrant experiences from developing countries, the West African immigrant women see an opportunity to redefine a Black identity that is more cosmopolitan, international, boundless, and borderless. And at times, these identities are different from the ones that have been defined by American-born Blacks.

A major source of the women's identity is the common experience of international migration. This identity seeks to create a cultural space where West Africans as a group can affirm and live out the true meaning of their Africanness. In the mixing and blending of cross-national identities that are created and shared as the women foster bonds with one another emerges a new Black identity that seeks to use migratory experiences to achieve cultural, political, and economic empowerment. This empowerment sometimes takes the form of an unorganized but collective effort to resist the negativities often associated with blackness in the United States. The women reject current and historically entrenched notions about Black people in general. And they, like their African American sisters, remain firm in their determination not to have their cultural and ethnic identities defined for them by outsiders or those who have not experienced what it means to be Black in white-privileged American society.

On the whole, the West African women remain very content about the economic niches they are carving for themselves and the opportunities that have opened up to them following their migration.

However, like their African American sisters, they perceive that they cannot accept the pervasive and entrenched discriminatory and stereotypical attitudes that denigrate them on account of their ethnic, racial, gender, and class identities. Subtle remnants of *de jure* and *de facto* discrimination are still etched in the minds of the immigrants. The women's subjective identification with Black America is based upon the shared cultural meanings that Black people in the diaspora form to represent multiple dimensions and strands of identities. For some of the women, this identity is also premised on the historical perception that America typically has not treated its Black citizens well. The immigrant women made specific references to the discriminatory practices that are still embedded in core institutions in the country, particularly in education, criminal justice, health care, housing, and the labor force. Their perceptions about what it means to be Black are not the same as how white Americans define blackness. There is a more positive subjective appraisal of blackness than the cultural negativities that Americans have come to associate with its Black minority population in general.

Persistent discrimination toward Blacks represents a deep-seated concern among the immigrant women. The way to counteract and minimize this discrimination, according to the immigrant women, is not via assimilation but through the formation of a new Black identity that is based upon a Black African ethos devoid of victimhood mentality and powerlessness often portrayed by Black cultural and social society. From their viewpoints, counteracting and confronting this perceived powerlessness involves embracing self-help and actualization, collective communal grassroots mobilization, and a deconstruction of white and Anglo domination and influence.

Total or complete assimilation is shunned even by those women who intend to seek citizenship or naturalization. Acquisition of citizenship is seen as a means to achieve cultural and political empowerment. But this empowerment is rationalized not in terms of a localized contestation of issues in American society but rather in Africa where these immigrants expect to return in the future. In this regard, the outcomes and manifestations of the identities that the immigrants construct are often designed to be played out in localized political and cultural spaces at home. Assimilation may be shunned because it may not provide the immigrant women with the power and status they would like to have in the United States due to their racialized status as foreign-born minorities.

Some of the immigrant women maintain minimum contacts with a cross-section of the host society. A common reason accounting for this is the women's perception that they continue to experience subtle and, at times, overt forms of racial oppression due to their race and ethnic background. Their lower to lower-middle class status does not offer them protection from persistent denigration and open attacks by anti-immigrant and organized hate groups. Many of the immigrant women prefer to form ties with other coethnic immigrants as well as their relatives and friends who are living outside the United States or in Africa. Forging strong transnational ties is considered important to the women. The women's perspective about racial and ethnic identity is a reflection of tribal or clan identity juxtaposed against the backdrop of a Pan-African identity and a mixture or blending of a cameo of identities formed and learned in America. Knowing that the majority of them will be repatriating to Africa in the future serves as a protective layer of additional security enabling the women to deal with racially motivated negative experiences that many of them reportedly face in their daily activities. Their gendered and racialized status forces them to strengthen the social interactions that the women establish with other immigrants who are underrepresented and racially subordinated by the larger dominant culture. Reliance on their Black African cultural identities and institutions enables them to form strong bonds to contest anti-immigrant sentiments and growing nativism designed to exclude non-whites and people of color, particularly Black immigrants, from the core society. The social spaces that these women create are intended to foster intraimmigrant belongingness and a sense of African cultural pride and heritage. Accenting Black pride and cultural heritage is simply a way for the immigrant women to create and bring social meanings to their varied immigrant experiences.

Understanding the processes involved in the immigrant women's formation of transnational modes of social integration is pivotal in mapping out how minority Black women negotiate and contest the male-dominated patriarchal structures that, for the most part, serves to deny women of color their place in American society. Their resistance to gendered oppression and social violence is manifested through carefully woven strategies emphasizing coalition building and economic emancipation for themselves and their children. The affirmation of this empowerment on the part of the immigrant women is testimony of their resilience and the strength of their ambitions to speak with one voice and with clarity concerning the multiple realities that continue to influence their lack of social, cultural, economic, and political power. Economic and cultural empowerments are the proven modalities that many of the women are utilizing to manifest their myriad and transnational identities in the United States. By creating and forging these transnational ties in the United States and beyond, these immigrant women are attempting to construct identities that are cross-cultural, dynamic, and fluid. The fluidity of these identities as they are constructed makes it somewhat difficult for outsiders to develop markers to pigeonhole and stereotype the identities that are formed by these women. Investigations into the expectations (psychological, philosophical, cultural, or economic) that serve as the underpinnings grounding these identities are warranted.

CREATING TRANSNATIONAL IMMIGRANT SPACES

One of the approaches to studying migration is the value expectancy model. This model posits that there are social-psychological motivations inherent in the formulation of migration decision making. This paradigm recognizes the importance of macrolevel or structural factors (income, labor force and employment variables, educational opportunities, laws regulating population mobility) and microlevel factors (family patterns, social networks, normative expectations, the social psychological motivations of migration, household dynamics) in forming and mediating the decision-making processes involved in whether or not someone should migrate. De Jong and Gardner (1981), Fawcett (1985), De Jong, Root, and Abad (1985, 1986), and Eades (1987) are the principal proponents of this approach.

This approach is relevant to the understanding of the transnational networks that African immigrants form to facilitate or influence the decision-making process in their migration from Africa to the West. For West African migrants, there is a value expectancy of migration. This value expectancy is based on what the entire extended family intends to accomplish when it sends its members abroad. The networks that West Africans form to implement various migratory strategies— usually by choosing to migrate to destinations where they have existing contacts, social networks, or family members—is also at the core of the transnationalized lives that have come to dominate the migratory culture of West Africans. Household formations and well-established traditional systems and patterns of family relationships have positioned West Africans to become active participants in the new global migration. Household and family resources are harnessed and collectivized to enable certain family members to be sponsored to travel abroad to attend school, find employment, and provide economic returns to strengthen the family and household economic circumstances. Schmink (1984), Pessar (1982), DaVanzo (1981), Portes and Bach (1985), and Buechler and Buechler (1987) argued that the household unit as an agency of economic production allocates its resources in such a way as to maximize the productive capacities of the family unit.

Information flows about employment prospects, visa regulations, costs of living, and what life is like from the migrant-receiving locations are transmitted home via these transnational social networks operating at the familial level. The migrations of whole family units to the West and their settlement in several European countries as well as in the United States are intended to meet the long-term economic needs of household members. For West African immigrants, this is often accomplished via remittance flows from the migrant destination to the migrant-sending countries. These remittances that many West African families have come to rely on are sent home from several transnational locations to extended family members. Remittances may be used to meet consumption needs or to sponsor other family members (Fawcett and Arnold 1987). The expectations regarding the need to provide economic support for relatives at home are a normative and culturally institutionalized facet of African migration cultures. Without the economic support through remittances, many of the immigrants' family members would not be able to afford the barest necessities of life. Sending money home is an obligation, a civic responsibility with a spiritual overtone. In sharing their means with extended relatives at home, no matter how small, the immigrants are fulfilling a spiritual duty that is imposed upon them by the departed ancestors as well as the living: the imperative to share one's means and gifts with all. In this regard, remittances become blessings. People are encouraged to gift in spite of the imperfections in the system (for example, gifts or remittances may be channeled for wrong uses). In the giving of their means, the benefactors gain the favor of family here and those already departed. The giver is accorded honor, gratitude, and blessings by the community of extended kinfolk. Giving and supporting extended relatives at home is also viewed by the immigrants as a way to transform society and culture in the home country. In this regard, some of the women view themselves as change agents, using their resources to leverage and clamor for change and, at the same time, to realign and redefine social expectations while affirming new modalities of social and cultural activism and incorporation.

Whether they confine their migration internally to Africa or move to other worldwide destinations, West African women do not sever links with their countries of origin. Home affairs are cherished and celebrated even from great distances away. The home country is seen as the ultimate place to return to, irrespective of prevailing adverse economic, political, or social conditions. The interconnectivity with home is also buttressed in cultural and normative beliefs that affirm the spiritual meaning of home to all immigrants. In essence, these immigrants have left home without abandoning or severing ties completely. A unique feature of African émigrés in general is their strong commitment and attachment to their respective homelands. No matter how poor the countries they leave behind, African immigrants express a sense of nationalism and continental pride that is unrivaled. This interconnection is both spiritual and economic. Spiritually, Africans believe that home is where the ancestors are buried and that the blessings from the ancestors are bestowed on all who live in the same spiritual realm. Among the Akans of Ghana, for example, the spirit or soul (*ntoro*) and the blood or consanguine (*mogya*) relationships are linked via spiritual ties between the living and the dead. Traveling abroad and forgetting about the world of the ancestors is seen as denying them respect and reverence. And as a result of this abandonment, the material and spiritual blessings of the living can be withheld. That is why most African immigrants living in the diaspora like to go home regularly, if possible, to pay homage to the ancestors and the living and to solicit their blessings for economic prosperity in their new lives abroad. Libations may be poured in honor of immigrants who visit home. Food may be prepared and extended relatives invited.

When West African immigrants create transnational identities in foreign lands, they often rely on the goodwill and spiritual gifts of clan and tribal members to provide them with security and protection in all their daily activities. When they accomplish a feat, no matter how small, the immigrants make it a point to share this with their relatives back home. This is done to show appreciation for the magnanimity and generosities of the living and the dearly departed. Even the transnational and cross-border identities formed abroad are designed to show the immigrants' deep-seated belief that community goals are fostered in a spirit of altruism—that individuals standing alone cannot gain mastery over all the problems confronting the group. It is group and collective mobilization of resources that ensures success and social well-being. This consciousness is etched in the minds of West African and African émigrés in the Black diaspora in North America and elsewhere. The same consciousness is woven into the fabric of African societies.

The transnational posture of the women immigrants serves as a bridge between their new societies and their home countries of origin. The growing diasporic mobility of African women has led to the establishment of transnational networks of African communities worldwide. Through these networks, African communities and collective identities representing the panoply of African cultures have been created and recreated in immigrant-receiving destinations worldwide. Networks of mutual support that form along national, ethnic, religious, professional, or class lines serve as a reminder to the women of the need to maintain their common unifying purpose—to enhance their standard of living by capturing the economic benefits conferred to migrants who engage in international migration. Through their newly formed transnational identities, African female immigrants worldwide are able to define and develop proven strategies for coping with the uncertainties of traveling abroad. The gendered immigrant identity that is based on kin group membership and collective diasporic experiences is manifested among the immigrants as a community that transcends nationality, ethnicity, language, and culture. The fictive and affective bonds and alliances forged in the new transnational networks authenticate who these women are and their sense of being, dreams, aspirations, and hopes. At times, these communities and networks serve as facilitators, assisting disaffected and marginalized immigrants to navigate the thicket of institutionalized racism and discrimination in the West by invoking group help as a strategy to mobilize economic, cultural, and psychological resources to ensure collective empowerment.

As they weave common tapestries that define the contents of their gendered roles and foreign-born statuses, these African immigrant women strive to abolish artificial and geographic distances between them and their relatives or other contacts living in various parts of the world. The contours that define how these transnational immigrant networks operate are deeply rooted in the women's sense of shared destiny, history, and common hardships. More importantly, because these transnational networks tend to highlight group solidarity and collective action, as opposed to individualism, they tend to develop and maintain a unified voice in response to marginality, alienation, or, as stated, discrimination. A transnational identity is a social asset designed to maximize the migratory experience and give a voice to the cultural presence of the Black African female immigrant. For many of the West African immigrant women, being in America is considered a temporary sojourn and is tantamount to a self-imposed exile. The transnational relationships that these immigrants establish with other relatives who are scattered all over the world is a symbolic manifestation of how temporary places of abode (away from home in West Africa) are created to anchor the exiled identities of the immigrants. Living in these transnational corridors can be construed as living in exile, as expressed by Afkhami's (1994) account of women living in temporary exile.

The social and cultural realities of maintaining a transnational focus can prove challenging for some of the immigrant women. A case in point is Theresa, a Senegalese immigrant who left behind a large extended family in West Africa when she immigrated to the United States. Every month that she gets paid, Theresa finds herself struggling to pay her bills and remit home at the same time. She has taken on two jobs to meet this challenge. At the time of the interview, she was contemplating adding a third job. The transnational interconnection between home and the host society is maintained by the flow of highly valued Western-made material goods and trappings to relatives at home. On their part, relatives at home are eager to receive the regular remittances. The relatives come to see the profound effects of international migration in their own lives. Some of these families may use the remittances to install utilities at home (notably, electricity and pipe-borne water), buy a car or TV, access telephone services, or renovate the family residence. As demonstrated earlier, for nonimmigrant families, these material symbols may provide the motivation to push the young to migrate.

For children of school-going age in the predominantly rural and agricultural areas, continued economic support from America may mean that one will not have to toil and labor on the family's farm since the remitted funds are also typically used in hiring farmworkers to supplement assistance from the family. This may free up children's time to concentrate on their schoolwork. Economic assistance is sent home from multiple destinations to the families at home. "A little bit from each family member living and working abroad goes a long way in changing the economic conditions of relatives living at home or who have migrated to other parts of the world for the same reason I am here in America," Theresa said. The transnational lives of these immigrant women are intertwined and neatly woven into the fabric of West African and American societies, respectively. At times, the interconnections of the social and cultural networks may span across entire continents and regions of the world. As one immigrant confirmed, "These networks exist, in part, to enable and empower people (immigrants) to deal with the temporary and permanent forms of social exclusion, discrimination, and inequalities that are systemic in American society and elsewhere. At another level, these networks are intended to alleviate the economic plight of millions of people back home in Africa."

In maintaining the connections with their home countries, while at the same time forging an identity in their new locales, African immigrant women find themselves having to balance expectations emanating from their diasporic identities and from the pressure to provide economic support to their extended relatives back home. Balancing these expectations is daunting because it means that at any given point in time, the African immigrant women living in the West must live in two or more worlds at the same time. Though far away from home, several of these women indicated having to make economic decisions that would potentially impact the lives of both the young and old in Africa. These decisions include issuing specific guidelines as to how the remittances they send home should be used: whether to pay for the school fees of the children in the extended family household; who to consider for sponsorship to the West; which of their elderly relatives should be given a monthly allowance; what to use remittances for; and how to remit and how often.

These immigrant women not only seek to build transnational bridges and networks to connect them to their homelands but also to redefine how Blacks, as a group, are portrayed and resented by the host societies. A significant feature of the women's transnational gendered identities is the systematic deconstruction of negative labels and stigmas commonly associated with Blacks of the African diaspora in the West. Social and cultural definitions that cast Black people negatively are rejected by the women as oppressive and counterintuitive. The women celebrate their blackness and femininity by elucidating its invigorative power in assisting them in defining a space for discourses that serve their collective empowerment. In their worldview, historical and cultural manifestations of the Black experience in the West have yet to assume full-fledged visibility and presence. The marginality of Black ethnicity and the institutionalized forms of stereotypes and prejudice that sustain the denigration of Blacks operate in a closed spatial environment where notions of blackness are fixed. Some of the immigrant women see their role and place in American settings as a fresh opportunity to develop and affirm newer modalities of Black diasporic consciousness that transcend race and ethnicity. The gradual fulfillment of this new consciousness is approached by an emphasis on collective empowerment and responsibility and at the same time an acknowledgement that portraying a victimhood mentality inhibits any effective coalition and bridge-building involving groups with similar interests but different gender, class, racial, ethnic, or national backgrounds.

The negative images often associated with a global Black identity has come to mean that peoples of Black African descent (wherever they are found) must negotiate, renegotiate, and, at times, collectively resist entrenched and oppressive racial and ethnic ideologies. The women find themselves rejecting the stereotyped behavior typically defined of Blacks in the diaspora. The social and cultural displacement that some of the women feel living in the West is tantamount to what one of the respondents described as "being a captive to the structures of institutionalized oppression." Their individual and collective goal is that African cultures and Black people in general ought to be contextualized within the framework of Afrocentrism and panblackness. For these women, a theoretical and psychological paradigm that affirms their essence as cultural nurturers is pivotal in how they go about constructing transnational gendered identities associated with being Black. African culture provides them with a frame of reference from which to evaluate and create a cultural prism for the elucidation of self-awareness, cultural production, and psychological and spiritual well-being. Reflecting on their foreign identities, gendered status, and class relationships in the United States, many of the Black immigrant women remain recognizant of the poignancy of patriarchal systems that have pigeonholed them and disavowed their multifaceted roles in the world.

The patriarchal systems that are also firmly entrenched in the West remind the women of a similar structure that they left behind in Africa. Some of the women spoke eloquently about the sexual violence that some of them had experienced prior to their emigration to the West. Whether as young girls or adult women, the immigrants decried the maltreatment that some of them had experienced at the hands of fathers, male associates, brothers, husbands, and patriarchal-dominated institutions such as law, health, political, and education systems. From the immigrant women's perspective, the vestiges of the sexual victimization of young girls in Black Africa persist today, and, despite the global attention to the problem, many of the countries in the subregion have yet to formulate or implement robust measures to ameliorate the sexual victimization and also the enslavement of young girls.

Memories of the sexual exploitation that some of them experienced at the hands of men continue to dominate how the women construct notions of sexual identity and womanhood. For those who have managed to survive sexual victimization, there is a sense of fear, trepidation, anxiety, and lack of trust of African men, whether they encounter such men in the United States or at home. The plan of action for surviving the brutalizing effect of sexual victimization primarily consists in the formation of strong networks, acquiring economic independence and self-sufficiency, and a strong commitment empowerment through education and economic independence. Transnational networks provide channels of global communication that reflect immigrant women's growing sense of positive self-awareness and self-worth. The markers of positive self-worth and identity are often interlaced with a strong attachment to the core principles of Afrocentric and Pan-African perspectives that view Africa as the epicenter of cultural and historical renaissance. The women continually strive to appropriate for themselves and their children a hybrid identity that borrows from every corner of the Black world diaspora. For some African immigrant women, appropriation of multiple ethnicities and identities becomes the fulcrum around which culturally defined notions about their blackness and Africanness are affirmed or given a centered location and resonance.

The immigrant women's diasporic experiences become a visible manifestation of cultural protest that is designed to bring the dynamism of Black African cultures to center stage in the Western world and at the same time give it a cultural revival. The immigrant women strive to represent every positive aspect of Black culture and identity. In the identities they project, there is recognition of the importance of work, family life, the love of children, the well-being of others, and, above all, a deep-seated resilience and fortitude that obstacles can be overcome with group or collective spirit. Their cultural traditions continue to offer them with coping strategies to confront and deal with the incessant and negative commentaries they come into contact with regarding their Black descent. Pride in the richness of their heritage and traditions encapsulates them from what are otherwise constant barrages against Black societies.

In general, the formation of gendered identities among the immigrant women is conditioned by the notion that, somehow, being white and the myriad of identities associated with it are usually not seen as contestable. In their view, white ethnicities are often seen as absolute or nonproblematic. The same, however, cannot be said for people of Black African descent and ancestry in the United States. Some of the immigrant women decried the cultural casting of Black women in general as functionally illiterate, more prone to be on welfare relative to whites, and likely to engage in prostitution to support their drug habits. While the source(s) of this portrayal can be traced in part to the media and to lingering discrimination, the immigrant women also expressed concern over the portrayal of Black women by Black male hip-hop artists. As one of the immigrant women pointed out, "There is so much self-hate and poor self-esteem among Blacks themselves, particularly rap musicians who often will use sexually explicit language to describe the women in their lives, irrespective of whether they are their mothers, grandmothers, girl friends, or sisters. How anyone can dehumanize another being and use such offensive language is beyond me. Most of us from Africa cannot understand why Black leaders sit by and let this victimization and woman-bashing go on for such a long time, all in the name of making money. The moral compass of the community has eroded."

According to Georgina, a Liberian immigrant woman living in Omaha, Nebraska, white America is not entirely to blame entirely for the media's inaccurate and disparaging or negative portrayal of Black people. She explained that

> the negative portrayal of the identity of blackness in the U.S. is also attributable to Blacks who sit on the sidelines and allow a few in the Black community to gradually destroy the rich cultural heritage and traditions about community, religion, and family life held by the majority of Blacks throughout the world. In city after city, Blacks continue to embrace the culture of urban hip-hop music to the point where some of them begin to take on the beliefs and the values of the rappers. In my household, this sort of rubbish is not tolerated. Most of my female friends do not like this at all. This is not the identity we want to present to the world as Black folks. I agree that hip-hop is a cultural form designed to depict the struggles in the community. But it objectifies women as sexual commodities. This is how children learn at an early age to disrespect women. Later, this same disrespect is extrapolated to include other authority figures.

For Georgina and the rest of the immigrant women, there is consternation about the impact of urban Black minority hip-hop culture on the influences of their children. "Shielding our children from the corrosive impact of urban rap music is very difficult because we are also part of that community," an immigrant parent asserted. The desires of the immigrant women are that their children will be selective in terms of the aspects of hip-hop culture that they embrace, and being mindful that they do not completely abandon the legacies and traditions their parents brought with them from Africa. As another immigrant woman affirmed, "Some of our children use the urban culture as a marker for defining their blackness and Africanness. However, what I tell them is to continue embracing racial and ethnic identities that are global and transforming. This means that their identities must reflect the transnational experiences forming the basis of their migration realities in the United States."

For African immigrant women, the formation of a transnational immigrant identity centers on an important cultural and economic issue. This is symbolized by the need to create (or re-create) economically self-sustaining cultural communities comprised of networks of fellow émigrés who are joined by a common continental heritage and legacy. The common ground is to foster bonds of collective destinies and shared essence to ensure survival in the host society. The formation of transnational identities among African immigrant women tends to consist of three groups. These groups are: fellow immigrants from the immigrant country of origination, immigrants from other African countries domiciled in the same location, and, lastly, other people of Black African ancestry in the diaspora, especially American-born Blacks and others from South and Central America and the Caribbean Basin countries. Transnationalism among African women immigrants in the host societies takes on the form of a Pan-African identity whose goal is to link all of the peoples in the Black diaspora. Included in this group are native-born Black Americans, Black Canadians, and Blacks of British nationality. Having multiple links in the chain of transnational networks ensures that contacts are formed to serve as conduits for employment, psychological support, benevolence, legal aid, and collective security. International migration gives agency for the women to straddle multiple cultures.

An important facet of the transnational lives of the women immigrants in the West is the continuous struggle to find cultural and political representations to anchor their multiple and complex identities. Many of the women encounter cultural alienation while domiciled in the United States or the West. Constantly cast as Black outsiders, the immigrant women learn to come to terms with the predefined roles and identities that define their blackness. Being defined as Blacks and as outsiders limits their coordinated access to cultural and political representation. Some of the immigrant women contest the hegemonic ordering and institutionalized mechanisms of controls in Western societies that refuse to acknowledge the contributions of peoples of Black African descent to the development and progression of world cultures. A strategy for contesting this unequal power relationship consists of two approaches. The first is to rely on their own institutions imported from Africa to give meaning to their identities in the United States. But this strategy does not address how the immigrant women contest their marginalized status in various cultural institutions and key areas of the U.S. economy. Second, the immigrants have to rely on American institutions for jobs if they are to meet their economic needs. A way to confront this challenge is by engaging in multiple secondary migrations as well as engaging in continuing education at community colleges to upgrade their credentials. The immigrants are always searching for locations in the United States where they can enhance and facilitate their economic advancements without having to endure negative social stereotypes. A common practice is to have multiple immigrant families and groups congregate in specific employment domains. Once a sizeable number of immigrants gather together, they begin to form channels of communication to provide economic and psychological support to one another. In other words, the immigrants forge close-knit contacts and relationships with each other to provide access to, and information about, possible jobs.

For some of the women, the competition for jobs is very intense because they have to compete with other immigrant women from Southeast Asia, Eastern Europe, and Latin America. At times, some of them cross ethnic and national immigrant lines to foster relationships and networks with other immigrant groups. By developing networks with Hispanic and Asian women's groups in the United States, the West African immigrant women are able to expand their base to enhance their employment prospects. Since most of the women perform jobs where they are susceptible to frequent redundancies and chronic layoffs, the maintenance of these transnational immigrant networks becomes significant because they influence how soon an immigrant is able to find new employment when necessary. For those immigrant women who do not possess valid working papers, the relationships forged within this informal network are pivotal. The networks may provide the immigrant with access to recruiters and employers who do not check immigrant work papers. It may also facilitate access to the underground economy where identification cards can be purchased. This kind of group support is critical to the survival of many immigrants, not just those from West Africa.

For West African immigrant women in the United States, the formation of civic and grassroots movements that seek to address gender-specific issues related to the migratory experience is another channel used by the women to create their immigrant identities. Pressing issues such as violence against women, access to health care, equal pay, sexism in the workplace, and structural impediments that hamper the advancement of women in the workplace resonates as core issues influencing the women's quest for inclusion and acceptance into the body polity of American social and economic affairs. Some of the women believe that coalition building and the collective mobilization of resources is important in the women's attempts to speak with a collective voice in addressing their needs and giving them a place at the table of decision making. For West African immigrant women, this form of collective mobilization is not a new phenomenon. At home in West Africa, most of them lacked the social and political power to contest or effectively respond and mount challenges to matters affecting them. Their powerlessness is evidenced by the fact that they are often the victims of unfair land tenure rights, which give men unfettered access to land acquisition and property ownership rights.

In the educational arena, boys continue to receive priority when it comes to a family's investment in the postsecondary education of children and dependents. The opportunity to be in America has changed some of these dynamics among the immigrant women. Many women are involved in women-only network groups and social organizations to agitate for measures to improve upon the lives of immigrant women in the United States. Again, these networks may span national boundaries. Additionally, family members from other parts of the world are usually involved in the strategies of empowerment by contributing money or providing resources (information) to help the immigrant women negotiate their inclusion into the affairs of the host society.

Formation of Cultural Communities in Minnesota

During the past quarter-century, the counties surrounding Minneapolis-St. Paul have become a destination for immigrants from all over the world, particularly from war-torn East and West Africa, the Middle East, and the former Eastern European countries. The primary reason for choosing Minnesota is not hard to trace. With a buoyant economy, the state has one of the lowest unemployment rates in the nation (unemployment averages less than 4 percent per year for the last decade). The dozen counties surrounding the Minneapolis and Saint Paul metropolis are ranked among the fastest growing and most livable areas in the country. The state's public K through 12 educational institutions are persistently ranked in the top ten across the nation. Moreover, Minnesota has a reputation for being a liberal, pro-welfare, and low crime rate state, with state-funded programs for children's health care and a progressive political and social ethos based in the traditions of Hubert Humphrey, Walter Mondale, and Paul Wellstone. Many Somali, Ethiopian, Sudanese, Hmong, and Liberian refugees now call Minnesota home.

Shona came to the United States as a refugee. She fled from Liberia during the reign of President Taylor. Shona fled to the Gambia and sought a safer haven in that country. From there, she traveled to Cape Verde and applied for a visa to enter the United States as a refugee. Church groups, particularly the Lutheran church, got involved with her situation and assisted her in filing for asylum status in the United States.

Once Shona's status was adjusted to enable her to become a permanent legal resident, a new outlook dawned in her migratory experience in the United States. Recognizing that education is a proven means for achieving social mobility and advancement in the United States, Shona enrolled at Normandale Community College, where she pursued an associate degree in accounting. She carried a full load of classes every semester and also worked as a student assistant on campus. Because she was a refugee with legal status in the United States, all expenses associated with her education were paid by a government grant. Three times a week and on weekends, she worked in a UPS center at night. Some of Shona's relatives from Liberia who had emigrated to Norway and Sweden would send her money to augment her wages. "The assistance that I receive from Scandinavia is an investment in my future. I will pay it back one day by providing support to other relatives at home or abroad. I have a brother in the United Arab Emirates (UAE.) He works in construction. He sends me money often," said Shona. This generous support from extended family members who live outside the United States reinforces the West African immigrants' strong ethos of collective empowerment as opposed to an individualistic approach where one keeps what they earn to themselves. This altruism has become a major feature of how immigrants from Africa have managed to weather and deal with economic shortcomings.

Among West African immigrant, the definition and formation of transnational identities are carried out with one key principle in mind—the need to maintain and sustain an interconnection with extended family members and networks of friends and associates who are scattered all over the world. Concerted efforts are made on the part of these women to maintain these networks because they assist the immigrant women in broadening their international migratory experiences. Maintaining contacts with extended kith and kin also serves a functional purpose by enabling the women to tap into resources that have no geographic boundaries or limits. The goal is to ensure that there is always a place somewhere other than the current place of residence that the women can call home. And though Africa features prominently in the women's definition of home, one of the manifest consequences of international migration to the West is that it has afforded the women the chance to create various nodes of social contacts that are formed to provide multiple layers of security in case economic and cultural opportunities wane in one location. Many of these women are prepared to move to another country should they begin to encounter difficulties for which they cannot find solutions. To most of these women, the notion of place is amorphous and fluid enough to incorporate other destinations into their international migratory schemes. For the immigrant women living in the United States, nodes of social contacts exist in Italy, Denmark, Sweden, the Netherlands, Australia, and Canada. For those living in Canada, nodes of extended family contacts are established in countries such as Australia, Germany, France, Hong Kong, and the United Kingdom.

MANAGING FAMILY AND HOUSEHOLD ECONOMIES IN TRANSNATIONAL LOCALITIES

Work, household organization, culture, and gendered identities intersect to give context to how the immigrant women marshal collective resources in the management of their households. Paid work outside the home is the principal form of labor force participation among the women. Although some of the women operate ethnic stores catering to African and Caribbean immigrant communities, by and large, such economic activities are pursued in conjunction with paid public or private sector employment. Irrespective of their occupational status, work is viewed as pivotal for survival in the West. Work and occupation is organized around specific gendered assumptions held by the women to the effect that complete reliance on a male figure for sustenance is inimical to total autonomy and the independence of women. Family relationships and the internal dynamics shaping these relationships are structured in such a way as to provide leverage to the income that the women bring home from work. An emerging trend among these women is that a majority of them have managed to become less dependent on their male counterparts or partners for economic support. In holding multiple jobs, the majority of these women have, over time, gained power in family decision making regarding household management of finances.

The case of Grace and Efi illustrates how the West African women use their familial-based transnational connections to better their lives. Both Grace and Efi (immigrants from Sierra Leone) came to the United States from Germany, where the two of them had an uncle who was a businessman. The uncle had sponsored them to come to Frankfurt to assist in the management of an import-export business. The two women came to the United States to visit another relative but overstayed their visas. When IRCA was promulgated, Grace and Efi were able to legalize their status. The two women received a lump sum from relatives in Germany, France, Britain, Malta, and Canada to start a business in Omaha. "This was a cooperative venture. We could not have made it if our relatives outside of the U.S. had not contributed," Grace said. After a successful start, the two women expanded the business, adding a catering unit that employed other immigrant women from Africa. Efi and Grace recently sponsored two West African women living in Bahrain to come to the United States to work as professional chefs. The two women are related to Grace and Efi, and their addition to the catering business increased the income from their business. These enterprising women created a successful business while managing their individual households and raising their children. The children also take turns working in the business after school hours, during weekends, and when school is not in session.

At the time of the interview, Grace and Efi were in the process of providing financial support to assist another relative living in Toronto, Canada, in opening a West African restaurant to serve the thriving community of African immigrants in that community. Grace and Efi frequently travel to Africa to purchase goods and items to sell in their store. Efi's mother recently arrived in Omaha to help raise Efi's third daughter while she devotes all her time to their business. Having female relatives outside of the United States who can be sponsored to come and work in the family's business or help raise their children have allowed Efi and Grace to have little overhead cost. At the same time, it has allowed the women to have enough resources to assist others start their own ethnic stores. When I enquired about whether Efi and Grace are going to sponsor male members of the family to join them in Omaha, Efi laughed and said, "The men don't fit in properly because they tend to be wasteful of family resources; focusing mainly on their economic need and often neglecting to take care of children and sharing with the less fortunate members of the family. I would be skeptical to sponsor a male relative. But the women are assiduous and will use whatever they earn here to provide for all their children, including those at home in Africa." This form of commitment to the well-being of relatives at home is significant because it results in the transnationalization of the lives of people at home who will otherwise remain perpetually impoverished in the absence of state-directed economic assistance. International migration touches every aspect of the lives of the poor in Africa. For those who have relatives living and working abroad, migration offers hope and fresh opportunities to alter or transform the landscape dominated by economic miseries and deprivations.

Some of the women have transformed their income-earning opportunities to their advantage by ensuring that the entrenched vestiges of male dominance that had characterized their spousal relationships during the early stages of migration are minimized. To maximize resources and reduce the amount of money spent on services such as day care and babysitting, female kin living in the household or nearby in the same community will often share essential domestic responsibilities, including cooking meals, transporting children to and from school, and buying provisions. These shared interhousehold responsibilities among female kin members have solidified the bonds that exist in the immigrant women's households. In instances where gendered expectations regarding the need to balance work and childrearing roles has had a deleterious impact on male-female relationships in the household, a common coping strategy among the women is to mitigate potential alienation by establishing shared households (nuclear and extended) comprised of female kin members who share costs and responsibilities. Some of the women might also establish bonds with female nonkin who reside elsewhere but in the same community. As a result of this cooperative spirit, some of the immigrant women are able to minimize the deleterious effects of economic hardships. There is a strong ethos not to become dependent on social services and welfare agencies. When the women fall on hard times and need economic assistance, the preference is to tap into the goodwill and magnanimity of the African immigrant community. The women are part of the elaborate and highly structured mutual aid and benevolent societies that African immigrants form to cater to the economic, psychological, legal, and even spiritual needs of their members.

In female-headed immigrant households, cultural expectations related to family organization, work, and household management are sometimes fraught with problems. The women often encounter difficulties in balancing multiple jobs and raising their children at the same time. While this problem is unique to a majority of the immigrant women, it is more acute in female-headed households that have no extended family members or male partners living in them. In a few instances, women indicated that they prefer to live by themselves or away from male partners or relatives. According to these women, having their male partner live elsewhere is an economic strategy designed to ensure that husbands or male partners who are financially irresponsible do not squander the meager resources generated by some of the women who work two or more jobs. The perception of these women is that they would be financially worse off if the husband or male partner resided at home. In these cases, as the women point out, whatever money is earned and brought home goes directly to support the children and assist the women in meeting other household financial obligations.

To offset the economic cost of managing their households, some of the immigrant women have sponsored elderly relatives to come to the United States to offer mainly psychological and economic support. The incorporation of elderly immigrant matriarchs into the transnational migratory process among West African women residing in the United States and elsewhere can be viewed as a rational and calculated act designed to provide economic empowerment to the immigrant women in the management and organization of their households and family networks. When both professional and nonprofessional West African immigrant women sponsor elderly matriarchs to come and join them in the United States, the goal is to tap into their rich reservoir of childrearing and socialization skills. The matriarchs bring with them a wealth of knowledge about how to effectively raise children and manage household economies. They extend these nurturing and caregiving roles to both young and adults alike. Culturally, they connect young family members to the past through storytelling. The average age of the matriarchs living in the households of West African immigrant women is sixty-nine years old. The majority of them (74 percent) arrived in this country during the last ten years. Less than 10 percent of them work outside the home. The elderly matriarch's sojourn may not be confined only to the United States. At times, they travel to other Western countries where there are other family members in need of assistance for someone to take care of their children or manage the household. It is therefore not uncommon to have one matriarch shuttle between the United States, Canada, and Great Britain where relatives are domiciled. Their roles in transnational migration are pivotal in bridging intergenerational cultural gaps between themselves and their grandchildren. As transmitters of family cultural heritage and traditions, these matriarchs assume an important niche in linking children and grandchildren to affairs in the country of origination. In essence, their presence ensures the continuity of African traditional lore and culture in the homes of the immigrant women.

For some of the elderly matriarchs, living in the United States is a necessary evil. On the one hand, they consider themselves very fortunate to be able to contribute their time and cultural skills to ensure that the households they live in with their grandchildren are well cared for. Residing in the West has definitely improved upon and enhanced their material well-being, giving them access to a broad range of consumer goods they did not have access to in West Africa.

However, some of them consider life in the West as alienating and marginalizing. Limited to small social circles, usually made up of other immigrant women, the immigrant matriarchs often find themselves unable to tolerate feelings of alienation from the core body polity of their host societies. Language barriers have impeded their access to social services and government agencies. Frequently, matriarchs are reluctant to deal with social service agents. Coming from countries where the delivery of social services to the elderly is nonexistent or very poor, some elderly immigrant matriarchs find themselves relying on their children to assist them in navigating the social services thicket in the United States. Not used to sharing their personal information with agents of government who they consider to be outsiders, elderly immigrant women do not receive the services for which they are legitimately qualified. The result is that they must rely on their adult children for financial and social support. Even when they do receive social welfare assistance, the form of assistance is usually limited to health care and public transportation.

Finding themselves in a strange and foreign land where they are marginalized and culturally alienated, the West African immigrant women adapt to America by relying on their creative identities to enable them to survive and accomplish their dreams and goals. This strategy has worked because it models the women's identities on two basic principles. First, it has enabled the women to retain their immigrant heritage and cultural legacies. This cultural heritage is premised on the belief held by the immigrant women that continued self-improvement and mobilization of family and kin group resources are vital in ensuring social and economic advancements. Second, it has enabled them to define their identities in such a way to incorporate other identities formed by other immigrant groups in America. This dual identity allows the women to develop institutional networks that transcend ethnic, class, tribal, and national affiliations. Moreover, the values and norms upon which the immigrants' transnational identities are underpinned are flexible enough to allow the learning of new identities or the blending of old identities with newly learned ones to ensure their continuity in the racial, class, and ethnic stratification of a pluralistic American society. These modified familial roles may distinguish the immigrant women and their families from normative American familial systems and institutions.

The immigrant women have not only become creative and adaptive, but more importantly, they have maintained very dynamic identities that will continue to serve them well in decades to come. This adaptation is not unique to West African immigrants. Immigrants from all corners of the world who come to America recognize one imperative in the formation of immigrant identities: that immigrant adaptability, acculturation, and assimilation are not linear experiences. For some groups of immigrants (particularly those of European descent), the structural and individual determinants of identity formation and racial and ethnic politics were influenced, in large part, by their economic, political, and cultural incorporation into the body polity of American society. The same cannot be said for the new wave of immigrants who are currently arriving in the country. As for other minority and non-European immigrants now coming to the United States, there is consternation about institutionalized policies and political imperatives that consciously seek to exclude new immigrants from gaining full access to the promises that America has to offer.

Like their Black Caribbean immigrant counterparts domiciled in the United States, these West African immigrant women understand the economic and political implications of living in globalized economic and culturally structured systems. As a result of their migratory experiences, they have come to understand the cultural and human capital that is at the center of the worldwide spread of capitalism and the impact of such processes on the lives of women. As a number of scholars have found, immigrant Blacks from Africa and the Caribbean continue to play significant roles in the new systems of cultural and economic production in terms of the identities that they aspire to create in transnational spaces (see, for example, Foner 1979, 1983, 1985; Glantz, 1978). Through the migratory experiences and the strong work ethic and cultural capital that many of them bring to the United States, these immigrants are closing gaps in economic inequalities and at the same time exploring creative ways in harnessing their potential resources to lift and empower themselves and their fellow Africans at home in Africa. Erasing the economic disadvantages they encounter as a result of income, gender, class, ethnicity, and employment differences with the main society poses strong challenges as well as opportunities for several of the immigrant women. And though they may lag behind other minority or immigrant groups in the country in terms of income earnings and do encounter discrimination (Dodoo 1991a; Farley and Allen, 1987; Lichter 1989, and Kaufman 1983), their dogged determinations, collective energies, enterprise, sense of altruism, and cultural capital (Sowell 1981; Glazer and Moynihan 1963) has enabled them to become active participants in the continued definitions and redefinitions of what it means to be Black in America.

As the migration of Black Africans to the United States unravels, research scholarship focusing on the communities and relationships that immigrants forge among themselves and with the host society becomes pertinent. This research will have to reconceptualize how Black immigrants in general are going to adapt their rich cultures to form newer race and gender-based ethnicities and identities in the United States. A beginning point of this investigation is to develop more robust sociological theories of international migration to examine the transnational familial networks established by Black immigrants. These familial networks, it should be noted again, are not passive agents in the lives of the immigrants. The kin-group-based familial networks may serve as a buffer, providing an anchor while insulating the immigrants from the uncertainties of what it means to be a Black immigrant and a foreigner. The ability to harness the resources of all members of their families and provide mutual assistance to those in need has fostered and solidified bonds of altruism among the immigrants. These bonds are structured to recognize that group-defined goals and expectations, rather than individualistic goals, are important in mapping out the various trajectories that the immigrants must follow if they are to become successful in America. And becoming successful is not solely defined in terms of material acquisition. Becoming successful in America is also measured in terms of being able to assist in providing the economic needs of family members in Africa who are faced with unimaginable poverty and deprivation.

CHAPTER 6

GENDER, MIGRATION, AND WORK

Farming is what I have always known. When I arrived in America,
I was offered a cleaning job at K-Mart which I did for a while. But
the job was not rewarding. So when I found this job on the farm, I
was very happy. The job is hard but I enjoy farming. We start work
very early in the morning and rest during the afternoon. In the
evening, we do a little bit more. I have adequate food to feed my
family. And I also like the pace of farm life.

—Hanna, a Senegalese immigrant

Though we are surrounded by urban communities, we try as much as
possible not to emulate urban culture. We have to live like villagers
who are surrounded by impersonal urban cultural lifestyles. This is
the only way we can ensure the survival of the networks that we form
to protect us.

—Antu, a Liberian immigrant woman

The migration literature abounds with extensive evidence about the
experiences of Mexican and Hispanic migrant farmworkers in the agricultural belts of the United States, particularly in the Southeast and
the mid-Atlantic, the Midwest, Texas and the Southwest, California,
and the Pacific. During the 1930s, the United States put policies in
place to attract predominantly cheap Mexican and Hispanic labor to
the country. Migration across the border from Mexico was encouraged by the U.S. government under its *Bracero* program. Hundreds
of thousands of Mexicans streamed north across the border to work
on American farms. For agribusiness, the steady supply of cheap labor
was an economic boom, enriching scores of agribusiness and food
processing companies in Florida, Texas, California, North Carolina,

and Georgia. Migrant farmworkers from South and Central America make up the bulk of U.S. agricultural farm labor. Contract labor, chiefly illegal aliens and undocumented workers from South America, came to the United States to look for work. Over time, Hispanics have been successful in carving a niche for themselves in the agricultural and food processing sectors throughout the country. Paid minimum wages, discriminated against, and sometimes exploited and made to work under poor sanitary conditions and subjected to unfair labor practices, the bulk of the migrant Hispanic farmworkers continue to come to the United States to search for better economic standards of living. And despite numerous attempts on the part of the government to minimize the flow of illegal workers streaming into the country, including migrant farmworkers to the United States, the public remains skeptical about policies to control the border.

As a group, African immigrants do not have a long history of working in the migrant farm labor economy in the United States. But at home in Africa, women play pivotal roles in both the formal and informal sectors of Africa's economy. Millions of women have carved exclusive occupational and work niches in virtually every aspect of economic and cultural production. Through work, women are able to define their roles and places in social productions.[1] West Africans are very hardworking people with a strong work ethic. As they continue to strive to attain economic independence and raise their standards of living in the United States, every form of employment is considered attractive and important. No job is ever turned down or looked upon with disdain. The perception among the majority of the immigrants is that Americans are unwilling to perform some of the jobs that the immigrants perform, particularly agricultural farm work and food processing. Many of the West African immigrants who live in the United States consider themselves fortunate to have a job.

Migrant farm and agricultural work, including food processing and meat packaging, is tedious and physically demanding work. But the income that West African women immigrants earn goes a long way in supporting them as well as their relatives at home. For several of the West African migrant farmworkers, migration to the United States and the opportunities to work are sometimes viewed as strategies to link entire households and family networks to international labor centers not only in the United States but also in other developed countries. Family members join the stream of international migrant farmworkers with the goal of eventually combining their resources to undertake economic projects and other business initiatives in the migrant country of origination. These individuals and their family members may circulate not only in the United States but also in Canada. Some of the migrant farmworkers started working in Europe and the Mediterranean before arriving in the United States. These women view transnational migration as a strategy implemented to minimize family poverty and enhance the well-being of the entire family unit. As Agrawal's (2006) work affirms, migration among Third World women is the vehicle for achieving sociocultural and economic autonomy not only in the host society but also in the country of origination. This autonomy is aimed at positioning migrant women to contest patriarchal systems of gendered inequalities. More importantly, the driving force behind migrant women's search for economic autonomy is to confront their abject poverty and low economic status, which is the prime cause for women's migration in the first place. As Arya and Roy (2006) found, among Asian women, the driving force behind their decision to migrate is to ameliorate the economic deprivations and poverty associated with the lives of rural and urban women in Asia. Arya and Roy's findings are not limited only to Asia. The underlying reasons for migration among Asian and African women are similar: to search for better economic livelihoods.

The group of West African immigrant women doing farm work in Minnesota, Missouri, and Nebraska can be divided into two groups. The first consists of the women who work almost year-round on the farms and are nonseasonal. These women live with their children and family in and around the small towns where these farms or food processing plants are located. Most of them have valid work authorization papers and have been living, on average, for eleven years in the United States. Almost 65 percent of them possess secondary-school credentials they acquired from West Africa prior to their migration. The rest of the West African migrant farmworkers completed basic primary and elementary education prior to their arrival in the United States. Several of them entered the country to reunite with relatives and attend school, but most had to drop out due to their inability to pay for their tuition and other educational expenses.

Hanna's family exemplifies the first group of immigrant farm women from West Africa. A native of Senegal, Hanna farmed in rural Senegal before coming to St. Louis to join relatives. In Senegal, her family cultivated yams, peppers, tomatoes, maize, and groundnuts. "Farming is what I have always known," Hanna said. Explaining her current employment situation, she stated, "When I arrived in America, I was offered a cleaning job at K-Mart which I did for a while. But the job was not rewarding. So when I found this job on the farm, I was very happy. The job is hard but I enjoy farming. We start work very early in the morning and rest during the afternoon. In the evening, we do a little bit more. I have adequate food to feed my family. And I also like the pace of farm life." On the weekends when she is not working, Hanna takes some of the produce from the farm where she is employed to the local farmers' market. While not bustling with activities such as the markets she was used to while living in Senegal, the Saturday farmers' market has enabled Hanna and her family to connect with and become part of her community, make new friends, and at the same time identify with her farming roots. With time, she and her family have been successful in growing some fresh African vegetables like okra and eggplant, which West Africans use in making stews and soups. "I find the Saturday markets enjoyable because it brings me face-to-face with a cross section of society. It connects me to the community. It gives me a visible presence. Whenever I am not able to attend due to illness, my customers become curious and ask when I will be back," she said.

The second group of immigrant women consists of the seasonal migrant farmworkers who come to Missouri, Minnesota, and Nebraska only during the harvesting season in late summer and early fall. From here, many of them will continue to Illinois and Indiana to harvest soybeans and fresh vegetables. They usually do not form a close network of migrant farm families, as they tend to be more transient. Their ties to the community tend to be fleeting and they will usually not go out of their way to expand their social circles and networks in the community. Every summer and fall, six immigrant families from Togo come to a farm near Omaha. At the time of this study, it was their sixth year of coming to Omaha. In Togo, the women cultivated groundnuts, cocoyams, and cocoa. In the Midwest, they assist in the harvesting of cucumbers, tomatoes, beans, and other vegetables. The proprietor of the farm provides them with a place to live, which is located on the farm. Most of the women and their children are undocumented and the fear of immigrant raids by law enforcement authorities often dominate their conversations. The self-anointed leader of the group is a thirty-two-year-old mother of three children, Sita. Her migrant farming experiences have taken her to a number of states, notably Maine, Vermont, Idaho, Washington, Oregon, and California, and also Georgia, North Carolina, and South Carolina. "We came to the U.S. via Belgium initially and subsequently to the Province of Saskatchewan, Canada where we were employed as farm laborers. The owner of the farm where we worked was a French-Canadian who took delight in the fact that all of us were very fluent in French," Sita said. When the proprietor of the farm sold his farm to a Canadian subsidiary of an

American agribusiness company, Sita and the other five immigrant women crossed the Canadian and U.S. border, entering the country illegally. Once in the United States, they sought farm and agricultural work, which Sita said was not difficult to find. Her three children have been born in either Canada or the United States. Today, avid farm migrants, the six Togolese women traverse the country working for small and large agribusiness establishments. "The work is physical and enduring. In Togo, we used cow dung and horse manure as fertilizers. We used hoes and cutlasses. No tractors. No mechanized farm equipments. Every aspect of the agricultural process was done by hand. But here, farming is hard but enjoyable. It feels very good to be doing a job we did before. Above all, we get paid very well. The tools and the equipments help a lot," Sita confirmed.

Connie and her sister Edwina are both from the Mende tribe in Sierra Leone. The two women fled the country during the turbulent civil war and came to settle in Nebraska. They both arrived in the United States in 2000 on a visitor's visa but overstayed their visas. Their initial goal was to file for refugee status, but after consulting with an immigration attorney about what the process would entail, the two women rescinded their plans and decided to find work in the underground economy. When they heard through a friend and family associate that a rancher-farmer was hiring in Nebraska, Connie and Edwina went and filed an application. To their surprise, they were hired the same day and given a place to stay on the farm. They were afraid and skeptical that the farmer would report them to the immigration authorities after he discovered that they were not authorized to work in the United States. Both are paid $10 an hour, with lunch provided by the proprietor of the farm. Part of their responsibility includes milking cows every morning, helping in the harvesting of corn, and cleaning the barns. The two sisters work alongside four Somalis refugees, two Hispanics from Mexico and Honduras, and a Romanian. According to Connie, working on this farm provides them with job security, as there is always ample work to be done on the farm. "The work is plentiful but tedious. The reward is tolerable. I never dreamed I will find a job in the U.S. that pays $10 an hour considering I do not have valid work authorization. We fill a void in this society. Most Americans are not willing to milk a cow at sunrise or very early in the morning. I enjoy doing it because without this job, I will be somewhere struggling economically in Freetown, Sierra Leone," Connie affirmed. Having worked on the farm for a couple of years now, Connie and Edwina are convinced this is the best job they will ever have in the United States. "The farm proprietor and his family are all very caring folks. They take very good care of us, providing us with lessons in farm safety and how to ensure an accident free farm operation. They also provide us with annual bonuses and time off when we do not feel well. Above all, we have free food. We raise our own chickens and turkeys. We have learned how to make cheese as well. We are almost self sufficient by depending on the land for our livelihood," Connie continued.

Some of the West African migrant farm women are not as fortunate as Connie and her sister Edwina. In Austin and Worthington, Joyce and Femi work at a meat processing plant. The two Ivorian women have valid work authorization papers. The hourly pay is good, at $11.50. The two women had come to Minnesota during the early 1990s, went to school for a while, but dropped out after encountering financial difficulties at a vocational school. The money they were supposed to have received from the Ivory Coast to pay for the cost of their education never materialized. A Somali friend introduced them to a Hispanic supervisor who recruited workers for farm and food processing establishments in southern Minnesota. Joyce was hired by a farming establishment near Austin. Femi got a job with a turkey farmer in Worthington. By all accounts, the two West African women were living their American dreams. But with time, more and more Hispanics have been coming to the farms and the food processing plants in search of employment. According to Femi, most of the Hispanics are willing to work for far less than $11.50 an hour. The result is that the two West African women have had their hours reduced considerably and the unallocated portion of their time allotted to Hispanic migrant farmworkers. With children to support, the two West African women are finding it difficult making ends meet. Femi has taken a second job as a janitorial assistant. "My preference is to work on the farm," she said. However, Femi and other West African farmworkers must now compete with Hispanic migrants who are settling in the agricultural and food processing towns in southern Minnesota. This results in the depression of wages on the farms and food processing establishments. Recognizing the competition with Hispanic migrants, Femi stated,

> We were here first. We were paid well then. Not any more. Now some of the farm owners are using day contract labor because it maximizes their overhead and profit margin. The farm management have become very selective as to who they hire. The Hispanics have taken over the farm jobs. There is not a single native-born Black or American Indian working here. A few Africans came here recently from Illinois after hearing they could earn about $12 an hour. But they have all gone back

now. I will uproot in the near term and head to Oregon and Washington where I hear the wages are good and the working conditions also very good, even for those who do not possess valid papers. I hear the farmers treat their workers very well. But my children have had enough moving around.

Despite the tediousness of farm work, the occupational and safety risks, the low pay, poor working conditions, and the lack of fringe benefits, the West African women immigrants are exploring ways to create agencies to improve upon their conditions of work and mobilize for collective action. At the moment, several of them have joined with Latino and Mexican farmworkers to better understand how the forces of globalization have shaped the economic outcomes that many of the women describe as unfair and exploitative. For many of them, there is recognition that being drawn into the international migratory flow of cheap labor weakens their ability to mount any effective mobilization to contest the economic- and labor-related issues confronting them as women, foreign-born, Black, and mothers. For those who engage in organized resistance and mobilization for collective action, their future, and that of their families, becomes threatened as they may face repercussions in the form of job loss. This renders them unable to support their families. For those who have children to support, the outcome is dire and many end up having to depend on other immigrant families for economic support. Irrespective of how they perceive the exploitative outcomes of their work situation, the narratives from the women suggests that employment provides the women with the agency to contest and gradually erode the patriarchal authority structures that have dominated their lives in both West Africa and the United States. For these women, therefore, occupational or labor force participation may serve as the catalyst for redefining not only gendered roles, but, more importantly, for forging new transnational identities—both in the United States and at home—to effectively deal with their economically subordinate roles.

FOSTERING KINSHIP BONDS TO OVERCOME ADVERSITIES

Despite their relatively few numbers and the fact that they are spread out in small farming and food processing towns across the Midwest, many West African women have managed to form strong networks that offer economic and psychological support for the migrants' families. A distinguishing feature of the social organization of the migrant women's lives is illustrative in the statement made by Antu, one of the migrant farmworkers in Missouri: "Though we are surrounded by urban communities, we try as much as possible not to emulate urban culture. We have to live like villagers who are surrounded by impersonal urban cultural lifestyles. This is the only way we can ensure the survival of the networks that we form to protect us."

Coming from countries with differing social structures and differing cultural and normative value systems, these women tend to emphasize their class status over their national origins. Class, after all, is one of the salient traits other than their West African roots that they all share in common. In emphasizing their common class membership, the women are able to gain an understanding about the imperative of engaging in collective economic enterprise to ward off or minimize economic problems that some of them encounter as farm laborers. They cooperate by providing financial assistance to other women in need. Helping other women to meet their economic needs is not confined to the boundaries of the farm or the food processing plants. It extends to relatives at home in West Africa. Recently, the women combined their resources to assist one of the women from the Gambia in paying for funeral expenses of a sister. In addition, the women have set up an emergency fund to which monthly contributions are made by everyone. Every three months or so, the money saved is given to one family to use as they see fit. This is a way to ensure that the women will have the resources to purchase expensive items by paying cash rather than buying on credit.

This cooperative spirit and bonding is also intended to safeguard the women from hostilities and racial confrontations they face in the small and isolated rural towns where these farms and meat packaging businesses are located. Collective security is emphasized, and when they venture out to town on weekends, the women normally go in groups. The women have reported assaults and racial slurs. According to one of the women, many of the people they encounter perceive that they are taking jobs away from Americans. But the reality, as one of the farm migrants stated, "is that most Americans are not willing to work farm jobs. There is a hog farm nearby. All the workers are either Hispanic or African immigrants. Occasionally, you come across a few Eastern Europeans."

From their perspective, the formation of kinship bonds has been facilitated by the rotations from one farm to another, a common trend among West African immigrant women. Some of them have worked as migrant farmworkers across the entire Midwest, often moving from one farm to another and from farming to food processing and vice versa. In moving around, they come to encounter immigrants from the region and elsewhere from Africa. These encounters have often resulted in relationships and friendships, including the establishment of an informal and loosely structured economic and social network to look after the interests of the women and their families. Similar networks based on kinship and national groupings have been noted among Sudanese immigrants that have settled in the United States and Canada.[2]

The women often gather together in each other's homes with their children, trading stories about life in West Africa. Whether the activity is cooking, sewing, knitting, or telling African folklore to the children, the women are all united in a common purpose—to use the income from their farm work to raise their living standards and that of their children and extended family members. There is a high sense of loyalty, solidarity, and camaraderie among the immigrant women. Living in small rural towns has also brought the women together to confront alienation and isolation. As one of the women mentioned, "The town folks here are not very welcoming. Our children are often taunted, ridiculed, and sometimes harassed at school and at the supermarkets. We never let the children go to town alone. Some of the Whites admitted that they have not seen or interacted with Black folks before, particularly Blacks from Africa. I was referred to as a roach by a store clerk who admonished me to go back to Africa because in her mind, I have no business being here."

There is no systematic effort on the part of some of the women to become integrated in the social and cultural affairs of the farm towns. Considering their small numbers and their minority, foreign, economic, and class status, many of the women prefer not to engage in any interactions with the rank and file of the farm towns. This form of isolation is purposive. It is designed to keep a social distance between the immigrants and the community in the hope that it will minimize fears and apprehensions regarding the presence of the migrant farmworkers in these small towns. The goal is to never call attention to their presence in the community. The only relationships that the women form are with other migrant farmworkers who are Africans, Hispanics, or Eastern Europeans. But the intrarelationships that the West African women form among themselves are considered high priority.

A sense of altruism permeates the conversations of these women, and there is an unwritten norm that every women and her family is going to be supported and catered for when times become rough and families are faced with dire economic hardships. Long-term plans about the prospects of repatriation often dominate the conversations of the farm women. They stress the necessity of ensuring that they will have something to fall back on when they are no longer able to do farm work and can focus on returning home to West Africa. Plans are discussed about building a home, starting a new business, or how to save and raise the capital needed to start a business venture, no matter how small, somewhere in West Africa. Their energies and resources are steered in the direction of home. Long-term plans and expectations reflect the urgency and imperative of reconstituting their lives upon their return to Africa. One of the women reported on the support and encouragement they give to one another to manage their resources well, by living frugally and committing their savings toward the realization of their hopes, dreams, and aspirations in West Africa. "I am building a house in West Africa. It is going to be a beautiful house. Every month, I remit home for this purpose," this farmworker affirmed.

The education of their children is a major preoccupation of the migrant farm women. The value of education and doing well in school is stressed. Even on the farms, time is set aside for the children to do their homework. Time is also set aside for studying. One parent went to the extent of stressing the difference between doing home-work and studying. A persistent approach to studying, this immigrant affirmed, "is what transforms a child into a scholar. Doing homework only ensures that you can pass a test. We ensure that our children set aside time to do their homework, and then learn something new. We enjoy having them around while we work. But we do not want them to do this kind of job. They do very well in school. The teachers are perplexed. They always highlight the fact that these kids excel despite the status of their parents. The secret is to motivate them to do more than what is required." Together, the women take turns taking their children to school, checking their children's homework, and attend-ing parent-teacher meetings. Playing is encouraged and adult supervi-sion is provided. Merely milling around on the farm or at home on weekends and school holidays is frowned upon by the immigrant farm parents. Every play time on the farm or at home is taken as an oppor-tunity to teach some of life's lessons.

On one of the farms, Stella, an immigrant from Ghana who has ten years of service as a migrant farmworker successfully convinced six other West African women she worked with to combine their resources to hire a tutor to assist some of the migrant farm children do their homework. As Stella said, "Education is priceless and we have to encourage our children to excel in school and achieve enviable educa-tional credentials. That is the only way these children will have a good future in America. Though most of their parents are illegal aliens, the children are bona fide American citizens. They will be living in this country when their parents return to Africa, perhaps. As Black children, their only hope for a better life in America is quality education. We all share in this belief. Pursuing education will minimize some of the negativities that otherwise will surround their blackness."

As they toil on the farms, the languages and cultures of the women are filled with vivid images and representations of African music, folklore, and mythologies. When farm work becomes strenuous and taxing, solace is sought in telling stories about famous African statesmen and women. Tales are told about animal fables, a popular one being the story of *ananse* (the spider). A group of women huddle under a tree to share some sugarcane one woman had brought to the farm earlier. Later, I came to learn the cultural symbolisms behind the chewing of the sugarcane from one of the immigrant women: "Chewing sugarcane is a way to boost sugar intake and quench thirstiness. Sugarcane that is sweet will fill your belly. It gives you energy. This makes you drink more water to prevent dehydration. It also makes you feel less hungry." Singing while they work is an important medium of communication and channeling anger and joyfulness at the same time. The songs and stories are carefully chosen and they often reference courage, bravery, and the need to persevere. A call and response song immediately rallies everyone, no matter the level of tiredness. A new burst and surge of energy is seen, often reaching a crescendo in laughter, occasional sobs, and cheerfulness. One woman attempted to explain this in her own words. Work, she said, "exemplifies the African principle of self help and survival. To work is to toil. Back home, we toiled but had nothing to show for our hard work. That is why some of us are here. In our work, we find dignity and self worth. We are not alone here. Our families in West Africa are solidly behind us, supporting us through their prayers. I know because I feel a spiritual connection. I even feel my grandmother's presence. She is guarding me here."

The farm environment is the space where the women construct, blend, or mix their different unique identities, vent their anger on a wide range of issues, particularly about their colonized status, violence, sexuality, poverty, exclusion, and visions for better and brighter futures for their children. Examples of the shared meanings of work among female immigrants can be discerned in the migration literature. Reeder's (2002) account of Sicilian women affirmed the bonding and cooperative spirit that women immigrants forge to confront economic hardships and gendered inequalities emanating from male out-migration. Vecchio's (2002) account of immigrant women's work in Wisconsin, Mahler's (2002) account of Salvadoran immigrant women, and Guglielmo's (2002) research on proletarian feminism among garment workers in New York speak to the issues emanating from how women have historically used migration to create new spaces where shared interests and cooperative alliances are relied upon to create economic and cultural opportunities for women.

Deeply embedded in the meanings the immigrant women construct about work is an understanding that the migratory process offers another opportunity to become, to ensure survival, and to transcend the myriad of blocked opportunities and spatial limitations that have come to dominate the West African political and economic landscape in recent times. The imperative to survive and overcome economic hardships and adversities is primary. Secondary, but of immense significance, is the need to mobilize to overcome everyday hardships emanating from being in a new environment far away from home. In a sense, these immigrant women were defining themselves by their work and pride, their songs, and their hopes for a better tomorrow. Watching the immigrant women work served as an illustration of the hard-work spirit of African women in general. The colorful scenes created by these women all over Africa when women sell their wares at markets such as Salaga, Makola, and Kejetia in Ghana are legendary. Here, one sees the vitality and resiliency of African women, their brawn, and their tenacities as they work to make a living, sometimes not being mindful of the foul stenches from the uncovered gutters meandering through these markets. For these women, work and life are intermeshed. Each fulfills a sustaining role by affirming a belief in the need to gain mastery over problems while confronting new challenges. Trading affirms the role that millions of African women play in the economic and cultural development of their respective countries (see, for example, Snyder and Tadesse's (1995) account of the role African women play in national development). For each of the migrant farm women, the meanings associated with doing farm work are varied. From the perspective of one woman from Togo, farm work is a form of resistance. This resistance is directed toward the men (husbands and male partners) who have wrecked their lives by claiming to hold on to patriarchy. To another woman, doing farm work is the result of the failed regimes at home that have squandered opportunities and caused a deficit of hope. Farm work, to another woman, is a way to replace the anger and the near hopeless conditions she faced at home in West Africa. To yet another woman, farm work is to show gratitude to the few Americans who always treat them very nicely, never exploiting them but always showing them respect and dignity because they work hard to produce the food they eat. Even in the midst of the difficulties and hardships some of the migrant farm women encounter, it became clear from their narratives that the women intend to create new aspirations in the new spaces made possible by migration. Being categorized by the rest of society as lower class is not seen as debilitating. Instead, as one women echoed, "work is empowering. Work gives you the ability to find happiness and at the same time overcome economic hardships and struggles. It gives you the means to provide for my family."

IMMIGRANT WOMEN AND CLASS FORMATIONS

As a group, the African immigrants who come to the United States tend to bring with them certain cultural advantages (human capital) which may facilitate their social and class mobility. Forming class and occupational alliances based on work is nothing new among African immigrants as a group. Throughout the region, these class formations (sometimes based solely on gender) are central to the understanding of migration, gender, and cultural spaces. Dodson (2000), Vletter (2000), and Crush (2000) have documented the formation of broad-based class structures that migrants in the region of Southern Africa, including South Africa, often create to anchor their migratory lives in new locals. Coming from societies where educational attainment is considered a determinant of social status, several of Africa's best and brightest are coming to the United States to pursue cultural goals, pursue higher and advanced education, and, at the same time, to achieve intergenerational mobility. Many of them enter the United States embracing the ethos that people get ahead in America primarily due to their own abilities, merit, assiduousness, luck, and support from one's social networks. Coupled with this is their belief that structural changes in the American economy necessitate a well-trained labor force and, in particular, people who have functional skills and formal credentials to market.

The belief of America as an open society, coupled with the conviction that the global marketplace is constantly evolving and requiring that workers attain higher standards of education, has served some of the West African immigrant women very well in this country. They are already used to living in social systems where merit and educational attainment trumps tribal, clan, or family affiliations. Their pre- and postarrival educational attainments have propelled a growing number of them into the new Black professional and middle classes in the United States. Those of them with graduate and postgraduate credentials are carving niches for themselves in professional and non-professional roles across the country. African immigrants are now joining the ranks of Black doctors and physicians, lawyers, dentists, accountants, pharmacists, college professors, nurses, scientists, engineers, school administrators, public schoolteachers, and social workers. A large number of them have also joined the ranks of occupations like law enforcement, retail sales, electricians, assembly line workers, and small-business proprietors.

A significant transformation has occurred in the skills composition of the West African women who have migrated to the United States. In West Africa, some of the women worked as secondary school teachers, civil servants, nurses and allied health workers, and physicians. By African standards, some of the women could be considered middle class and relatively better off economically than their counterparts who did not possess secondary-school-leaving certificates, diplomas, or university degrees. With the exception of the doctors, some of the women have engaged in continuing education that lasted for an average of three years. Subject and disciplinary areas are carefully chosen to ensure employability upon the completion of studies. Business, computer sciences, general technicians, nursing, and teacher education are common areas of specialty. To minimize cost, the preferred choice of educational institutions for pursuing continuing education is the small- to medium-sized institutions of higher learning, including technical, vocational, and community colleges. These institutions are preferred by the immigrants because they offer numerous programs of study leading directly to employment or the licensure to practice or work in specified vocations. For those women who pursue postgraduate education in the sciences, particularly in health-care-related fields, absorption into the labor force is facilitated by the high national demand for workers trained in virtually every aspect of the sciences.

Clara is a West African immigrant physician now working with a major regional hospital in the Midwest. Her initial ambition was to go to medical school in West Africa. Even though she was able to gain admission to the university, she was selected to matriculate in biochemistry instead of her choice to study medicine. Upon the completion of her baccalaureate degree, she went to Canada, where she pursued a masters degree in microbiology, after which she applied and was accepted as a medical student in the United States. After the completion of her education, for her internship, she chose a rural community hospital near St. Louis, Missouri. Clara is currently working as a physician in East St. Louis, where she serves a predominantly poor Black and Hispanic minority population. "Without the medical services we provide, most of the poor and minority patients will have to find a doctor far away from their homes. The job is rewarding and it comes with the recognition that we are saving lives and making a difference in the overall quality of life of the community. When parents bring their children, they often tell them that they too can become a doctor," Clara stated.

Using any objective or subjective measure of class and occupational prestige, Clara is a successful professional immigrant and can be considered part of the new Black professional upper-middle, if not the upper, class. According to Clara, the majority of her schoolmates in West Africa have left to the West, particularly those with credentials in science, engineering, health, and computer software. As Clara ascertained, for many West Africans who enter North America to pursue graduate education, obtaining a visa is not often stringent. This is not the case among those who do not possess postsecondary credentials at the time they apply to go to the United States. For Clara, the connecting point in her transnational migration is her educational skills and credentials: "I have relatives who did not finish secondary school. Some of them have been trying to secure a visa to the U.S. for the past decade or so without any luck. The only way for some of them to enter the U.S. is to find their way out of West Africa to the Middle East, then to Europe, then possibly to the U.S. It took a friend of mine nine years to finally enter the U.S. She had to travel to Libya, Romania, and Germany before making it to the United States." For West Africans yearning to come to the United States without certifiable skills, the journey to the United States is often tedious and circuitous. But if they are successful in entering the country, their future prospects are brighter.

Despite her high level of educational and professional attainment, Clara remains leery of racial and ethnic discrimination on the job based on her gender and racial status. "I find that my White patients and some of the hospital staff always second guess my decisions. As if I don't know what I am doing. I often find it uncomfortable when they reference the poor delivery of health services in Africa. I feel a sense of accomplishment but professionally, I remain very isolated from my peers at work. I attribute that to racial and ethnic differences," Clara hinted. In the nice suburban subdivision where she lives, Clara reported experiencing similar negative racial and ethnic hostilities. "My status as a doctor does not insulate me from the realities of racism and anti-Black feelings outside the hospital," she referenced. Clara continued to elaborate on the intersections of race, ethnicity, gender, and class in structuring her conceptions about what it means to have a Black immigrant identity in the United States. She explained,

> To the people I meet on the street, my blackness is seen as my distinguishing trait. And with this blackness comes all the negativities associated with being Black in America. Sometimes, the problem is my gender. I do encounter sexual hostilities and what I consider to be very disrespectful behavior from some Blacks (particularly men) as well. I was told once by two Black men that I cannot be a physician. Some think I am a physician's aide. I get this at the hospital too, among people who do not know me. To be Black and successful to some is an anathema. It is alright to be White, female, a physician, and a professional. But not when you are a Black African immigrant. Unfortunately, some Black people believe that as well.

While her educational and occupational background does not insulate her against the pervasiveness of racism and gender discrimination in the United States, Clara remains hopeful about the future. She finds comfort in the fact that continued opportunities for more and more minorities and a vigorous stress on educational achievements will continue to swell the ranks of the Black professional class. She expects that as this class continues to form, African immigrants will become a part of this bloc because of their strong commitment to postsecondary and postgraduate education.

Clara's professional and class status mirrors that of Jennifer, a Liberian professor and educator at a Midwestern college. Like Clara, Lucy had a university degree from Liberia and from Britain before coming to the United States to pursue her doctorate in a social science discipline. She received a research assistantship that waived her tuition during her studies. The assistantship also provided a small stipend to meet her living expenses. "The stipend was not much but I managed to send a portion home every month for five years until I finished my doctorate. I felt this was an obligation because by comparison, I was better off than a vast majority of Liberians, my immediate and extended family members included," Lucy continued. During the dissertation stage of her doctorate, her advisor recommended Lucy for an instructorship. Lucy was assigned to teach two sections of an introductory class to gain teaching experience. According to Lucy, the opportunity to teach marked the first steps toward becoming an American citizen. "I was grateful for the chance I got. At home, people are known to pay bribes just to get a professional job. Here in America, I felt like it was my merit that opened the door for me to become a professional," she stated.

The teaching opportunity enabled her to develop and hone her teaching skills. Fortunately for her as well, she benefited significantly from the research apprenticeship and the professional and research relationship she had with the chair of her dissertation committee. The two were able to publish research articles in peer-reviewed journals by the time Lucy completed the doctorate. Armed with teaching and research experience, Lucy applied to several colleges for a job. She knew the process would be tedious and financially daunting since she was not a permanent resident. But she persisted in the hope that she would find an employer to sponsor her for permanent residence. Lucy's application for a teaching appointment was successful, and following an interview, she secured a job as an assistant professor in a tenure-track position. Her institution applied for a permanent resident card on her behalf, paying all the associated costs. "I was very lucky indeed. The institution really wanted me. I was one of three minority faculty recruited that year. The other two were Chinese and Korean professors. My credentials were the selling point in my hiring," Lucy indicated.

Recognizing that the prerequisites for tenure and promotion (effective teaching, research, and service) can be daunting for Blacks and women, Lucy continued to develop her teaching and research skills. Her strategy was to wean herself from her dissertation advisor by publishing on her own. She revisited some of her graduate school papers, revised or rewrote them altogether, and modified parts of her doctoral dissertation for publication. At the same time, she developed new courses to broaden the curriculum in her department, bringing technology to bear on her teaching, and attended training seminars on effective teaching and communication. For Lucy, the process was demanding. Even after successfully achieving tenure and being promoted, Lucy feels a sense of alienation and finds that her academic credentials do not offer her any sense of fulfillment once she steps outside of her academic and structured university environment.

Like Clara, Lucy feels that her identity as a foreign-born Black female and a professional is overshadowed by the different trajectories of race, ethnic, and gender relations in the United States that she must construct and negotiate. While she finds some measure of comfort in the university environment, this level of comfort is replaced by consternation, and at times fear, when she steps outside of the campus environment. She stated,

The academic environment insulates me from the everyday realities of what it means to be Black in America. I had little or no sense of what the typical Black person goes through. On campus, one feels protected from the sometimes-harsh realities of life on the streets, particularly for racial minorities. The university campus is a comfort zone for me. My security is shattered once I am off campus and people use derogatory words and treat me condescendingly because of my accent, skin color, or gender. I have sensed and experienced rejection even by other Black women simply because they prefer to see me as a privileged person. When I speak and communicate effectively, I am rebuffed as trying to be white, unfortunately by Blacks. It is somewhat unfortunate that my Black skin does not offer me any protection from subtle abuses, even from Blacks.

Despite her favorable outlook about the racial climate on her campus, Lucy remains apprehensive about hidden and subtle forms of racism at her university. She continued to elaborate on her lived Black immigrant women experiences stating that

Some of my white colleagues speak to me at times using Black, urban, hip-hop language, often expecting that I will speak back to them in the same style. This is demeaning. Not being a native-born Black makes it difficult to experience the full range of blackness. There is even a sense that I am considered threatening. Some of my own colleagues perceive that I am too elitist and aloof from the everyday struggles of the average Black person on the street. On days I do not bring my lunch and end up eating on campus, I notice that the Black students even segregate themselves according to whether they have been born in Africa or in the U.S. Occasionally, I have joined the table of both as a way to bridge the divide, albeit to no avail.

Lucy finds that despite experiencing isolation and alienation on campus, and having to deal with students who perceive that her knowledge base is not the same as her white counterparts merely because of her skin color, she feels relatively secure on campus, though sometimes skeptical of both her liberal and conservative colleagues in academe. "Academe provides a false haven for dealing with and confronting issues of ethnicity, gender, and class. Differences are respected and tolerated. But under that tolerance is a veneer of entrenched conservatism and lack of respect for issues affecting minorities in general. Some on campus are not too pleased about the growing presence of international students from Asia and Africa on campus. Some of the Black students feel out of place in the classroom where they are surrounded by the majority white students," she reported. However, as she pointed out, "the academic workplace is an infinitesimal aspect of my total world. Faced with insecurities and lack of acceptance from the community, I cannot help but confine my social circle to a small group of international intelligentsia that I have come to know mainly on campus and throughout the world. The identities and relationships that I forge and maintain with them have kept me grounded in my Africanness and blackness. This worldview enables me to cope with the fact that I am not totally embraced or accepted by the larger Black community."

From both Clara and Lucy's perspective, being Black is not sufficient to become part of the Black body polity in the United States. "To be Black is not to belong except at home in Africa. Here in the U.S., you occupy and represent an alien or foreign status. Even when you have proven yourself that you are capable, responsible, law-abiding, and honest, your blackness still trumps any qualities you may have," according to Clara. For Lucy, there is a sense of being culturally dispossessed. "The only way to deal with this problem is to concentrate on home in West Africa, even with all its problems. At home, you are always somebody. You are beautiful and valued. You do not have to shy away from your blackness," Lucy suggested. As they strive to deconstruct the negative notions associated with their blackness, these professional women nonetheless recognize that having an immigrant status enables them to develop an attachment to two societies—one distant and thousands of miles away, the other, closer but yet still very far away because of the isolation and alienation they continue to encounter. Their entry into the pulse of that community reveals that they must embrace certain unspecified cultural notions as well as have certain experiences directly related to the Black experiences in America. She articulated the subtle dimensions of these cultural notions and the lived experiential realities of what it means to be Black and foreign in America by positioning her Black struggles within the civil rights movement and Black agitation for emancipation. As she recounted,

> I did not match or participate in the civil rights movement. I was not here in this country then. I did not have water from hoses sprayed on me by the police. Neither was I beaten by a policeman's baton. Those who endured these struggles and hardships paved the way and matched for some of us to be here today. Scores died in the process. But I feel that I am also enlarging the Black fight for justice through my teachings, the mentoring and raw support I give to our Black students, through the numerous letters of references I write for our Black

students, including my push for them to stay in school beyond their bachelors, or simply talking to employers about the job prospects of our Black students.

This form of role modeling is equally significant because from Lucy's perspective, "this transcends race, ethnicity, gender, and class. It is a way to help people in general to recognize their capabilities and thereby assist by showing them some of the time-tested and proven ways to achieve their fullest potentials. It is a way to enable people rather than disenabling them by dwelling on past vestiges of inequities and exclusions."

In some ways, Gen (another West African immigrant woman) represents the embodiment of the rising African immigrant middle class in the United States. An immigrant from Senegal, she came to the United States purposely to pursue her lifelong ambition of becoming a nurse. Though she could have pursued this dream in Dakar, her parents sent her to the United States twelve years ago. Upon the completion of her nursing training, finding work was not very difficult due to her nursing credentials. Being a registered nurse, she found herself highly marketable. After just two years of working at a large midwestern hospital, Gen decided to join the military. For two years, she served on a naval vessel in Asia before returning to the United States, where she was assigned to a veteran's hospital. While in Korea, she started an online graduate course in social work, which she had completed at the time of the interview.

For Gen, the opportunity to serve in the defense of the country is a way to express gratitude for what this country has given her. Like her West African counterparts, Gen feels very much as ease and personally content to be living in the United States. "I never thought I would be serving in the U.S. military. But I have gained so much from this country. I like my job. The pay and benefits are great. I find the commitment of the military to equal opportunity matters to be progressive. Your skin color or gender does not give you automatic coronation to be the one to be chosen to perform the job. Your merit does. They have leveled the playing field for minorities. The rest of society has yet to reach that standard," according to Gen.

As a civilian, Gen remains skeptical about race and ethnic relations and the role of minority women in society in general. Despite her strong civic and pro-American stance, Gen finds that she still has to negotiate and renegotiate social acceptance as a citizen. "People disrespect you for being a Black woman. They make your blackness an issue. This makes it possible for them to look down on you. I am followed whenever I go to the store to shop, as if I am going to steal something. My children experience the same mistreatment. They are stigmatized even before they get to say a word. Their teachers do it, the police are equally guilty, and the media feeds into this at times by shinning light on Black youths, often depicting some of them as wayward and disrespectful," Gen indicated. And as a foreign-born Black woman, Gen finds herself always having to answer questions about her nativity and having to respond to suggested notions about the differences between her and other Black women in America, particularly native-born Black women. "You speak very properly; you are well-educated; you are not as loud and confrontational as other Blacks; you comport yourself very well; you seem relaxed; always smiling; and not wearing anger in your intonation"—these are some of the subliminal nuances interlaced with hints of racism and gender discrimination that Gen often encounters from the public.

From her perspective, Gen vociferously detests these condescending treatments and finds it very offensive, if not abusive and disrespectful. Gen expressed anger and resentment toward the general society for its lack of willingness to identify with issues facing Blacks as a dark spot on a country that is otherwise the envy of the rest of the world in terms of standards of living. Gen believes the purpose of some of these undercurrent hints of racist statements coming mainly from some whites Americans designed to

> divide Blacks into two groups—the good and bad Blacks. The intent is to separate, not to unite people. For those deemed as good Blacks, the system showers praise and adulation often holding them up as the standard, sort of like the model minority. For the bad Blacks, the customary belief is that they are always crying victim, often quick to lash out at white society for oppressing Blacks and showing no initiative to lift themselves out of their economic and cultural morass. The ploy is to mask the real issues facing Black people and solidify the belief that these problems are self-induced in which case the government or American society in general cannot be blamed.

Ultimately, such an approach, as Gen cautioned, "shows a complete misunderstanding of the diverse background and multiple experiences that Black folks from all over the world bring to the U.S. Sometimes, it is too easy for those not familiar with Black culture to aggregate blackness rather than finding the time to understand the subtle differences. Taking the time to learn about culture and differences within specific cultures to understand commonalities and differences are critical. Black folks do the same thing by often referencing ethnic and racial group features to categorize people."

Like other immigrant groups that have settled in the United States, West African women follow different tracks to express their migratory hopes and dreams. As shown, some come to pursue academic goals. Others come because they are forcefully uprooted and displaced by wars and civil strife. Still others come purely to find work, with no stated intentions of going to school or reuniting with relatives. Others certainly come because of educational opportunities they find in America. These immigrants are by no means monolithic in terms of their motivations to enter the United States. Differences in the impetuses driving their decisions to migrate are thus discernible.

For other groups of West African immigrant women, their lives in America are shaped by one driving force—the compelling need to work multiple jobs. Education, while valued and considered an asset, is hardly embarked upon due to structural issues such as their lack of valid legal residence status, transportation problems, lack of money, and the belief that education can sometimes be a waste of time and effort, particularly if one's goal is merely to seek a sojourner status in America and ultimately repatriate, taking with them their savings to start a business in West Africa. This group of African immigrants may be described as opportunistic immigrants who engage in targeted migration to fulfill a specific need or goal. Always concerned about possible arrest and deportation, these immigrants live secluded lives by limiting and carefully selecting their bonds and associates. Monies earned working in the underground economy are sent home to forestall their loss due to the high risk of deportation and arrest. The money transferred home can potentially alter the social and economic circumstances of the affected immigrants. It positions them to become part of the business and entrepreneurial class in West Africa where selling, trading, and merchandising have become major cogs in the retail and wholesale sectors of commerce. Often lacking the credentials needed to gain access to the high-paying jobs with fringe benefits in the United States, some of these women often become part of the working class poor, at times members of the permanent underclass. By limiting their social circles and networks to carefully selected friends, some of them are not able to tap into the wide range of economic and cultural opportunities to enhance their migratory experiences. It is not uncommon to find three or four women from the same countries or tribal affiliations with similar experiences sharing an apartment.

Sefiaa, a working-class West African immigrant woman living near St. Paul, considers herself part of the working and poor class. She came to the United States from Ghana on a visitor's visa but over-stayed her visa. In Ghana, she was unemployed. She did some sewing to support herself but her meager earnings could not sustain her. She petitioned a school friend already in the United States to send her an invitation letter with which she was able to secure a visa. Upon arrival, she tried her hands at several jobs, including dishwashing, cooking, and janitorial services. Sefiaa did not pursue postsecondary education in the United States. "I felt it would be a waste of time and resources. I just want to work and raise enough capital to take home to start a business. That is the only reason why I am here. I know of several women from Africa who are doing the same thing," she said. Almost seven years after arriving, Sefiaa is still washing dishes and doing odd jobs here and there. She takes solace in the fact that her employment has been consistent and, with the exception of a two-week absence from work due to health concerns, she has practically managed to hold on to her jobs. "I am making progress toward my goal," she said. "I will soon be gone, amnesty or no amnesty. I transfer more than 80 percent of my wages home. That leaves me very poor. I live from hand to mouth. Sometimes I don't even have enough to pay my rent and other bills. I do not have any children to support. I don't like where I live." She decried the filth and disorder encroaching on her community. "The whole place is going down. Homes are in need of repairs. There is a lot of criminal activity going on. Young men deal-ing drugs and gangsters always disrupt your sleep at night firing guns. This is not living. It is hellish. But I blend in very well. There are Haitians and other African women around the neighborhood. They are my friends. We get together often and tell jokes and stories about home. And we support each other financially and psychologically," according to Sefiaa, whose long-term goal is to build two houses in Africa. One will serve as her primary residence. She will lease the other and use the rent to support herself.

For this West African immigrant woman, the achievement of her American dream is going to be manifested in her ability to marshal the resources to re-create her life back home. She has full intentions of repatriating to West Africa, where she hopes to enjoy the fruits of her labor and hard work. She articulated goals and aspirations in the following statement:

> I will be somebody when I go home and set up a small business. Here I am nobody. I am referred to by the 'n' word sometimes. They think I am making money because I am working all the time. I am just like them, struggling. I will go home. I am building a house for myself. It is going

to be nice. I have shipped some home furnishings. I do not have a car.
I rely on public transportation. I do have a car that I shipped home. I
could leave today, but I am trying to finish another house.

For Sefiaa, her personal safety and security are major concerns. But
she remains undaunted. Like Clara and Lucy, she is able to find her
identity and place among other Black coethnic immigrant women
who have come from the developing world to the United States, particularly from the Caribbean and South America. "We protect and
look out for each other. We do not bother anyone. I would not be
able to survive without these other immigrant women. We laugh and
cry together. They know all about me. We help each other. The children know that they come here and will be fed and made to feel comfortable. They are always in and out of the immigrant homes around
here. We share a strong cord. Even some of the African immigrant
men don't understand. Some of them are simply wasting time here.
But the majority are good people," according to Sefiaa. By bonding with other immigrant women, Clara, Lucy, and now Sefiaa, are
all affirming a bold commitment to find creative ways to unburden
themselves of the years of economic suffering they endured living in
West Africa and at the same time create new spaces to anchor their
evolving gendered, ethnic, and class formulations and identities. For
all these women, work is the agency of empowerment despite their
concerns about experiencing cultural alienation or marginalization on
account of their ethnicity and, perhaps, their gender.

The migration of West African women to the United States is still
evolving. Preliminary analyses of the form and nature of this migration suggests that economic factors are pivotal in delineating the factors
that spur this movement. For a growing number of women immigrants
from West Africa, farm labor employment has become the dominant
form of economic participation in American society. To the immigrant
women, these jobs are plentiful but the labor to meet the demand is
often scarce because some Americans are not willing to do these laborious jobs. Hence, the increasing number of women farm migrants who
are able to find jobs on these farms even though they may not possess
valid and legal work authorization documents. To the farm proprietors
and owners of the food processing plants, the availability and steady
supply of labor is critical for their financial bottom line.

West African immigrant women become part of the epiphenom-
enon of the continued global circulation and transnational movement of labor, mainly from the less developed to the developed
countries. The high demand for farmworkers in the agriculturally

rich states in America is fueling the movement of masses of unskilled youth from Africa and Latin America to the shores of this country. The need for American growers to maintain their competitiveness on a global scale also means that for those from developing countries who are willing and able to make it to the United States, the prospect of securing employment is high. Many of the West African women who perform farm work have completed secondary education. They are better educated overall than their Hispanic migrant farmworker counterparts. And like Hispanic migrant farmworkers, the West African women view farm labor as attractive, offering wages that by American standards is pittance. However, in forming their rationalization to come to the United States, the low wages in the agricultural sector do not thwart their migratory plans. The wages they receive from doing farm work put the immigrant women ahead of their counterparts at home. To most of them, this is what is important, and regardless of how much they earn in America, these women find a way to share their meager wages with relatives back home by sending regular remittances to family members.

Migrant women farmworkers do not view farm labor as an undesirable, low status, physically unbearable, and less prestigious job, as most Americans do. Yes, farm work is not for the faint of heart, and the income they receive, however meager, is seen as relatively better than what they are accustomed to earning in West Africa. Moreover, one finds that despite the low pay, the fact that one may often find multiple family members all working on the same farm means that the women are able to mobilize and marshal their earnings to meet their collective as well individual needs. Mobilizing their households and economic resources also ensures that during periods of unemployment and ill health, there are available resources to cushion the effects of short- and long-term absence from work. By American standards, most of the West African migrant women farmworkers can be classified as poor. However, their cooperative and altruistic spirit has enabled a majority of the immigrant women to live in households where their total income earned exceeds Black American households that are female-headed or that lack two income earners.

The existence of a nonfarm professional class of West African immigrant women is reflective of the continued rise of a new cadre of Blacks whose levels of professional and educational attainments are equally noteworthy and inspiring. While this group of West African women in the United States does not have the same visible professional status of Asians, their growing presence in occupations such as medicine, health care, professorships, science and engineering, business and accountancy, the military, school administration, and teaching deserves public attention. A growing number of African Blacks have achieved professional statuses that are exemplar, particularly those in academe, the sciences, engineering, medicine, and allied health. As members of the new Black middle and middle-upper classes, these immigrants are redefining and recreating a new Black identity that is not only cosmopolitan but equally transnational. For the women, this new form of identity transcends the historical and traditional stereotypes based on the unequal mistreatment of women in African societies as a whole. For these women, the opportunity to work on a farm or have a professional status has far-reaching social and cultural consequences and implications beyond the borders of the United States. It signals to the patriarchal-dominated systems from where these women have come from that West African women, irrespective of their educational or class status, can carve occupational niches for themselves within the nexus of the new global movement of skilled and unskilled labor.

The bias in U.S. immigration policies favoring those with skills will continue to serve West Africans because as a group, immigrants from Africa tend to possess secondary and postsecondary credentials at the time of entry into the country. As stated, their post arrival educational attainment positions them also to become even more competitive in the labor market. The continued growth in the number of West African women specifically and African immigrants in general cannot be excluded from the ever-increasing phenomenon of the brain drain leaving the continent in search of better economic and cultural opportunities. In the formulation of national and international policies to manage this new form of labor flight, one must not only look at the traditional or classical theory of the push-pull factors of migration. Instead, a broader perspective that incorporates the transnational exigencies created by the demand for skilled labor worldwide may have to be ascertained and the consequences of such exigencies assessed for their theoretical and policy implications.

For some of the women, ardently pursuing occupational and educational goals is designed to promote social mobility and advancement. Education brings added value to the immigrants' access to occupational opportunities. This facilitates the possibility that the women will become incorporated into core sectors of the labor market. Having pursued advanced education may also increase the possibility that a family member already in the United States can file for permanent resident status for the purpose of reuniting with relatives already in the country. Reunification with extended family members who are permanent residents or citizens of the United States will continue to be the most common way for some of the immigrants to sponsor family members to join them here in the United States.

Irrespective of their occupational and class status, West African immigrant women are not unanimous in their perspectives on how international migration has changed their lives in the United States. Even with a common economic agenda of continuously seeking ways to improve upon their lives and, by extension, the lives of their relatives at home, West African immigrant women generally acknowledge that they are shaped by the persistence of racial, ethnic, class, and gender discrimination in the United States. The effect of this chronic problem is that when they frame and define their identities, these women tend to opt for a broader panethnic and transnational occupational and class status that transcends American notions of what it means to be Black. The women's notion of occupational and class identities are informed by a new cultural orientation anchored in self-actualization, self-help, and a commitment to the principles of economic collectivism and altruism where family, community, and personal responsibility are fostered. In this ethos and belief system shared by the immigrant women, government becomes a facilitator, not a provider. Coupled with this is their firm belief that civil rights are necessary and vital to ensure individual and group security, equal protection, and access to opportunity. These, as the women affirmed, are the recipes key to building a multicultural and diverse society. In essence, the widely held notion among the women is that blackness is a phenomenon that is not limited to or defined by geographic space. Blackness, they reason, should not be confined to a specific location or experience. Blackness, to these women, takes on global nuances on its own, sometimes through shared meanings and experiential essences. These global nuances and genres of blackness cannot and should not necessarily be defined and articulated exclusively by the American experience. Instead, it ought to be defined by the local and international communities where the Black immigrant diasporic experiences are manifested in their diverse cultural and social totalities.

INTERNAL MIGRATION: STILL SEARCHING FOR OPPORTUNITIES

West African immigrants are always searching for better work opportunities wherever they may be found. Economic and cultural characteristics of different towns, cities, and states are frequently compared for their comparative economic advantages to see which locations provide the optimum benefits for their households. Upon their arrival in the United States, many Africans settle in the cities and towns of those states that have large immigrant and minority populations. The residential settlement patterns of African immigrants are no different from those of recent migrants arriving in the country. African immigrants prefer to live in or near large metropolitan communities located on the eastern and southern seaboards of the United States. New York, Pennsylvania, Virginia, Florida, Massachusetts, Georgia, and North Carolina have historically attracted the largest share of new immigrants from Black Africa. Texas, Illinois, California, Minnesota, and Indiana continue to experience an influx of new émigrés from the African continent as well.

Among African immigrants in the United States, there is a prevailing sentiment that one does not simply drop anchor in a specific location and exclusively confine their immigrant experience to that community. African immigrants are constantly on the move in search of opportunities beyond the traditional locales where they initially settle. The prospect for better employment opportunities is an important determinant of the geographic and spatial settlement patterns of the immigrant women. Irrespective of their educational or professional status, many of the immigrant women (75 percent) prefer to live in U.S. cities with sizeable Black and immigrant population enclaves. The preference is to live closer to kith and kin so that they can tap into social and economic networks to ease the transition associated with their new statuses and roles in the United States. The primary motivation for selecting a place of residence is to facilitate the chances that the women will remain connected to ties with other immigrants while fostering affiliations that permit the continuity of kin relationships from the country of origin. The decision as to where to settle is instrumental and purposive. The goal is to take advantage of economic opportunities and at the same time maximize social and cultural capital while fostering solidarity with extended family members and other immigrants of the African diaspora.

Upon their original residential settlement, secondary migration becomes very common among African immigrant women. When they move away from the primary or initial place of settlement, the goal is twofold. The first is to reunite with other family members in order to take advantage of better job prospects that will improve upon their standards of living. The second is to seek better educational benefits and opportunities for their children away from densely populated urban centers with large pockets of minority populations. Even though housing affordability and the desire to find quality education for their dependents were identified as reasons for engaging in secondary migration, the need to live in close proximity to family members or social networks outweighs the affordability of housing.

Within the professional and managerial West African immigrant class, family contacts and the need to stay closer to extended relatives outweighs the cost of housing as a determinant of secondary migration. Secondary migration is therefore seen as an income-maximizing behavior designed to enhance professional development and to improve upon overall immigrant human capital attributes. Despite the fact that many of the women (particularly the migrant farmworkers and those working in the janitorial and cleaning-related sectors) have yet to attain income equalization with other immigrant groups, such as Latino and Asian women, many of them engage in continuing education to bridge their income gap with other minority groups and to improve upon their overall standards of living. Ultimately, several of these women will capitalize on their education by moving to cities and towns experiencing economic growth. The purpose of such a move is to enhance the prospects of earning higher wages. Their ability to close the income gap is going to be influenced by how the women are able to cope with, and overcome, discrimination and structural economic disadvantages (poor housing, lack of health care resources, inadequate savings, and high costs of education). As Dodoo (1997, 529) reported, there is still a high level of quality characteristics that some African immigrants and refugees bring with them to America, including, at a minimum, secondary-level educational credentials. For those who do not have marketable credentials, efforts are usually made (as already specified) to pursue secondary and postsecondary education to improve upon their employment prospects and the chances of earning lower-middle to middle-class wages.

To maximize their economic resources and capital, some of the women have started moving to destinations in the interior of the country, particularly to North and South Dakota, Montana, Nebraska, Kansas, Minnesota, and Missouri. The secondary migrations are from the densely populated Atlantic and Mid-Atlantic seaboard states and cities to the interior and mountain states, particularly Colorado and Wyoming. Their internal migratory patterns mirror that of the rest of America as a whole and often involve migration to the sun-drenched cities and states. This includes immigrant-rich states like California, Texas, Florida, Arizona, Nevada, and New Mexico. Another aspect of this migratory trend is migration from New York, Pennsylvania, and New Jersey to destinations in Virginia, the Carolinas, Georgia, Florida, and Alabama.

Among the immigrant women, the purpose of internal migration is to take advantage of the relatively low cost of living, particularly housing and burgeoning economies. While some of these areas may not boast of a large, diverse Black minority population (particularly those areas that are not in the southeast), many of the immigrant women who moved have done so in response to economic and structurally induced forces. The preference is to live in close proximity to racial and ethnic minority populations. However, this is not the sole motivating reason behind secondary migration. For some of the immigrant women with professional and postgraduate credentials, the westward migration is facilitated by employment opportunities that they were able to secure before embarking upon the move. For others, secondary migration is motivated in part by the opportunities to enjoy the wide and open landscape, including the immense recreational and outdoor opportunities offered by these places. In immigrant households with dual incomes, secondary migration to destinations with burgeoning economic opportunities has ensured the social mobility of some of the families. Once they achieve middle-class status, many of the immigrant women continue to work very hard and, in some cases, may even work overtime and night shifts to boost their earning potential. In the short- and long-term, their collective embracement of a strong work ethic and commitment to family, coupled with a cooperative spirit, continue to serve these women very well as they weave their immigrant tapestries in the United States.

As they engage in secondary migration, some of the women begin to recreate new ethnic, gender, and class identities in their new locales. The creation and formation of new roles and identities begin with the establishment of a cultural community based on Black African immigrant social and cultural ethos. In Minneapolis and Saint Paul, Fargo, Bismarck, Billings, Omaha, and St. Louis, some of the immigrant women are beginning to carve cultural niches for themselves and their children by establishing African stores to market Black ethnic and cultural products. In their new migratory experiences, the women do not have to accompany their spouses or male partners or stay behind until arrangements are made for them to be "sent for" to join a male partner. The decision regarding when and where to settle is handled by the women themselves without any of the strictures of patriarchy that had previously dominated their lives. They may consult with or share their migratory goals with male partners and solicit input but are certainly under no moral obligation or compulsion to accept their advice or input. This is because in the new global migration where their educational qualifications and labor market transformations have empowered them and placed them in charge of their own economic destinies, some of the women find that they do not have to kowtow to their husbands or defer to them in matters involving economic decisions.

Carving social and economic identities and roles in the Midwest and other frontier areas has not been easy for some of the immigrant women. For some, life in the American Northern Plains is characterized by seclusion, marginality, and, at times, a sense of feeling that time and life are frozen, unchanging, and devoid of a Black African presence. But the cultural and social constraints or impediments associated with living in places with little or no Black African presence is not construed to be disenabling. Instead, migration to the plains is viewed as the cultural repositioning of Black African ideas and ideals characterized by the need to redefine and bring new meaning, difference, and content to what it means to be Black in a white majority society.

For the women with children, internal migration is also seen as an opportunity to better the lives of their children. This is accomplished by moving to communities and locations with quality public schools as well as places that have lower crime rates. Once they migrate to these places, the immigrant children, just like their parents, do tend to experience cultural alienation. But the benefits of raising their children in quality school districts and in communities that have low crime rates trumps the cultural alienation that many of the women reported to be experiencing. Moving children to quality education and life in low crime communities is part of the cultural repositioning to remap the future of their children by laying the stress on educational attainment. One immigrant woman from Togo provided a rationale for moving her two teenage sons to a small community about an hour's drive from St. Louis: "We moved because some of us were beginning to see the negative impact of urban culture on the children. It was very difficult to get the children to listen to you because there were so many pressures they were dealing with not only at school, but also at the malls, the basketball courts, and even in the streets near home. No area was safe for them. I decided to move because my cousin did so two years ago and that changed the outlook of her children completely. I am hoping the same for mine." This Togolese immigrant woman described the quality of educational resources in her new suburban community: "The schools are great. They really teach the kids something. I can see a difference already though we have not been living here for long. There is accountability. Expectations are well-defined. Yes, a few troubles here and there on weekends when the kids are off from school. But these pale in comparison to what we experienced before moving here."

To minimize the effects of cultural marginality in unfamiliar cultural locales, some of the immigrant women maintain a network of links with relatives who are domiciled in other parts of the country. In Omaha and St. Louis, some of the immigrant women talked about starting an immigrant newsletter to serve as the voice of the growing West African immigrant communities in these cities. In addition, to remain connected to their cultural heritage, visits are frequently arranged to bring relatives and friends who often come to visit and in some cases elect to stay permanently. A subtext in the formation of cultural identities among the women is buttressed in the affirmation of not just African values and beliefs, but also the articulation of a new cultural framework that posits a place and space for the expression of cohesive national and international identities based upon the celebration of blackness.

When they engage in internal migration within the United States, it is very significant for some of the immigrant women to continue to stress an African ethnic and racial orientation anchored in the cultural heritage and traditions that many have imported to the United States. Through these ethnic and racial creations, the women are able to form and express their unique identities while at the same time exploring ways to engage in the affairs of their respective communities. Membership in the community and the fostering of bonds with groups and networks is the principal channel for asserting group cohesiveness while at the same stressing an individualistic normative orientation and belief system. In other words, there is recognition among some of the women immigrants that the community is the site for cultural, civic, economic, as well as political, engagement. By participating in the affairs of the community, the immigrant women are able to define and implement strategies to ensure their eventual integration in the community. At the same time, the conception of the cultural community as a site for the mobilization of collective resources to achieve collective goals is defined in such a way as to allow the immigrants to create their own sense of individuality in such a way to recognize personal traits, values, and customs unique to their migratory circumstances in the United States.

The links that are fostered with relatives and friends are so strong that they help maintain cultural continuity even though one may not always be surrounded by people from the same ethnic and clan affiliations. The new cultural transformations and identities being forged in the plains states by the immigrant women is akin to what Aime

Cesaire referred to as "Presence Africaine"—the celebration of the totality of the experiences that shape and define the contours of Black African identities. The articulation of identity is often blended with cultural constructions of nationalism among the women. Nationalistic fervor is often asserted by the immigrants to give substance and discourse to the historical realities associated with their status of having origins in nation-states that, from a Euro-American perspective, are often relegated to powerlessness and political and economic marginalization. Collectively, West African immigrant women believe that the definition of an identity that reflects their sense of who they are as foreign-born Blacks, immigrants, and women, is best articulated or rationalized within the broad spectrum of the interactions of gender, ethnicity, and class relationships in the United States. To escape from the negative stereotypes frequently associated with being Black in the United States, the women often find themselves affirming their West African ethnic identities and strong feelings of nationalism.

As a group, the West African women have managed, in less than a generation, to achieve economic advancements that their relatives at home can only dream about. By all accounts, the future prospects of this group of African immigrants appear very bright and promising. Relative to Asian immigrants, their incomes are still low, but over a period of time, many of the West Africans are able to combine total family resources to mitigate the shortfalls in their income earnings (for a comprehensive account of minority immigrant earnings, see Dodoo 1991b). The primary reasons behind their successes can be found in the vitality of the immigrant women's kinship and familial networks, coupled with the strong desire to always find ways to improve upon their educational credentials. For many, educational credentials brought from home and improved upon in the United States have been the single most important factor contributing to the improvement of their employment prospects. For those women who entered the United States with postsecondary training, the community colleges and technical schools in their respective districts have been the linchpin in the slow but gradual climb up the class and income ladder for many of the women. Their flexibility to disperse themselves through the vehicle of internal migration to states and cities with booming economies to take advantage of better labor market conditions has also propelled many of the immigrant women to middle class status. In forming the calculus of their migration, the economic opportunities and advantages available in a place is given a higher premium than the ethnic or minority composition of the population. This means that some of the women are willing to move to towns and cities in the country where Blacks are generally underrepresented or not represented at all.

Finally, it bears noticing that the professional niches that West African immigrant women carve for themselves are geared toward maintaining a transnational cultural identity that is designed to be fluid to permit movements within and outside of international labor market centers. For those women who are able to afford the costs associated with traveling between the West and the countries of origination, many forms of transnational identities are formed to reflect the multiple and complex forms of circulatory migrations that are commonly found among West African immigrants as a group. Immigrant women with resources travel back and forth between home countries and the Western labor and economic centers. As they travel to and fro, business and investment decisions are formed and implemented. Many take advantage of liberal investment schemes put in place by West African governments to lure business and investments to the region. The result is that small-capitalization business ventures and schemes are formed to reflect the transnational identifications that these women have established in multiple domains.

Maintaining linkages with the home country ensures that when they establish businesses, family members who stay behind can assist in the day-to-day management of these businesses. Despite having a low racial, ethnic, and class status in the United States, several of the women are able to transform their lives by forming intricate networks of transnational and occupational ties to leverage the benefits of their migration and at the same time create better economic opportunities for them at home in West Africa. An understanding of the gendered contexts of these transnational movements and their implications for international development in West Africa as a whole is sorely needed. The continued incorporation of West Africa immigrants into the global labor market has already created a culture of foreign travel and migration among many West Africans. I expect thousands of young women from the region to join this mass migration in search of work and economic opportunities. The resources that these migrants forward home are fast changing the lives of families, communities, and the nation-states, raising the possibilities that the pathways for economic and industrial development in the region may be mediated by international migration and the creation of transnational systems of economic interchanges and transfer of human capital.

CHAPTER 7

RETHREADING FERTILITY
DECISIONS IN NEW SETTINGS

I have had three children in addition to my first two since grandma joined us here. All I do is to go to work. She takes care of everything and everybody. She is even encouraging me to have more children in the hope that I will have another boy.

—Margaret, a Sierra Leonean immigrant

I can only afford to raise two children. We made a decision not to have any more children. We have been practicing contraceptive use since we both came to the U. S. A large family size will stand in the way of the quality of life we want for ourselves and our two children. It is purely an economic decision. We are not going to burden our two children with our subsistence in time of old age.

—Abena, a Ghanaian immigrant

Immigrant fertility behavior is an important aspect of immigrant life and culture in the host society. In the United States, immigrant fertility is a hotly contested political issue. Framing the fertility debate is the widely held alarmist conception that new immigrants from the relatively poorer countries of Latin America and Africa are pronatal. Anti-immigrant groups have framed the discourse on Latino and African immigrant fertility and reproductive behavior by stressing the economic cost of providing social services (welfare, education, housing, and health care) for the dependents of both legal and illegal workers in the country. In addition, a high birthrate among immigrant minorities is also viewed as culturally oppositional to the dominant society's reproductive behavior. Cultural representations of Black and Latino women on welfare have been constructed in such a way to portray the women's reproductive behavior as being out of step with the national norm. In California, the push to pass Proposition 187 was designed in part to withhold prenatal, educational, and social services support for Black and Latino immigrants who are undocumented. Former California Governor Pete Wilson pushed for the curtailment of social services for illegal immigrants and their dependents. At the national level, the welfare reform legislation of 1996 also sought to cut the educational and health care services states provided to the children of illegal immigrants. Before and after 9/11, the national discourse on immigrant fertility has become more pronounced and scathing, driving up nativistic sentiments and immigrant-bashing.[1]

Not much is known about the fertility and reproductive patterns of Black West African immigrants entering the United States. A central question is the impact of international migration on the fertility choices of West Africa's newest immigrants in the United States. Are there any specific norms and values related to fertility and children in American society that West African immigrant women have or are learning from their American counterparts? How firm are the immigrant's attitudes and values regarding fertility issues? Are there certain lingering cultural norms related to fertility that the women imported from Africa to this country? Does the onset of fertility reduction occur immediately following migration or is there a lag period? Answers to these questions are important in shedding light on the trends and sociocultural processes involved in the transitioning of immigrant fertility from high to low birthrates.

For some of the immigrant women, the timing of fertility, norms related to fertility decisions, perceptions and attitudes relating to the calculus, benefits, and the costs of having children are likely to be framed within the immigrant's perspective(s) regarding the outcomes of the migratory experiences. For others, decisions regarding fertility may be framed by referencing normative beliefs and values regarding fertility that have been learned prior to migration. The reference point for fertility decisions may come from parents, tribal beliefs, religious practices, economic exigencies, and the general environment regarding the cultural and social-psychological factors germane to the specificities of fertility behavior. All told, micro and macro factors often converge to explain fertility choices. Fertility behavior is indeed a complex process to understand, and, sometimes, attempts toward the unraveling of the nuanced contexts of fertility behavior or its proximate determinants may end up raising more questions than providing answers.

NORMATIVE CONTEXTS OF
FERTILITY IN WEST AFRICA

In traditional African cultural systems, a high premium is placed on children. There is a conscious desire on the part of families to have many children. This pronatal culture is pervasive in rural and urban parts of Africa. Children are seen as blessings from the ancestors. When children are born, elaborate festivities and rituals—popularly known as outdooring or child-naming ceremonies—are performed to symbolize the continuity of life and to solicit the prayers of the departed ancestors to ensure the survival and prosperity of the new-born and their family. These outdooring or child-naming ceremonies are sometimes lavish. Women clad in white sing and dance to pacify the soul of the newborn. In some societies, the celebrations assume pomp and pageantry when the first born is a son. In the Ga-Adangbe nation in Ghana, elaborate celebrations await those women who have their twelfth child. The mother's status is elevated in the eyes of her peers and community of kin group. A sheep is slaughtered in order to symbolize her feat. In the northern tier regions of West Africa where Islam is the dominant form of religious practices and orientation, very large families are also the norm. Household sizes are large, and male children often spend their time herding cattle and cultivating the land, growing millet, rice, and sorghum. Literacy levels remain very low despite mandatory laws requiring parents to send their children to school. The infrastructure remains poor or nonexistent; so are standards of living that continue to lag behind the southern regions of West Africa.

Within the traditional system, the more children families have, the more they command respect and prestige. Status in the community and the number of children one has sired is an affirmation of power and virility. At the economic and community organization level, children are considered assets. They are incorporated into the system of division of labor and provide assistance to their families. At an early age, children who live in the rural and agricultural areas assist parents with weeding farms, hoeing, planting, and harvesting of crops. Family size may also influence the acreage or hectares that a family is able to bring under cultivation. Children are integrated into social and economic production.

In the urban centers, children assist family members in trading at the markets, engage in head-portage retailing, or provide care for elderly parents and grandparents. Some of the children earn wages, which they contribute toward the total household income. These income-generating activities are sometimes performed in addition to attending school and helping with household chores. The high demand for children cuts across social class, income, and educational profiles. Moderate economic and cultural progress has provided incentives to a growing number of educated, middle-class, and moderate-income Africans to lower their fertility, but in the main, birthrates still continue to be very high among rural, low-income, low-class, and low-educational segments of the population, even in the midst of declining infant mortality. Cultural and social norms and beliefs about fertility choices (the preference for sons, prestige, the need to satisfy or please the ancestors, and quest for status) may impinge on the decision to have many children.

Having more children is also seen as an investment in the old-age economic security of the parents. Normative expectations are structured in such a way as to allow children to provide for the economic needs of aging parents who do not have access to national insurance schemes for senior citizens and the elderly. The peasant and agricultural mode of economic production makes it relatively easier for extended family members to take care of their elderly members. Most families in the rural areas cultivate their own food and engage in animal husbandry and livestock activities to augment family income and resources.[2]

For the many West African immigrant women who have settled in the United States, the opportunities afforded by migration continue to have a significant impact in shaping their standards of living and life-course expectations. Economic and cultural opportunities have facilitated normative changes in the lives of many immigrant women. Exposure to new ideas and new ways of thinking about family formation and the role of children has created some metamorphosis. Coming from societies in West Africa where large family size is the norm and where a high premium is placed on the number of children that families have, some of the women find themselves redefining the contours that shape fertility behavior among women in West Africa. One aspect where this change is noticeable is fertility behavior, family planning, and a new orientation regarding what constitutes the ideal family size. Nearly 80 percent of the immigrant women indicated that they came from a large family size (six siblings). Another 12 percent have seven or eight siblings at home. Only 8 percent reported having more than eight siblings. Declining infant mortality rates in the West African subregion in general has yet to translate into reduced fertility rates on the part of families. Pronatal cultural and social norms still persist despite the low standards of living, substandard nutrition, poor health conditions, and poverty. In both the rural and urban areas, some families still hold on to the belief that not all the children they have are going to survive beyond the age of five; thus, the imperative to have many children so that even if one, two, or more should die, families will still be left with children who survive. For some families, the decision to have many children is calculated to ensure that no matter the health problems that children face as they grow up, some of which may lead to death, there will always be some children left at home, which mitigates the dishonor or shame that often comes with childlessness.

Following their migration to the United States, some of the immigrant women now look back on the system of social and economic production involving children as exploitative and inimical to the overall well-being of children. The separation made between the worlds of adult and child work is sometimes blurred by the glaring poverty and economic malaise confronting the family unit. Every available hand and assistance that can be offered by anyone and everyone in the family unit is tapped to the maximum. Whether on the part of adults or children, idleness has economic implications in such economies; it may affect total family income and make it difficult for parents and guardians to pay children's school fees, buy school uniforms, or pay for medical expenses. Existing laws protecting child labor and stipulating the mandatory education of minors are therefore overlooked. According to one immigrant,

> A major problem in urban West Africa is the vast number of children who have been brought from the rural and agricultural areas to serve in domestic roles often by working as maids and 'house boys' in the homes of their extended relatives. While some of these children attend primary and middle school, a majority of them terminate their education before they reach the secondary or tertiary levels as their involvement in household chores and business activities leaves them little or no time to study and prepare for competitive qualifying entrance exams to enable them attend secondary and postsecondary institutions. Abuse is pervasive and the lack of coordinated institutional structures for handling cases of abuse means that many child abuse victims are not brought into the open let alone have their circumstances resolved.

In spite of their trepidations and concerns about the economic hardship a majority of them had to confront growing up, several of the women feel that the cultural emphasis placed on hard work, discipline, self-empowerment, education, strong kinship bonds, and communal altruism prepared them for life in the United States. For a Westerner looking in, the cultural norm promoting child work with the goal of enhancing the family's economic standing may seem harsh, cruel, and misplaced. But as one immigrant woman attested, "Such practices have become part of the globalized economic system and poorer families are compelled to utilize the human resources of its entire members."

For nearly all the immigrant women, large family size at home in West Africa was not viewed as an impediment to economic and social advancement. Poverty and relative deprivation is not as pernicious as it is in some societies as the majority of the people share in the same circumstances and status, and gaps in inequality and access to resources are not as varied as they are in other cultural systems. Children are raised not only by their biological parents but also by extended family members. Economic assistance for raising children may come from other relatives who at times may pay for the education of their nieces and nephews. In exchange, these children assist in household chores or in the management of a small business establishment. Young boys and girls are sometimes sent to live with uncles, aunts, and grandparents who provide for their education. More economically successful family members who live in the urban centers often invite children of their siblings to move to the city and come and live with them. Multiple families sharing in the raising of children may enable these families who are related by blood and marriage to minimize the economic impact that families face if they raise their children on their own or unassisted by extended relatives.

Though infant mortality rates are gradually declining in West Africa due to improved access to health care, the explanations for having a large family are usually not framed in solely economic terms. More often than not, cultural reasons are also used in justifying increased fertility or the need to have a large family size. Several of the immigrants referenced how fertility rates had increased in their respective communities at home during times of economic depression, agricultural failures, and natural and or man-made disasters. Following their migration to the United States, some of the women do not abandon the cultural and normative beliefs that they associate with fertility prior to their migration. The results of the focus-group sessions showed that among some of the immigrant women, the economic benefits of living in the United States offers the possibility to implement the cultural and normative expectations associated with high fertility. The opportunity to earn relatively higher wages in America may be used in justifying the reasons for high fertility. When they compare their standards of living in the United States and during their stay at home in West Africa, some of the women believe that they are in a relatively better position to respond to the cultural and or economic expectations of high fertility. Their higher incomes relative to what they earned in

West Africa, coupled with the practice whereby multiple families raise their children together may influence high birthrates among some of the immigrant women. Knowing that there are family members willing and able to step in and assist in raising children is an important consideration in fertility decision making. Though domiciled in the United States, the reference group used in forming and rationalizing decisions about fertility is derived from West African cultural and normative ethos. It can be surmised that the experiences and outcomes associated with international migration (opportunity to earn relatively higher wages, learn new familial roles and expectations, immigrants' exposure to new models of fertility practices in the United States) has had little or minimal impact in shaping notions of fertility.

In the rural and farming districts, having a large family size is considered an economic asset. As stated, children make significant contributions to household income. Children assist their parents and extended family members by providing valuable services on the farm, including land clearing, sowing, harvesting, and carrying farm produce to lorry hubs for transportation to the market centers. In the absence of efficient transportation, these children may be expected to walk for miles, carrying loads of farm produce to markets for sale. These activities are carried out in addition to household chores and school responsibilities. For some of the children, these responsibilities may also entail having to sell agricultural produce at the market. In the urban centers, children may assist both family and nonfamily members selling consumer wares on street pavements and in kiosks all over the cities. A number of them carry and walk long distances, hawking their wares at lorry stations, bus terminals, and at market centers. From their perspective, the nature of social organization and the informal nature of economic production facilitate the incorporation of children's services into the production process, thereby spreading the economic cost and burden of bringing up children to primary and secondary groups. The cultural emphasis is on the old-age security that children contribute to later on and provide for the care of elderly kith and kin.

Abena's perspective regarding fertility is illustrative of how some of the African immigrant women redefine and form new choices when it comes to family size. Abena is an immigrant from Ghana who grew up in a household that had twelve siblings. From her perspective, coming from a large family was an economic asset. It facilitated shared responsibilities and sacrifices toward the betterment of everyone. Family members made contributions to household budget, no matter how small the contributions. Describing the economic structure her household in West Africa, she remarked,

We did not have much. Everyone worked, no matter how small what they earned. The informal economy encouraged the practice of child labor. By American standards, we will be classified as living in extreme poverty. But it was not until we were all grown, working, and supporting our parents that I saw the importance of having many children. My parents don't have to worry about financial assistance. They get it from all of us. We contribute also to the financial needs of extended family members because of their help in taking care of us when we were kids. Now, we have become net contributors. We have paid back, with our labor and money, in a sense, what our parents expended on us. And as long as they live, we will continue to take care of them.

According to Abena, this form of family organization and production cannot be sustained in the United States due to the economic cost this may entail. Referring to her own two children and the cost involved in bringing them up, Abena and her husband made the decision to have only two children even though they are being pressured by relatives at home to have more. "I can only afford to raise two children. We made a decision not to have any more children. We have been practicing contraceptive use since we both came to the U.S. A large family size will stand in the way of the quality of life we want for ourselves and our two children. It is purely an economic decision. We are not going to burden our two children with our subsistence in time of old age," Abena acknowledged.

Responding to the decision some of her immigrant friends and relatives make to send children home to extended relatives to be raised (and to cut down on the cost of raising them in the United States), Abena remains ambivalent about the overall benefits and questions the economic and psychological effects on the children. "Some of the kids who were sent home that I recently met seem to be trapped in two cultural identities, often not knowing whether to embrace an African or American identity. For those of us who are undocumented and operate underground, having more than two or three children is not a wise idea due to the shifting nature of our status. I can understand why some immigrants will send their children home because the parents lack valid papers," Abena said. Aside from sending children home to ease the economic pressure of raising them in the United States, some of the immigrant women believe that once at home, these children receive other benefits. First, they learn about African cultural identity, which is different from the identities that Black children form and are associated with in the United States. Second, these children become well-grounded in primary and secondary education and are taught to view education as a means of self-empowerment and future economic well-being. Third, some of the parents believe that the children who are sent home develop and learn respect for authority figures in society, particularly parents and teachers. Upon their return to the United States, parents believe that their children are better suited to confront and deal with the negative images and stereotypes typically associated with Black youths.

The social networks comprising immediate familial and extended kin group members that the West African immigrant women form serve as an agency within which decisions about fertility can be rationalized or articulated. These networks serve as the fulcrum of immigrant life and culture in the United States. Through them, some of the immigrants are able to develop strategies to confront economic and cultural hardships, particularly finding employment, dealing with racism, discrimination, marginality, and also dealing with psychological matters such as stress and bereavement. Depending on its size and composition, it is within these networks that most of the women live, socialize, cater to their economic needs, and derive meanings from living in a foreign land. The women freely chat about themselves and their families, children, and husbands or partners. Perceptions and ideas about fertility, sexuality, intercourse, and pregnancies are also formed in these circles or social networks. For some of the women, these networks are not only their primary groups but also become their reference group for developing normative standards about what is expected of them not only by the host society, but more importantly, by their relatives at home.

For Gloria, an undocumented migrant farmworker, neither the costs associated with raising a large family nor her transient status serves as a disincentive to have fewer children. Using their familial and social networks, some of the immigrant women send their children away to live with immigrant relatives who are domiciled in Europe and the Middle East. Gloria and her husband have six children, all born in the United States. Two of the children are currently living in Denmark with Gloria's sister. Two others are living in Saudi Arabia with an uncle, with the remaining two living at home. According to Gloria, the decision she and her husband made to have six children was based on their belief that when these children become successful, they, in turn, will provide for their parents' upkeep. Gloria decried the use of contraceptives, casting her rationalizations of high fertility in religious tones. She stated, "It is not our place (me and my husband) to determine how many children we ought to have. Children come from God. It is the work of God. That is why we feel that natural fertility without the use of contraceptive is always desirable. Controlling fertility is tampering with the course of nature."[3] Her remarks are representative of other immigrant women who perceive that the costs of raising children in the West should not become the modality by which West African immigrant women view or construct notions about their fertility. Gloria's perspective on fertility is shaped by the belief held by some Africans that a household full of children bestows psychological benefits to the parents. Children bring psychological fulfillment and nurturing to parents. More importantly, the economic costs associated with raising them are not always borne by the biological parents. Some women do form loosely structured groups to enable them to offset the economic burdens of raising many children at the same time. As they interact among themselves, these women come to develop a group consciousness whose foundations are purely altruistic. The women pull their resources together to take care of one another. They derive a sense of honor and pride in assisting their fellow family members or friends. This is considered a religious obligation. In exchanging and sharing in both material and nonmaterial goods, these women are able to stay unified, an organic community and entity that is almost self-sufficient, though maybe poor by American standards. Their culture socializes them into the role of motherhood as an honorable trait. For some of them, motherhood is a duty, an obligation.

For those women who embrace an American ethos regarding how many children to have, subtle social pressures are used by extended family and nonfamily members to bring those women into conformity. Whether they come from matrilineal or patrilineal families, high fertility is construed as honoring one's elders and the ancestors. Some of the women immigrants are not so much interested in American culture and becoming completely assimilated. At times, they may even reject American consumerism and the idea that the American system does not allow for group consciousness but rather stresses individuality and choice. This, according to one immigrant, goes against how they have been socialized. Some of the immigrant women recognize that they do not have free agency or autonomy in matters regarding their fertility decisions because of being socialized into a strong kinship system. And even though their pro-fertility stance may have the unintended consequence of propping up the patriarchal systems of dominance and control over women, they ultimately rationalize that having children has a positive and enduring cultural legacy than any short-term benefits that men derive or gain by controlling women and children in West African society.

SOCIAL PROCESSES OF FERTILITY DECISIONS

The process involved in fertility decision making between partners is complex. These decisions are oftentimes deeply embedded and influenced by the social, cultural, psychological, and economic expectations regarding children and marriage. Integral to fertility decision making is the notion of exchange, sharing, or give-and-take between husband and wife (Bagozzi and Van Loo 1980). In this calculus, spouses communicate their desires about fertility. These desires are formed against the background of the spouse's economic status and the resources available to the household unit. The outcome and purpose of this exchange relationship regarding how many children a couple will have is to maximize the economic interests of both parties.

The rationalization and social construction of gender roles in society, particularly the social psychological benefits of having children and the status of women relative to men, are a few of the factors that weigh in making these decisions. A common belief is that irrespective of the circumstances and the dynamics defining and shaping how fertility decisions are made, the outcome should take into consideration what is in the best interests of all the parties, including the maximization of the needs of the children, if any. For West African immigrant women, the values and beliefs associated with fertility decision making have been formed prior to migration. According to the immigrant women, decisions about fertility (contraceptive use, timing and spacing of birth, how many children to have, and rules governing lactation) in West Africa were often made with little or no input from the women. This was particularly the case among women who resided in small, rural, and agricultural communities where male domination of women and children is commonplace. At times, decisions about fertility were discussed by the male partner and his relatives with the woman's input left out. From the women's perspectives, with the balance of power favoring men, fertility decisions in West Africa tend to be based on natural as opposed to controlled fertility. And while a majority of the women will prefer an environment in which controlled fertility was the norm, most of them find themselves unable to completely alter the balance of power regarding fertility decision making in their favor. Women are separated from this process, particularly if they are not well educated and gainfully employed. The calculus of fertility decisions was made to reflect the authority and status position of the husband or partner. Norms about fertility and its regulation are made by cultural agencies and authority structures outside of the household unit. Some of these women have little or no control and empowerment over their bodies. Among rural West African women who have completed secondary and or postsecondary education and are actively engaged in the labor force, their contribution to the economies of the household seem to be of less significance in the fertility decision-making process. Issues pertaining to women's fertility and health matters are oftentimes separated from other aspects of their lives, such as work, education, land tenure, and property rights. The situation is made worse for uneducated rural women in the farming communities. Their roles are largely defined as homemakers, in addition to being active in the production, marketing, and distribution of food. Family planning clinics may be available to some of the rural women, but usually they are discouraged, and at times sanctioned, by their partners and in-laws if they use contraceptive devices.

For immigrant women who lived in the urban areas prior to their migration (and were relatively better educated than their rural counterparts or worked in nonagricultural settings), the power to control their own fertility is minimized to a large extent by paternalistic norms and beliefs about fertility. Even though these women described their relationships with their partners as somewhat egalitarian, ultimately, decisions about the use of contraceptives and the timing of fertility or the number of children a family should have were all influenced by husbands. In the large urban areas where they have access to family planning resources, several of the women indicated that they were discouraged by their partners from using the services of government agencies to be fitted with birth control prevention devices. And despite having their own informal social networks where they exchanged information with other women about fertility issues, most of the women felt powerless or indifferent in engaging their husbands in a discussion about the consequences of high or low birthrates. Among the immigrant women who consider their gender roles as egalitarian with their husbands, perceptions about fertility involve an exchange process where the couples weigh the incentives and disincentives for high or low fertility.

Following their migration, a majority of the women (63 percent) indicated that they discuss issues related to the use or nonuse of contraceptive devices and family planning matters with their male partners. These discussions are often approached from the perspective that decisions about contraception have costs and benefits for the household unit. The data also suggests that couples not only consider the trade-offs of high versus low fertility but also implement or embark upon strategies to ameliorate the economic consequences or costs of having a larger family size. Where both couples work, saving money and the spacing of childbirth are ways that the women have been able to minimize the economic impact of having a large family size.

A central question in social demography is the question of what motivates the desire for people to have fewer children. One of the paradigms addressing this question is known as demographic transition theory. Using a classical approach, this paradigm, also referred to as the Princeton Project, modeled by Ansley Coale (1973), posits that economic development, modernization, high standards of living, improved social infrastructures, access to quality health care and nutritional standards, high rates of literacy, controlled urbanization, and changes in the system of division of labor and production from familial- to nonfamilial-based eventually results in the need for people to have fewer children. The emphasis of this model of fertility decline is on changes in the superstructure of society, particularly in the economic, social, and cultural institutions. This, according to the theory, creates new aspirations for people who now want better living standards for themselves and their children. In this perspective, emphasis is placed on the quality, rather than the quantity, of children. Having a large family size is seen as standing in the way of achieving a quality standard of living.

Writing about this perspective, Namboodiri (1980) noted that the transition to low fertility is accompanied by increasing differentiation and specialization, which transfers economic functions from nonfamilial and kin groups to larger and structured organizations. These structural transformations may be subsumed under the broader theme of modernization and development. From Coale's (1973) perspective, in an environment of decreasing mortality brought upon by economic and cultural development, birthrates can be reduced through rational and calculated fertility aimed at quality, rather than the quantity, of children. From Caldwell's (1978) perspective, children may become a liability rather than asset to their parents as the economic costs associated with childrearing may become an economic drag, which may lead to a lowering of the living standard of the parents. Ultimately, as Caldwell (1978) argued, the transition from high to low fertility is accomplished via social structural variables such as rising levels in education, incomes, and a general increase in economic standards of living and overall well-being.[4]

Other competing models of demographic transition are the Easterlin (1978) and Becker (1974) approaches to fertility reduction. Easterlin emphasizes the role of values and socialization in explaining the motivation behind fertility reduction. He postulates that the availability or the lack of adequate resources is central to the formation of aspirations, goals, and values. Applied to fertility behavior decision making, the Easterlin approach suggests that the number of children that are born to couples is influenced by the parents' resources relative to their aspirations. This means that parents' rationalization of their desired standard of living relative to the quality of life they want their children to have is what determines fertility behavior. Becker adopts the "new home economics" approach in explaining fertility behavior. In this model, the time, taste, costs, and the parents' desired standard of living are assessed in making decisions about fertility. Parents will have fewer children if they desire a high standard of living for themselves and their children. The emphasis is on the maximization of the utility (measured in terms of economic well-being) of the entire household. The Easterlin and Becker approaches, including the demographic transition models, have been the dominant paradigm in explaining the decline in fertility in developed countries. Their theoretical and empirical saliency and authenticity or applicability in explaining fertility behavior and decision making in the less developed countries have been mixed.[5]

The demographic perspectives on fertility decision making can be modeled and applied to the experiences of the West African immigrants. It bears stating that social, economic, and cultural traits of this migrant population are significant in unraveling fertility behavior. Looking at the age at which they migrate to the United States, one finds that West African immigrants tend to be very young. The age selectivity in migration is well noted. In the new global migration, a majority of those who risk and undertake the journey to the developed countries usually tend to be very young, in their early to mid-twenties. Most of them are well educated and are looking for better economic opportunities relative to what are available to them in their respective countries. This is the time in their lives when the young migrants arriving in the United States establish permanent or temporary contacts with their Western host societies. New ambitions and aspirations are formed. These new identities sometimes represent a fusion of ideas, beliefs, and norms that the migrants bring with them to their new environments. Some of the new migrants are shaped by the culture of their new surroundings. For many of the new immigrants who form the new transnational and global migration to the United States, the opportunity to migrate is seen as a form of economic and cultural self-improvement and empowerment. Migration is seen as a vehicle for achieving intergenerational social mobility with the ultimate goal of raising not only the migrant's standard of living but also that of their family (extended or nuclear). Migration is also seen as a way of tapping into the global mobility of labor from periphery to core countries and vice versa. The benefits that accrue for prospective migrants are shared through remittances, the exchange and transfer of innovative ideas and the learning of new roles, specializations, and division of labor. The changes that migrants learn through contacts with their host societies are also seen as having an impact on their values and normative belief systems. Given the micro and macro changes in ideas and ideals that accompany the transnational and global migratory experiences, it is possible to conjecture that with time, the fertility behavior of the migrants may mirror that of their host society. That is, as immigrants come to see the benefits that may accrue to them from reduced fertility, their values and belief systems regarding large family sizes will undergo a transition as well. The continued economic and cultural empowerment garnered via the structures of international migration will feature prominently in unraveling the proximate determinants of fertility behavior among African immigrant women.[6]

Nearly 76 percent of the immigrant women left home in their early to mid-twenties. Another 15 percent were between twenty-six and twenty-nine years old prior to leaving home. Only 9 percent of the respondents were thirty years old and above at the time of their emigration. The age structures of West African women immigrants who are arriving in the United States are similar to those of the other new immigrants. With respect to West African women, a distinctive feature of their migration is that they are less likely than Asian or Latin American immigrants to have been married at the time of their migration to the United States. In cases where they are married, the West Africans are more likely than Hispanic or Asian immigrants to leave their children at home. This is particularly the case considering that most of them enter the United States in a stepwise fashion where they have to travel to, live, and work in three or four countries before entering the United States. In this regard, children are seen as stumbling blocks in the chain migratory process. Husbands and children, if any, can be sent for later.

The diverse patterns of their migrations to the United States have a propensity to cause a delay or postponement of marriage and childbirth for some of the women. For those women who entered the United States directly from West Africa (32 percent), the median age at marriage was thirty years old, compared to the median age at marriage of about twenty-five years for urban women, and twenty-two years for rural women in West Africa. About a third of the women (32.2 percent) did not enter the United States directly. The immigrants who comprise this group initially left West Africa and traveled to a second destination or country outside of Africa, and, in some cases, to a third country before migrating to the United States. Another 25 percent started their immigrant journeys from West Africa and traveled to live and work in different countries before finally arriving in the United States to reunite with relatives and spouses. On average, it took some of the women about six years before finally arriving in America. This circuitous and chain mobility has implications for fertility behavior. For those women who were not in marital unions as they engaged in the stepwise or chain migration, having children had to be postponed or delayed until they reached their final destinations. Plans for marriage may also have to be put on hold during the period of migratory transition if the final destination or the last leg of the journey is filled with uncertainties and apprehension about what will transpire upon arrival in the host country. For those who had marital partners waiting for them in the United States, the timing for having children was delayed after the immigrants had secured employment documents and found a job.

Delayed marriages and pregnancies among some of the West African immigrant women are attributed to labor force participation and career aspirations. Like their Black American sisters, West African immigrant women have a high rate of labor force participation. Traditionally, Black women have always worked to contribute to total household income irrespective of their class, occupational, and educational background. Father absence from home is a prime motivation to seek employment to support children. The majority of legal and undocumented West African immigrant women work outside the home. Most of the women reported working very long hours to ensure their economic survival and also to save money to assist relatives at home. A number of the women (about 27 percent) indicated that they had to postpone marriage and pregnancy during the period when they were pursuing economic goals. Working second and, in a few cases, third, jobs is very common. Becoming fully incorporated into the labor force and working multiple jobs is seen as the primary motivation that formed the decision to migrate in the first place. Among some of the immigrant women, active labor force participation may overshadow fertility behavior, including the timing and spacing of birth. For those who have a high rate of labor force participation and who are without the kin group and social network support to assist in the raising of children, a conscious decision is frequently made to delay marriage and childbirth and also to limit the number of children born to the household to less than three. In a number of cases, work and the economic benefits that it may bring is seen as being more significant than the number of children born.

As a result of their migration to the West, some of the women have been successful in avoiding the social pressures or stigmas often brought to bear on childless women of childbearing age in West Africa. According to one immigrant woman from the Ivory Coast, extended relatives back home have ceased pressuring her about the need to have children. According to this immigrant, this pressure gradually "eases with the regular remittances I send home. My extended relatives have arranged for me to adopt a child. Meanwhile, they keep stressing the need to continue working hard and not to give up any opportunity to work a second job. And I don't mind because I am able to assist in raising my nieces and nephews at home. The pressure to have my own children will be greater if I were living in West Africa. Living in America has shielded me somewhat from that expectation."

Intermarriage between some of the West African immigrant women and non-West Africans (particularly Blacks from the Caribbean Basin and, in a small number of cases, intermarriage with white or native-born Blacks) significantly alters the fertility behavior of some of the immigrant women. These women described their relationship with their spouses as more egalitarian, with household responsibilities split equally. Structural assimilation and integration into the dominant culture seems to have occurred in this subgroup. This assimilation is manifested in the fewer number of children (less than two) born to these blended families. These households, unlike other West African immigrant households in the United States, are more likely to have only nuclear family members residing at home. Kin group members may live nearby but they do not share the same residence. Contacts and social networks are primarily with white Americans and although these women interact with other West African female immigrants, the networks of friends are also professional households and are carefully chosen. The average age at marriage among this subgroup is 33.5 years old. The wives in these households usually hold college or postgraduate degrees and are more likely than other West African immigrant women to be employed in managerial and professional occupations.

Predominantly suburban, some of the women had embraced Western ideas and norms even prior to their migration to the United States. Back home in West Africa, most of them had grown up in nuclear families and had attended preparatory schools and matriculated from a college or university prior to their arrival in the United States. Contraceptive use is a very common form of fertility regulation among these women. They have expectations regarding the spacing and timing of fertility. On average, the spacing between each birth is over two years, compared to one year for immigrant women of a lower socioeconomic status. The decision to space and time fertility is purposive—it is to allow the parents to set aside ample resources to meet the needs of each child. It is also a way for these immigrant women to pursue career goals without sacrificing employment promotion and loss in wages and salaries during the period preceding and immediately following the birth of a child.

Immigrants' legal status may also influence the decision of whether or not to start a family. This was certainly the case for a number of women who had recently migrated to the United States. According to Femi, "Not having any form of valid employment documents, legal or illegal, makes it difficult to plan ahead or manage a stable household with young children due to the uncertainties and apprehensions associated with deportation and or arrest." For Femi, this meant that she had to put her marriage plans on hold. Femi got married when she was thirty-two years old. The husband was forty-two. Both had been living in the United States for twenty-three years without valid papers. A few years ago, Femi's husband entered the immigration lottery system under the diversity program and was selected to apply for permanent residence. Only then did the couple start having children.

Immigrant couples that do not possess valid working authorization permits may sometimes separate by living in two different households. This split or separate household model is designed to ensure that both couples are not arrested at the same time for deportation by immigration authorities. If one parent is arrested, the remaining parent will assume responsibility in taking care of the children. Mami Esi, an undocumented immigrant from Ghana, maintained a separate household. Two of her five children are living with their father, who had his own apartment in another part of town. Of the three remaining children, two were living with Mami Esi. At the time of the focus-group interviews, the fifth child had been sent home to Ghana to be raised by Mami Esi's grandmother. She and her husband practiced family planning by using contraceptives. Though she would like to have two more children, she agrees that the extra financial burden this will put on them does not warrant the benefits they will derive from having more children. However, like some of the immigrant women, her perception is that cultural pressures and norms operating in her extended family unit trump the economic disincentives in having a large family size.

The opportunities to negotiate egalitarian relationships with their male partners, coupled with the women's ability to influence and participate in household decision making, have had a significant influence on the fertility behavior of some of the immigrant women. Irrespective of their socioeconomic status, the majority of the women (56 percent) reported that their desired family size of two children is based on their perceptions that having a large family size (defined as four or more children) may impede the high standard of living that these women want for themselves and their children in the United States. Having more children means that the women cannot travel home often, save enough money to buy land in West Africa, build a home, or start a business. While the justification for having fewer children in the United States is largely influenced by economic reasons, the data from the immigrant women suggests that the economic effects of large family size on family finances can be mitigated by sending children home for short or longer periods of time depending on the age of the children and the presence or absence of a male partner. For nearly one-third of the immigrant women (32 percent), the costs and resources associated with having and taking care of a large number of children is not seen as an impediment to economic advancement. As stated, through their kin and familial networks, some of these women have managed to minimize the economic impact of raising many children by adopting a number of strategies, chief among which is sending children home to West Africa to live with extended family members and even close friends. While at home living with family members, these children are educated at prestigious private preparatory schools. The expectation is that after they have completed secondary school, they can reunite with their parents and attend a college or university in the United States. Another strategy for coping with the economic impact of raising many children is by establishing a shared residence with other immigrant women who live together and share household expenses, particularly the cost of food, clothing, and accommodation. It is therefore not uncommon to find two or three single women from the same ethnic or national origin sharing a home with multiple rooms that is being rented or is being purchased. The residence members may take turns babysitting, shopping, preparing food, and taking children to school. This arrangement also frees up the time of some of the women to work multiple jobs or to pursue further education if they so choose.

Among some of the immigrant women, opportunities to tap into the intricate social and kin networks that most of the immigrant women establish in and outside of the United States may also affect fertility behavior. As indicated, matriarchs play a big role in immigrant family organization. Matriarchs or grandmothers are typically sponsored to come and assist with childrearing responsibilities. In those immigrant families where there is a matriarch or grandmother, the number of children living at home exceeds five. This does not include those children who have been born in the United States but have been sent home to West Africa or to other regions of the world to be raised by other relatives. Explaining her relatively large family size, Margaret, an immigrant from Sierra Leone, stated that without the assistance provided by her grandmother, she would not have had five children. Explaining her fertility choices, Margaret noted, "I have had three children in addition to my first two since grandma joined us here. All I do is to go to work. She takes care of everything and everybody. She is even encouraging me to have one or two more children in the hope that I will have another boy. But that will be too many children given that my husband does not make good income. Economically, we are stretched to the limit as things stand now." According to Margaret, while economic factors weigh in the decision to limit the number of children to five, cultural factors and norms operating in her village in Sierra Leone oftentimes compels her to discuss the possibility of having more children. Margaret stated, "Though I have five children, most of the women I grew up with have six or more children. These women are accorded respect and prestige in the village. When I informed one of them that I have had an intrauterine device (IUD), she expressed her concern that I am embracing western ideas. Her statement concerns me a lot and I think about it almost everyday. If I do have another child, I may have to send that child home to be cared for by close relatives." The prevailing cultural and normative belief about children in Margaret's village is that the initial costs of having and raising many children do not outweigh the cultural belief held in her village that ultimately, these children grow up and become contributory members to the families' overall economic well-being.

The findings in this chapter suggest that international migration has altered, albeit in a minimal way, the fertility behavior of some of the West African immigrant women in the United States. As they gain social mobility and become actively involved in the labor force, or pursue education or career objectives, some of the immigrant women are increasingly shifting their pronatality and premigration cultural and normative beliefs about large family size to fewer children, even though the decline has yet to affect all the different groups that have migrated to the United States.

Educational attainment, household composition and structure, income, length of stay in America, and immigration status converge to influence the motivation and decision making regarding the desired number of children or optimum family size. Among the respondents who were studied, the premigration and postmigration educational credentials appear to influence the decision to have fewer or more children. For those women who had completed secondary, technical, or vocational education in West Africa prior to their migration, the reduction in family size appears to be have occurred less than a decade following their arrival. A decline in the number of children living in the households formed by those immigrants who have pursued and attained college and university credentials postmigration was evident. Among the immigrant women who have recently migrated from West Africa with less than primary or secondary educational credentials and have yet to pursue postsecondary education following their migration, the data suggests that there is a lag effect on the perceived advantages of small versus large family sizes. In this group, birthrates still remain high relative to other fairly recent immigrant groups from Asia and Latin America who have settled in the United States.

Despite the above findings, the data also suggest that as a group, the West African immigrant women use various strategies to minimize the economic impact of a large family size on the standards of living and economic well-being of their respective families. Sending children home to Africa or to other parts of the world to live with relatives is a strategy sometimes used by the immigrant women to harness the economic and social resources of close relatives to defray the costs of childrearing. This strategy is usually implemented with the objective of minimizing the costs associated with raising a large family in the United States. The willingness of extended relatives living outside of the United States to share in the raising of children tends to promote high birthrates in some of the immigrant families. This finding suggests that microlevel factors (immigrant family's network of extended family relatives) rather than structural factors (economic labor force participation) are critical in delineating the determinants of fertility behavior of the immigrant women. Of particular significance is coresidence or cohabitation, where multiple West African immigrant families share a common household that is basically structured to allow for the collective mobilization of resources to face the social, cultural, and economic challenges associated with their marginalized status as immigrant minorities in the United States. These social networks prove to be particularly effective among the immigrant women who work low-paying, menial, and labor intensive jobs, including migrant farmworkers.

Birthrates continue to be relatively higher in West Africa than in almost every region of the world. Moderate improvements in economic development, cultural literacy, education, health care, and nutritional standards (particularly in urban areas) have produced only marginal effects on fertility rates. Rates of childbearing continue to be high due to the young age structure and the persistency of cultural values favoring pronatality. For the future, the fertility behavior of West African immigrant women is going to be influenced by the human capital characteristics that the women will continue to carve for themselves in the United States. For those who arrive in the United States with secondary and postsecondary credentials, it can be surmised that over time, their fertility behavior will undergo a transition to reflect their social, economic, and cultural capital acquired as a result of education, career aspirations, and economic incorporation into the host society. This means that one will expect relatively lower fertility among those women who enter with strong human capital resources.

Changes in the composition and size of the West African immigrant population coming to the United States will impact any shifts that may occur in the fertility behavior of the immigrant women. Waves of relatively more impoverished West African immigrant women are now entering the country as refugees or stateless persons seeking political asylum. This wave tends to be poorly educated, less endowed in terms of their cultural and literacy skills or human capital, and therefore likely to find the postarrival and adaptation processes more daunting and challenging. This group of women will continue to exhibit fertility behaviors that will not mirror the fertility behavior of prior immigrants from the same region. More importantly, their continued confinement to low-paying jobs and strong pronatal beliefs may lead to high birthrates. Exposure to new norms and values associated with the economic and cultural benefits of reduced fertility have been very slow filtering down among this subgroup. A strong sense of traditionalism, unequal and entrenched male dominance over the lives of these women, coupled with the relegation of women's roles to family household organization, converge to create an environment in which status and prestige become mediated through large family sizes. The involuntary nature of their migration forces some of the women to live in clusters and enclaves defined primarily by kinship relationships that were formed in West Africa and imported directly into the United States. Male members of the family are usually poorly integrated into household activities related to childrearing practices. Fertility decisions are entirely structured within social networks that are gender segregated.

The data suggest that discussions about fertility decisions in such households become nuanced by male superordinate status relative to the subordinate statuses of the women and children comprising the household. These households also tend to have matriarchs who favor large families. Family planning practices are therefore considered a taboo subject and even when such topics are broached, the male partners gain the upper hand. The bulk of household work is still carried out by women and children. Household chores are combined with paid employment outside the home. And poor language skills impede effective interactions with social service agencies. Mistrust for public officials remains strong, and even when there are legitimate economic needs, these needs have often been poorly communicated due to the unwillingness of some of the families to share personal information about fertility decisions with bureaucratic agencies. This factor may also explain the low rates of participation in continued education and schooling in general, which results in the inability to advance and gain social mobility. The economic and cultural incentives promoting high fertility may become more pronounced particularly in the case of those West African immigrant women living in households where the dominant form of religious culture is Islam. Such households also tend to have grandmothers and elderly refugees who emigrated with the family unit. The tendency toward shared residence with elderly in-laws often creates social pressures on mothers to have more children, with a particular preference for boys.

The fertility patterns of second-generation immigrant women (eighteen to thirty years of age) showed that their fertility behavior has yet to converge with the fertility of the American population. Birthrates remain high among the second-generation immigrant women (3.7 children per family). This finding holds for both second-generation immigrant women born in Africa and those who were born in the United States following the migration of their parents. This level of fertility is higher than that of subpopulation groups in the United States such as Latinos, Black Caribbean, and Asian Americans whose fertility rates average two children per household.[7]

Many of the second-generation West African immigrant women are in their childbearing years. Most of them are better educated, earn more than their first-generation parents, and have better access and information about fertility planning relative to their parents. Average total family income is $60,000, compared to $40,000 for their parents.[8] Despite their relatively higher social status compared to their parents, many of the second generation hold on to the fertility beliefs of their first-generation parents. Irrespective of their educational attainment levels, the majority of the second-generation immigrants embrace a large family size. Their fertility behavior is largely determined by sociocultural and psychological factors that are operative in West Africa rather than adherence to the norms defining fertility behavior in the United States. Several of them maintain close ties with extended family members at home in West Africa. These family members promote a culture of pronatality, often minimizing the economic costs of childrearing and deferring to matriarchs and elderly family members on matters of fertility behavior. As indicated, there is a practice of sending children home to be raised by relatives. This is a strategy designed to offset the high cost of childcare in the United States. Their cultural and social networks still reflect a strong African-based traditional system as these women continue to forge ties with extended relatives at home and at the same time limit their integration into the fabric of American society. These women rely on their own resources and social networks to assist them in navigating the complex vicissitudes of powerlessness and alienation. Having children is considered a key aspect of growing family economic fortunes.

For these women, access to contraceptive devices is not the issue. Using birth control still carries with it the same cultural taboos that are associated with contraceptive devices in the subregion of West Africa. The cultural pressures to have more children continue to persist among some of the second-generation immigrants, although economically, these immigrants and citizens of America tend to be relatively well-off than their parents. The age at first marriage for the majority of the second-generation immigrant women is twenty-one years old. The data reveals that most of these women (51 percent) had their first child at the age of twenty-two. At age thirty-five, nearly 65 percent of them have had three or more children. Only 15 percent of these women reported not using birth control and other contraceptive devices.

The number of children born to second-generation immigrant women married to a white American is comparatively lower (1.4 children) compared to those who are married to a West African (4.8 children). For those who are married to a spouse who is white, delayed fertility is typically the norm. Most of these women married when they were in their mid to late twenties. Their average age at first marriage was twenty-six years old. This group of women also indicated increased use of contraceptive devices relative to their peers whose marital partners are also from West Africa.

What emerged from the analyses is that the social contexts of fertility decision making among the immigrant women are varied and fluid. On the one hand, the immigrant women have managed to alter their premigration economic status and by all accounts have achieved social mobility in the United States. Several of the women are earning incomes that their counterparts in West Africa can only dream about. Their earnings have translated into better living standards than what they were accustomed to at home. In this regard, one could surmise that the women are achieving their economic aspirations. This social mobility has not, however, been translated into reduced fertility in the immigrants' households. Most of the women are overcoming the economic constraints that triggered their migration to the United States. What is clear is that the women still hold on to customs and traditions about fertility behavior and decision making imported from West Africa. The women consciously separate and demarcate their newfound economic accomplishments from their fertility decision making in terms of how many children to have. The extensive kin group connections that they foster with relatives at home and in other parts of the world means that even though they have left home, they never see themselves as isolated from home. The social pressures that promote pronatality are still transmitted via a network of kin group alliances and networks to the immigrant women. And most of the women are compelled to conform to some of these pressures even though they may not fully agree with the assumptions and principles. Despite being thousands of miles away from home, the women recognize that eventually they are going to repatriate home. Therefore, their cultural notions about fertility should not deviate remarkably from the norms and customs regulating fertility at home. Rather, fertility behavior conforms to predetermined cultural and normative definitions operative at home. West African immigrant women therefore find themselves playing and responding to a much broader social audience when it comes to fertility behavior. Fertility decisions are being made to reflect what extended families and relatives expect. This expectation is for the immigrant women to have as many children as possible irrespective of the women's economic and social positions in the United States.

The varied forms fertility decisions take are very complex and difficult to unravel or disentangle. Among West African women immigrants, it is important to stress that the social processes and dynamics involved in the making of fertility decisions are mediated and filtered through very powerful primary and secondary group relationships that the women have formed. And certainly, while economic factors have a significant role to play in these decisions, noneconomic considerations are of equal significance. Social psychological variables, attitudinal orientations, and imperatives regarding how children are viewed in West Africa are equally worth considering. Additionally, social exchange relationships within the broader contexts of familial

economic production and exchange of goods and services are important factors to consider in situating fertility decision making among
the immigrant women. While the women acknowledge that they lack
the agencies to be totally in control of their fertility decision making,
they also acknowledge that gender roles and the dominance of the
patriarchal system has yet to cause them to make a drastic reappraisal
of their fertility choices. The assumption they make is that while
some degree of role egalitarianism in their relationships with their
male partners can be discerned following migration, the extent of the
change is not robust enough to redefine their relationships with their
male partners when it comes to fertility decisions. For the bulk of the
women, when it comes to fertility decision making, it will take awhile
for the balance of power between the women and their partners to
reflect the new values and norms they have learned and continue to
learn in the host society.

For most of the women, fertility decision making based on the
Euro-American rational calculus, where couples focus on the economic consequences of a large relative to a small family size, is culturally viewed as inimical to the values that they have been taught
at home in West Africa. Only a minority of the immigrant women
fit their fertility decisions into the Euro-American model or calculus
of fertility control. As stated, among the women who constitute this
group, social ties to extended familial groups tend to be weak. The
family unit is more likely than the family of the other immigrants to
be nuclear. And attitudes and norms regarding antinatalist fertility and
their decision to have fewer children were formed prior to migration
to the United States. The women in this group are fully incorporated
and assimilated into American society and less likely to orient their
fertility decisions along traditional West African societal norms and
values. Having weak social ties with extended family members and
relatives at home, coupled with their high educational credentials,
may shed some light on the fertility decisions made by these women.
These women also view their fertility choices as a function of gender
role egalitarianism and the bilateral negotiations that they have been
successful in negotiating with their male partners.

The interplay of socioeconomic and cultural factors operating in
the United States and in West Africa converges to explain the fertility decisions the immigrant women are making. The nature and
form of the exchange relationship between husbands and wives are
of immense significance in explaining low or high fertility behavior.
Different households and family organization may respond differently
to the forces and constraining variables that shape fertility decision

making. The transnational and social networks that these immigrant women establish, particularly economic exchanges, are an important consideration in disentangling the complex and often evasive relationship between fertility behavior and migration. These networks may provide incentives or disincentives that family members incorporate into their rationalizations of low or high birthrates.

In the end, an approach that incorporates the importance of familial orientation and social psychological variables operating at the individual household unit may yield significant insights and understanding into how migration shapes the fertility decisions of the West African immigrant women. Understanding of the intraspousal relationships and changes in gender role relationships that occur as a result of international migration are needed to situate the proximate determinants of fertility among the new immigrant women. The experiences that the West African immigrant women garner while living in the United States are significant aspects of their migratory journeys. New lifestyles and life chance options are created in consonance with the fresh opportunities presented by migration. The total experiences emanating from international migration, coupled with the normative changes that this may bring, while significant, are not sufficient to completely alter the fertility behavior of the immigrant women.

Strong attachment to normative values and beliefs experienced and lived at home in West Africa prior to migration, and the continuity and maintenance of these values postmigration, are important considerations to take into account in mapping out changes in immigrant fertility behavior. Attitudinal changes, ties with the home country, gender role norms, the contexts of familial exchanges, and the cultures that underpin or define the benefits of large family sizes, particularly to social audiences at home in West Africa, are major factors to consider in understanding the fertility behavior of West Africans in the United States. For a majority of the West African women immigrant (62 percent), the boundaries of what constitutes family and household are rather fluid and varied. The tendency to share a common residence with other family members and at the same time live with and raise children who are not their own renders any systematic analysis of the structure and composition of the immigrants' households difficult to conceptualize. Cultural norms and customary practices dictate that they raise their siblings' offspring. Children born to both close and distant relatives are also configured and incorporated in the composition of family and household structure and organization. The sociopsychological satisfaction that some of these women derive from living with their own children alongside other relatives' children is immense.

This form of living arrangement does not fit into the standard model of household structure and organization in the West. But again, the women do not see raising children solely in terms of the economic cost and what they have to forgo to be able to afford these children. For these women, being a mother is broadly defined to include having to take care of other people's children as well.

CHAPTER 8

CONCLUDING REMARKS
AND LOOKING AHEAD

African women have become active participants in the new global and transnational migration to the major economic and cultural centers of the world. Explaining their own unique creations and re-creations of their migratory experiences via their own lenses and prisms is significant in migration studies. Sometimes overlooked in migration studies due to their powerlessness and economic vulnerabilities, African women are blazing the trail in cross-border population mobility. In the African context, the sea of change that this migratory behavior has unraveled is not only sociologically poignant and interesting but also transformative.

The forces underlying the migration of African women may parallel those of their male counterparts, but in several respects there are significant differences and variations in how African women's lives are altered following migration. As a group, West African immigrant women view the family and the networks of friendships and relationships that they form as a site for the cultural production of new roles designed to augment those they have imported from Africa. Their desire is to expand the global frontiers of Black African cultures by forging gender, racial, and ethnic alliances with other minority women. In so doing, these women expect to find common solutions to achieve economic empowerment and at the same time strengthen their cultural communities. This marks a significant racial and ethnic boundary crossing and shift for the West African women immigrants.

The shared essence, cultural closeness, and identification with other immigrant women are all geared toward the deconstruction of the notion of a monolithic and invisible Black culture. For these energetic women, migration facilitates and offers opportunities to affirm and

celebrate the varieties of gendered cultural kaleidoscopes representing the multiple cultures shared by these women. By their presence in
the new global migration, these women are weaving new tapestries of
identities that are challenging notions about Black African immigrant
women as passive actors whose lives are shaped and molded by their
male migrant partners. The migratory experiences that these women
garner enable them to renegotiate new egalitarian roles for themselves
and at the same time challenge the existing rigid boundaries of gendered relationships in African societies. The economic and cultural
benefits accruing from their migration are shared with extended relatives, particularly female relatives. Assisting other female relatives at
home is aimed at empowering young and adult women to better their
lives as they wrestle to find their niches in male-dominated systems of
cultural and economic production.

This book has presented a broad analysis of the migration of
women from the West African region to the United States. Certainly,
structural changes in public education and globalization have been
pivotal in defining the migratory streams of West African women to
the United States. The gradual weakening of rigid gender norms that
have confined African women to subservient roles in the past are being
replaced by a new cultural ethos that emphasizes the incorporation of
women into all facets of West African society. The economic, political,
and cultural conditions at the points of immigrant origination appear
more favorable to women today than they did just a few decades ago.
Improvements in technology, faster and efficient modes of transportation, and the flow of information between immigrant sending nodes
and the immigrant receiving points have facilitated women's access to
the resources they need to carve niches for themselves in the global
workplace. The expansion of low-wage industrial and nonindustrial
employment has aided the postarrival adjustments for many immigrant women coming from peripheral regions in Africa, the Caribbean,
Asia, and Latin America. The demand for service-related, low-skilled
workers in manufacturing, agriculture, hospitality service, and social
services all add to the myriad of conditions in the immigrant receiving countries motivating the women to come to the shores of the
United States in particular in search of better economic opportunities
for themselves and their families.[1]

The migration of African women is not just confined to the United
States. Scores of African women are entering the European Union and
Canada as economic migrants in search of work and better standards
of living. Others are entering to pursue cultural goals, mainly to continue their education, after which many, if not all, of them will end

up staying permanently. Included in the waves of African migration to the United States are those who are sponsored by relatives and those who are forced to flee as a result of being displaced or uprooted by the ravages of wars and political conflicts.

The migration of African women to the United States and other global centers of commerce, trade, and cultural opportunities have reached full maturity. Migration from West Africa is strongly influenced by persistent and grinding poverty. West Africans are coming to the United States looking for work in order to ensure their economic survival. Many of the West African immigrant women are coming to the United States on their own initiatives. Increasingly, as was demonstrated, a growing number of them are also relying on kin groups and extended family networks to come to America. They are forging a visible presence in the continued feminization of African migration to the United States. These women have made the choices to migrate with one principal objective in mind: to maximize their economic and cultural satisfaction in response to the pressing problems confronting many of them at home in Africa.

Based on the evidence provided, a portrait of Black West African immigrant women can be ascertained. This portrait is one that is based on the increasing role and visibility of West African women in the new global workplace. The portrait of West African immigrant woman is one that involves the multifaceted and unique Black cultural identities that the West African women continue to forge in the United States. These women symbolize the strong presence of West African women in decision making involving their extended relatives and familial organizations at home in Africa. Their multiple depictions converge to portray the migratory realities of a cadre of West African immigrant women who are poised for inclusiveness in the global labor scene, resilient and highly independent in their search for opportunities, and also knowledgeable about world and cultural affairs. Guarded, but at the same time flexible, to learn new ideas and embrace change, these women demonstrate the ethos of self-determination through individual and collective empowerments.

Despite recent crackdowns on illegal immigration in the country, the migratory experiences of these women confirms the prevailing attitude in West Africa that it is still possible to come to the United States and find gainful employment. The events of 9/11 have affected the selection of prospective immigrants who will be allowed to come to the United States to join friends and family members. On the streets of urban West Africa, mainly Dakar, Accra, Lomé, Abidjan, Freetown, Monrovia, and Lagos, young men and women still clamor and hope for the opportunity to come to the United States. Better means of facilitating the flow of information about their intended host society and the chances of finding employment trump any concerns the prospective immigrants have about how difficult it is to get to the United States. The opportunity to earn more money than what prevails in West Africa is behind the motivation to risk and come. Once they settle in the United States, the immigrants can send money home to assist relatives, build a home, or start a business.

West African immigrant women are recent additions to the remaking of the immigrant racial and ethnic quilt in the United States. A critical examination of their immigrant journeys show that despite having not been arriving in the United States for very long, the immigrant women have managed to achieve a respectable, if not enviable, social advancement and mobility that they could not have obtained in West Africa. Self-reliance, shared cultural and traditional experiences, and a strong emphasis on self-improvement through continuing education and an altruistic fervor to offer economic assistance to kinfolk have been pivotal in the advancement of the immigrant women in the United States. And while some of the immigrant women may initially find themselves struggling economically to make ends meet after their arrival in the country, for most of them, these struggles are ephemeral. Decisions about where and how to look for employment, where to live, whether to move to another city, and where to send children to school are all made within strong kinship and extended familial networks that the women have brought with them from West Africa.

The nerve center for the immigrant women is their kin group family lineage and the network of kin who come together to offer economic and noneconomic assistance to each other in times of need. The bonds and links that are forged among the kin groups are pivotal in the formation of Black African immigrant identities in the United States and elsewhere. These kinship networks have been successful in anchoring the immigrants to the social values needed to become successful in the host society. At the same time, they link the immigrants with affairs at home in West Africa. Kinship networks are replicated transnationally and are vehicles used by the immigrants to facilitate the formation of an immigrant cultural community to contest everyday challenges and issues unique to the immigrant experience. They also assist the immigrants in finding information about employment sources and serve to connect the immigrants with their respective homes in Africa. In this way, the immigrants are able to continue being active participants in the affairs of the home societies where the bulk of the immigrants will eventually repatriate.

The migration of West African women to the United States is a dynamic and evolving process. This process is just one aspect of the multifaceted transglobal migration of skilled and unskilled labor from the developing to developed regions of the West. The region of West Africa is a subordinate part of the larger system of advanced superordinate economic entities dominated by the capitalist, G-8 core countries. Principally spurred by internal forces—mainly economic and political problems—migration out of West Africa is expected to persist as economic conditions worsen, political institutions erode, and civic societies are stymied. Additionally, rising fertility rates, overurbanization, pressure on land, and environmental destruction will continue to push out West Africans who are desirous of a better life. The inability of the public and private sectors of West African society to create enough jobs to absorb the growing number of secondary and postsecondary school graduates means that scores of West African youths and adults will continue to look to the West, in particular the United States, to fulfill their economic goals.

As prospective migrants explore the multitude of ways they can enter the United States, family reunification will continue to be the principal form of legal admission into the United States, but with time, emphasis will be placed on admitting prospective immigrants with identifiable skills that employers need in the United States. This merit-based preference will continue to serve West African immigrants very well because of the selective nature of West African migration to the West. The majority of those who leave for the West have already completed secondary or postsecondary education. A growing number have credentials in technical- and science-related disciplines for which there is a high demand for workers in the United States. Also, the continued expansion of agribusiness establishments and the continuing reliance on foreign or guest workers in sectors such as food processing, landscape, construction, hospitality, and leisure will continue to attract urban West African youths to the United States and other Western destinations. For those who cannot enter the country using legal avenues, unconventional methods—particularly travel by foot across the Sahara with the goal of reaching the Mediterranean and subsequently crossing into the European Union—will become very common as more and more West Africans are pushed to economic despair.

Chain or stepwise migration will continue to increase as well, particularly for those who cannot obtain direct visas to the United States and to other destination points in the West in general. This type of interim and circular migration will ultimately challenge policy makers in the West African subregion to design and implement strategies to

discourage the youth in particular from crossing international boundaries without legal documents of entry. The governments in the region
must design and implement safe protocols of traveling for their citizens. This will ensure that prospective migrants are not subjected to
the nefarious practices of migrant smugglers and traffickers. This will
also ensure that migrants will follow proper procedures as they plan
for their migration. In West Africa, border posts, checkpoints, and the
screening of travel documents must be modernized with the installa-
tion of scanning machines that check the authenticity of travel documents.[2] Border security officials who provide aid and material comfort
to child sexual traffickers must be booked and prosecuted. This will
also entail the modernization of customs and excise checkpoints all
over West Africa. This is a gigantic undertaking for governments that
are reeling under the burden of fiscal shortfalls and more pressing
economic needs.

For those immigrant women with less than secondary school credentials, life in America can be tough. This group of immigrants usually
finds themselves working menial jobs, including farm labor. Though
they may make enough money to sustain themselves and their families, there is often not enough money left to remit home or to sponsor other relatives to join them in the United States. When they send
remittances, these remittances have averaged about $200 a month.
Part of the urban, Black, underclass poor, this class of West African
immigrant women tends to be young, live in substandard housing
in high crime areas, and embroiled in a cycle of poverty. For most,
the economic situation is dire. They often migrate to agricultural
and food-processing centers across the country in search of better
employment opportunities. Some are accompanied by their children.
Whatever economic gains they are able to attain via employment, the
benefits are fleeting as they have to find temporary places to stay, find
schools for their children, and for those not working with valid work
documents, there is further consternation about being found out by
immigration authorities and being deported.

Persistent problems facing this group of immigrant women include
discrimination, prejudice, and sometimes violence from both white
and Black Americans. These problems are exacerbated by the fact
that many of them are not documented and do not have legal status.
In working underground with false papers, many of them are at the
mercy of their contractors or employers who often threaten to report
them to immigration authorities if they fail to meet the expectations
of supervisors or foremen. Their inability to pursue postsecondary
education during the period that they are domiciled in the United

States is perhaps the most single factor that has thwarted their upward social mobility. Dependency on social welfare and public assistance is not widespread among this group of West African immigrant women. There is always fear about coming forward and applying for social services benefits. These women often rely on their own organizations to deal with economic necessities. Long term, while many of the immigrant women will consider repatriation, only few are able to implement strategies to achieve this goal. These strategies may include saving enough money to enable them have the capital to set up a business, build a house, or move an entire family.

As was expected, the majority of the women cited economic reasons (the need for self-improvement, to raise standard of living for themselves and their children, to earn higher wages, and to pursue education with the goal of finding better employment) as the main cause of their migration. Decades after achieving political self-determination from European colonial powers, several of the countries forming the West Africa region are still mired in economic morass, unable to provide for the basic needs of people, such as water, electricity, and food. Rising population pressures, human-induced ecological disasters, massive and unchecked urbanization, poor health care, and rising criminality combine to create hellish conditions for the bulk of the population. A small group of middle-class elites has emerged in West Africa, particularly among the ranks of senior civil servants, the business class, career military officers, doctors, engineers, and university professors. But they are overshadowed by the teeming masses of underprivileged urban and poor people who depend on less than a dollar a day to meet their economic needs. With worsening economic problems, most people leave and go abroad. The economic reasons for leaving are buttressed by the fact that the majority of the women, including immigrants as a whole, consider the United States as a land of opportunity.

In forming the rationalizations to come to the United States, the women, like other immigrants, are not dissuaded by the growing public antipathy toward immigrants and the difficulties that come with not having legal or documented status. The expectation on the part of the immigrants is that no matter how high unemployment rates are, and irrespective of efforts on the part of immigration officials to conduct raids and clamp down on illegal immigration, the question is not whether they will find gainful employment. Sooner rather than later, many of the undocumented immigrants are able to find jobs. Prospective immigrants remain cognizant of the thriving underground world of the undocumented and illegal immigrants in the country who are able to find jobs and who regularly remit to their relatives at home. Information and knowledge about employers willing to hire undocumented immigrant workers and fringe employment groups that are willing to match illegal immigrants with prospective employers are well known in immigrant communities across the country. The channels of employment information outlets for illegal migrants are also known by West Africans who visit bars, restaurants, and cafes throughout urban West Africa. The perception among most people is that jobs are plentiful in the United States and the West in general. One only has to have the will to work. Any other problems thereafter can be solved. The use of the term "economic migrants" to describe many of the West African immigrants is therefore appropriate and apt.

Although economic motivations dominate the reasons for migrating to the United States, political exigencies and instabilities (particularly the imperative to flee from the ravages of war and civil conflicts) are major factors in the migration of West African women to the United States. The persistence of ethnic conflicts and wars in the region has stalled development projects for countries that are already among some of the poorest in the world. Political and economic insecurities converge to drive out the well educated, resulting in the brain drain. When wars and conflicts have been waged endlessly, the victims have largely been women and their children. The result is disrupted lives and the foregoing of dreams and aspirations. Sometimes forced to flee only with the clothes on their back, these women and children have to depend on the international community for their personal safety and protection. This means that they have to travel on foot to safer havens where they are sheltered in makeshift tents. In many cases, such as the Liberians who fled to Ghana during the political crisis in that country, many of the displaced end up staying in the refugee-receiving countries for years, waiting for intervention by the international community to either find them new countries of abode or work to resolve the crisis so that they can return home. For most of the refugees, this becomes an endless wait for assistance, thereby further heightening their vulnerabilities and continued invisibilities in the host society. Oftentimes, cultural and economic barriers (language difficulties, lack of education, poor job skills) may thwart or inhibit their full integration into the host society, further causing their isolation or pushing them to the fringes of the host society.

The continuous political and economic malaise plaguing the West African region has fueled concerns as to whether it is possible to achieve stable regimes and a democratic civil culture. Failure of the postcolonial governments to incorporate ethnic and tribal minority groups into existing governance structures has worsened the outlook of future political and cultural reconciliation, appeasement, and pacification. In addition, political cronyism and the lack of rule of law have heightened the possibility that violence will become a permanent feature of the landscape of some of these countries in the future. Lack of trust in government and a pervasive culture of lack of accountability have added fuel to an already precarious situation. Holding on to power and denying the legitimate rights of the electorate to effect social change is adding to the woes of the people in the region. Under these trying circumstances, people look outside their home countries for social, cultural, and economic alternatives. Unless these issues are tackled, generations of West African youths are going to stream to the West, by whatever means necessary, to seek a better lifestyle.

Efforts to foster a climate of national, interregional, and international harmony and cooperation at every level of economic and political governance must be implemented to promote a viable and sustained sense of nationhood and citizenship in the West African region. The promotion of civic culture through public education will enhance the image of the region in the international community and help in promoting private entrepreneurial investments in core sectors of the economies of these countries. West Africans themselves are going to have to assume the mantle of leadership to ameliorate the mounting social, cultural, political, and economic problems facing the region. As Khapoya (1994, 216) noted almost a decade and half ago, "Africans have to take the lead in changing their social systems and improving their lives. They cannot sit on the sidelines and be spectators. Years of sympathetic words from the West, years of foreign aid of all kinds, and decades of expert advice from expatriates have not lifted many West Africans out of abject poverty." This means economic and political accountability must become part of the institutional life and culture of these countries if further deterioration of living standards is to be averted.

Immediately following the postcolonial period, several countries in the region were poised for political and economic self-determination. Several boasted of infrastructures and systems of education that were the envy of other developing nations in Asia and Latin America. Today, mainly due to mismanagement and lack of planning, the hopes and aspirations of millions in the region have been dashed. The dominance of the state in the planning and implementation of economic development projects will have to be supplemented with private sector initiatives and investments. The principal role of the nation-state is to create the necessary conditions that are conducive for both public and private economic initiatives to launch business and economic activities. It is pertinent for the West African nations to incorporate and integrate their diverse ethnic and cultural groups into the process of nationhood to ensure the establishment of civil order. Failing to do so will mean, once again, that thousands of West Africans will continue to look outside and away from the region for the fulfillment of their economic, cultural, and social dreams.

For many of the West African women who have successfully migrated to the United States independently, migration has provided them with a sense of economic independence and the freedom as well as the flexibility to foster more egalitarian relationships with their male partners. Opportunities to pursue continuing education, coupled with the ability to move to locations where they can maximize their earning possibilities, have been empowering for the immigrant women. Being prepared and willing to start at the bottom of the labor hierarchy at times has meant that most of these women are willing to adopt a long-term perspective while they seek new opportunities and explore creative ways of self-improvement and empowerment instead of reliance on the magnanimity of patriarchal relationships. The economic and cultural capital they have derived by educating themselves and managing their households with or without the support of male partners has strengthened their hands in the rearing of their children and in household decision making. It can be argued that the migratory process has created new possibilities and options for African immigrant women in terms of their familial structures and organizations. International migration has given agency and empowerment to the woman immigrant. It has also assisted immigrant women in defining new local and transnational spaces as well as places to contest traditional norms and patriarchal systems. Certainly, the narratives of immigrant women lend support to the notion that African women are yearning for new directions, new opportunities, and new connections to re-create better economic opportunities not only for themselves but also for their children. For most of the women, migration has become the facilitator, the medium for accomplishing and achieving autonomy and independence while challenging old and entrenched norms about the role of women in African society.

From the perspective of the women, international migration to the West is seen as very liberating and a way to assert autonomy, strengthen familial kinship networks, improve gender relationships, and at the same time confront the male-dominated constructions of economic, social, and political power that the women leave behind in West Africa. Their migration brings with it a sense of global awareness and the nurturing and promotion of gender and cultural identities that are cosmopolitan yet traditional in their commitment to, and affirmation of, African values. The vehicle of international migration is not perceived to be a destructive force that drastically alters their lives and the respective communities that they come from in Africa. The movement from the global economic and cultural fringes of Africa to the core economic centers of the West is not symptomatic of a clear break with the sometimes-overwhelming nature of African rural and traditional-based social systems. If anything, the women perceive that the experiences garnered as a result of international migration strengthen the traditional lore and norms underpinning the institutional framework of their respective societies. In this regard, migration is viewed as a vehicle for implementing social and cultural changes.

In replicating their cultural institutions and normative systems in the United States, the immigrant women often come to rely on the need to maintain the continuity of African traditions and cultures. The women's definitions of race and ethnic identity formation present an array of multiple and blended identities that are designed to reconfigure newer meanings of blackness. For the most part, these women are somewhat reluctant to embrace the negative connotations frequently associated with being Black in America. Black identity is reconstituted and reclassified by these women to represent and symbolize positive notions about Black roles in national and international affairs. In essence, these women refuse to be typecast in pejorative terms. Many of them affirm the rich traditional and cultural foundations of Black society and strive to find ways to empower themselves and to transform their local and transnational spaces. Some of them straddle between American cultural ethos, on the one hand, and a blending of African, transnational, and panglobal identities, on the other. They have latched on to the values of hard work and enterprise that they have imbibed from Africa. At the same time, they manifest racial and ethnic identities whose boundaries are not rigidly defined. Not being bound by one specific identity expression has enabled the immigrants to form panoplies of identities and at the same time embrace multiple cultures to anchor their lifestyles and global worldview. The ability of the immigrant women to forge panglobal identities will also be affected by American public attitudes regarding immigration and the policies and politics associated with who should be allowed to enter the country. On this issue, the ability of the immigrants to build coalitions with native-born Blacks, including other minority groups such as Hispanics and Asian Americans, will become critical in defining the future identities of the immigrants. The attitudes of Black Americans

toward U.S. immigration in particular, will play a major role in defining the outcomes of racial and ethnic incorporation of the new African
Americans.[3]

African-centered values continue to serve as the reference point
for evaluating immigrant behavior and expectation. Beyond this, the
immigrant women maintain a posture that is fiercely pro-Black while
rejecting racialized categorizations and formulations based solely on
skin color and place of origination. This is not to completely deny
the centrality of how skin color affects social mobility in a race- and
class-conscious society like the United States. These women manifest a range of Black hues, each one possessing a set of identities and
social expectations.[4] What these women often decry is the outright
subjection of people of darker complexions to an inferior status, which
may translate into the denial of equal access to opportunities. Having a foreign-born Black status does not insulate them from racism,
discrimination, and marginalization. Problems posed by these factors
are recognized but are never allowed to influence the choices and
decisions that they have to deal with. Ultimately, it is not clear how
the identities manifested among these women might change or be
changed by outside forces such as media and secondary-group cultural
influences. What is clear is that there seems to be recognition of being
different from Black America in terms of cultural values. Differences,
no matter how subtle, are not contentious to trigger or cause a rift
between these women and the rest of Black America. These women
consider themselves part of the growing population of foreign-born
Blacks who have joined to form part of the growing Black diaspora in
the United States.

Studies focusing on African migration to the West must reconceptualize and reinvigorate the field by coming up with fresh theoretical
approaches to position and extend the scope of coverage of diasporic
racial and ethnic identity formation among the immigrants. To date,
studies have focused on the racial and ethnic dimensions of Black
African immigrant identities. Examining identity formation is important and has added to our understanding of how these immigrants
compose transnational identities. The results from these studies have
also shed light on how Black immigrants from Africa construct and
conceptualize issues of race and ethnicity. It is pertinent for migration
studies to move beyond racial and ethnic identities by concentrating on aspects of identity formations such as class, gender, political,
and economic identities. Taking an insular and limiting approach to
identity studies (while fruitful and scientifically challenging) may also
cause the unintended devaluation and lack of acknowledgement of

the contributions that Black African immigrants and people of Black African descent make to American society and the collective human culture in general. For example, future studies can investigate how Black African immigrants engage in political activities and how they construct and articulate political consciousness. Such an approach is needed to gauge the perspectives of the immigrants in the political developments of their respective countries. Research could focus on how the immigrants create political cultures and organizations to contest political issues not only in the host society but also in their home countries. Equally important is how these immigrants form and express political alignments and rationalize various forms of political ideologies and philosophies. Adopting some of these approaches will not only expand the scope of immigrant identity studies but, more importantly, it will show that immigrants have a wide range of experiences, beliefs, interests, and motivations beyond their racial and ethnic identities. Studies are warranted to investigate the totality of the lived realities of Black immigrants as a whole.

The initial focus of migratory studies on the racial and ethnic identity fits in well with America's preoccupation with issues of race, skin color, and ethnic membership. It also fits in well with the dominant culture's racialized ideologies, norms, values and how notions of superordinate and subordinate relationships are formed and contested. But identities cannot be construed only from the perspective of a Black-white binary categorization or simply as a minority-majority construction. It is imperative for the debate on these issues to move to other spheres of immigrant activities and concerns. For example, a focus on political and economic identities may shed more light on how these immigrants form and implement various economic strategies to assist in the development of their respective nations. In essence, adopting a holistic approach to identity will diversify the field of migration studies and add to the existing theoretical lens through which to view international migration.

The decentering and shifting of migrant racial and ethnic identities to include broader areas of human activities is not intended to delimit and devalue migrant identity formation approaches along the continuum of blackness and whiteness. Rather, it is intended to show that there are other paradigmatic and theoretically salient aspects of identity studies needing the attention of migration scholars. Such an approach, if adopted, will recognize that immigrants are active participants in the affairs of their respective home countries, and the identities that they create to situate and express their experiences are indeed multifaceted and constantly shifting. For example, during focus-group sessions with the West African immigrant and refugee women, it emerged that the participants were not only interested in responding and reacting to questions about their racial and ethnic expressions, but also equally interested in discussing issues about the social, cultural, and political developments at home and the role and place of Black Africa in the world's geopolitical and economic scenes. The women indeed presented and portrayed a worldview identity that incorporated their notions about global poverty, the oppression of women and children, sexual enslavement, and how to increase the role of Black Africa in world affairs and raise the standards of living of its people.

Certainly, the way(s) that identities are construed and given relevance can influence how these other spheres of human organizations and activities are approached by the immigrants and given resonance. This reiterates the earlier assertion that identity expressions and formations among the immigrants are just cogs in the larger repertoire and perspectives that these immigrants define and articulate as they construct diasporic identities in the United States. Beyond their racial and ethnic identities, the ranks of the African immigrants consist of poets, engineers, teachers, farmers, doctors, nurses, homemakers, and social workers (to mention a few). Their formulation of racial or ethnic identities represents a small part of their lived experiences in America.

The process involved in international migration affects both sending and receiving societies. To date, several studies have focused on the impact of migration on host or migrant-receiving societies. For the immigrant-sending nations of West Africa, migration causes brain drain and stifles development. As these migrant-sending countries deal with economic and social development problems, studies are needed to examine the net impact of outmigration on national development and nation-building. Certainly, the migration of Africa's young and the well educated is bound to have a deleterious impact on the manpower and human resources of the migrant-sending nations. Policies are needed to assess the shortfall of the brain drain in key sectors of the continent's social structure, such as health care, education, science, culture, and engineering. The vast majority of those who are going to the United States and other Western nations have been educated by African taxpayers. Despite the fact that they contribute immeasurably to the social and economic development of their respective countries through remittances and investments, it is pertinent for their home governments to implement strategies to assess the overall costs of the brain drain. This will require a database or census of who has left and who might be leaving in the future. The absence of a database to provide information about those who are leaving or returning for resettlement means that the central governments of West Africa cannot tap and utilize the skills of its citizens to implement the task of national reconstruction or nation-building. It is equally significant for the governments of West Africa to launch an aggressive policy aimed at registering their citizens abroad. This can be accomplished under the auspices of the various diplomatic missions and high commissions or embassies located all over the world. Bilateral and multilateral arrangements can be undertaken with the immigrant-receiving countries to assist in the registration of nationals living abroad. Measures to incorporate the skills and resources of returning migrants will have to be incorporated into national planning and development schemes to facilitate the full involvement of immigrants living abroad.

Steps to ensure that returnees are assisted by their national governments in transferring their assets home are also warranted. Government planning directives to provide feasibility assistance to aid those returnees desirous of setting up small capitalization businesses at home must be promoted with vigor. These feasibility studies may include information about marketing, distribution, and the capital outlays needed for start-up businesses. If successfully implemented, these small businesses will provide private-sector employment rather than relying on current policies whereby governments are the major employers in West Africa. Private-sector investment and capital ventures may hold the key to opening up the economic potential of these countries rather than the overreliance on the public and state sectors that are currently mired in inefficiencies and prone to economic and political corruption. Government assistance must include the mobilization of local and international resources to create the infrastructural networks needed to provide economies of scale and comparative advantages for small businesses to produce and market goods and services for export and home consumption. This will have to include the construction of roads, bridges, schools, and the provision of water and electricity for rural and urban centers. Liberalization of tax laws and incentives are equally warranted to assist small-scale companies to get off the ground. This approach will have to include the creation of tax-free industrial zones to maximize the economic advantages of the small businesses and promote greater efficiencies.

Holistic and sustained measures are needed by the central governments of these countries to reform financial laws to make it possible for returnees to transfer their assets home without having to encounter bureaucratic hassles and administrative bottlenecks. Related to this is the critical need for the central governments to understand the push factors causing the exodus of both skilled and unskilled West Africans to go abroad in search of better economic opportunities. This must be backed by proactive policies to arrest and ameliorate problems of poverty and massive unemployment. The ultimate goal has to be geared toward population retention and significant improvements in the living standards of the people. This will take time and will also require drastic rebalancing and restructuring of national economic development priorities. By all accounts, a majority of the countries in the region have become migrant-sending or labor-exporting countries. Despite this trend, these countries have yet to derive significant economic outcomes from their citizens who have relocated abroad. The bulk of the remittances these migrants forward home are for consumption purposes. The efficacies of policies designed to channel remittances into nonconsumption or business creation activities must be discussed and the findings incorporated into national planning and development objectives.

To stem the tide of massive rural to urban migration of the youth and school graduates, the central governments must strive to make living conditions in the rural areas and small towns livable and self-sufficient. The creation of rural-based jobs will go a long way toward providing employment for middle- and secondary-school graduates. This will further assist in rural population retention and ease the current population mobility from rural to urban centers where housing conditions are worsening and employment prospects are dim for migrants. Easing the population pressure on the urban centers will go a long way in curbing urban sprawl, ecological and environmental degradation, the misuse of land, and other problems associated with the spread of slums and shantytowns. These slums have become an eyesore and a major urban and ecological disaster for many of the administrative capital districts of West Africa. Services such as trash and refuse disposal, lack of pipe-borne water, shortage of housing, and electricity are just a few of the problems facing the shanty towns that have developed around the urban fringes of West Africa's urban cities.

A sustained and measured approach will have to be undertaken to revitalize the informal sector of the economies of the countries as well. The goal is to create jobs for the poor and neglected urban masses that are eking out an existence on a little over one dollar per day. This approach will also have to be backed by a comprehensive policy toward providing job training for the youth and adult males who have thronged to the capital cities in search of nonexistent jobs. If carefully implemented, this strategy can stem the tide of young men and women who risk their lives trying to cross the Sahara Desert from West Africa in the hopes of making it to North Africa, the Mediterranean, the European Union, and possibly the United States. Campaigns to educate the youths and adults alike about the treacherous nature of crossing the Sahara on foot are sorely needed. This public education must be accompanied by an honest public discourse about the possibilities of making it in the European Union or the United States.

Etched in the minds of many in urban West Africa is the notion that jobs are plentiful in the West and that wages are relatively higher than in West Africa. While this is the case, what most prospective immigrants fail to recognize is that the cost of living is equally high in the West. For those who do not possess any marketable skill, the road ahead once they are able to arrive in Europe or the United States is going to be filled with untold difficulties and hardships. Some may be able to find employment as laborers working in food processing plants, agriculture, and in the hospitality services sector. For those African immigrants who possess skills in the sciences, particularly medicine and health care, engineering, technology, and business, the prospects of finding employment with fringe benefits are very good. Immigration laws across the West, including the United States, currently favor immigrants from Africa with skills who possess postsecondary credentials, preferably university degrees.[5] The fact remains, then, that international migration will continue to be an important aspect of Africa's present and future status. If they do not travel to the United States or other Western nations, Africans may choose to go elsewhere, possibly Asia. This process has already started with small streams of Africans migrating to China and other countries in Asia, particularly Japan, Malaysia, Singapore, South Korea, Taiwan, Hong Kong, and India. In anticipation of this possible shift in migration from Africa to the United States, some schools in Africa have started forging cultural exchanges with Asian institutions.

For the West Africans who have been fortunate to make it to the United States, adaptation and incorporation into American society have been facilitated, by and large, by the desire to pursue autonomy and independence, first for themselves and secondarily for their children. The primary source of their autonomy has come from their cooperative and communal spirit, coupled with the strong kinship and bonds of networks that they form among themselves in the United States in order to tame the economic and social vicissitudes that define the gendered contexts and meanings of their migratory experiences. In the process of affirming the gendered realities of their experiences, West African immigrant women have been able to demonstrate that while kinship relationships are critical in pursuing economic goals, community networks and cooperative spirit are equally crucial factors in helping immigrants and ethnic minorities achieve improvements in their standards of living. The strong desire to create and nurture self sufficient immigrant communities continues to dominate the lives of the West African immigrant women even after living in the United States for a long time. In general, the immigrant women perceive that they do not have the political and economic resources to ensure their full integration into American society. Nonetheless, they believe that the economic and psychological security that they derive from their immigrant social networks, clans, and subclans are not only self-sustaining but also intrinsically viable to ensure that their needs are met.

West African immigrant women have now joined and become part of the global demand for women's labor. This growth is due in part to the expansion of international capital and entrepreneurial activities throughout the world. As a group, these women are active persons who are searching for better economic opportunities to raise their standards of living. More research is needed to explore the increasing role of women in international economic production. Attention must be focused on the complex intrafamily networks that West African women utilize to implement international migration. Concerted efforts must be undertaken to explain in detail why these women are leaving their respective countries to join the international labor pool. There is the need to develop and formulate international protocols to safeguard the working conditions of these women to ensure that they do not continue to become victims of unfair labor practices and exploitation. Livable wages with benefits, parity with male workers, worker rights to unionize, medical leave, and occupational safety must be implemented to protect migrant workers from labor abuses. The organized forms of patriarchal structures that had thwarted the full incorporation of women in the global economic production process must be dismantled in favor of a more balanced and equitable economic system in which people (irrespective of class, race, ethnicity, or gender) can move freely and become active agents in their economic empowerment. It is pertinent to incorporate women's perspectives and issues into the structuring of work norms and regulations.

The unraveling of Black African immigrant women's identities is occurring at various sites of academic scholarship. Despite the fact that the majority of studies on the reconstitution and continuities of the neo-Black African diaspora have been investigated by demographers, sociologists, geographers, and ethnic studies scholars, there is a growing body of scholarship describing the contents of the Black diaspora coming from playwrights, poets, historians, musicians, and literature studies. It is vital to incorporate information about African migration and identity formations from these diverse sources to provide broad-based conceptualizations and insights about the transformative dimensions of international migration in shaping Black African identities in the West. This multidisciplinary approach can enrich and provide new theoretical paradigms for investigating Black African diaspora studies while at the same time bringing a meta-analytical theoretical and methodological framework to the many genres represented by Black cultures. This approach must also encapsulate the multiple dimensions of Black African exiles and their identities abroad.[6]

The composition of the Black diaspora in the Americas, Europe, and Asia have been submerged and peripheralized by the daunting economic and political challenges facing the African world today. Migration or going into exile is a product of these challenges. Understanding the subterranean visibilities and invisibilities of how Blacks reconstitute their identities in new settings can offer scholastic insights into how Blacks transpose or create African-based community organizations outside of the region. At the same time, knowledge gleaned from this approach may yield information about how Black-African-based community organizations and structures are contested by the host societies. In sum, the frontiers of Black African diaspora studies and its core components and underpinnings can be delineated using a cross-disciplinary perspective. The recent stream of African and Caribbean immigrants to North America provides an opportunity to study changing notions of blackness and its inherent differing and complex forms. The reconceptualization of what it means to be Black has to proceed with information culled from every facet and aspect of the Black experience globally. This will require a reflective understanding of global Black cultures and institutions and the historical, political, and economic forces that have shaped, and continue to shape, the internal dynamics of the Black world.

Notes

Chapter 2

1. See, also, Ould-Mey (1996), Takougang (1995), Oxfam (1999), and Batterbury (1998), and World Bank (1990–2000) for comprehensive summaries of socioeconomic, cultural, and political conditions in Africa.
2. See, for example, Kennes (1999), Ojo (1999), and Uka (1984) for a comprehensive discussion of the interplay between political and economic conditions in the developing countries.
3. For example, Apraku (1991), Gordon (1998), Konadu-Agyemang, Takyi, and Arthur (2006), Arthur (2000).
4. See Michael Kevane's (2004) explanations concerning how gendered relationships continue to affect development and economic issues in Africa.
5. See, also, Jonathan Crush's (2000) account of cross-border population mobility in Africa.
6. See, also, Amin's (1974, 1977), Arthur's (1991), Caldwell's (1969a), Todaro and Stilkind's (1981), and Zachariah's (1981) investigations into the structural determinants of regional migrations in Africa.
7. See, Docquier and Marfouk (2006), Phizacklea (1999), Campani (1995), United Nations (2006), Arya and Roy (2006), and Castles and Miller (1993) for a comprehensive overview of women in domestic and international migration.

Chapter 3

1. See Mabojunge (1970), DaVanzo (1976), Gordon (1998), Cohen (1992), Adepoju (1991), Watkins (1995), and Agyemang, Takyi, and Arthur (2006) for a discussion of the causes of African migrations to the West.
2. These problems are magnified by poverty, illiteracy, environmental and econological destruction, overpopulation, rapid urbanization, economic, and political corruption, and the ascendancy of militarism.
3. See, for example, Richter and Taylor's (2008), Aguilera and Massey (2003), and Curran and Rivero-Fuentes (2003) on the role of households and family networks in migration decision making.

4. See, for example, Arthur (2008) for a discussion of the importance and uses of remittances in African migration.

5. See, for example, Harris and Todaro's (1970) and Caldwell's (1969b) explanations about the incongruence between rural poverty and underdevelopment in triggering rural to urban migrations in the less developing countries.

6. This term is often used by West Africans to describe the waves of immigrants from Ghana who fled the country to find better economic opportunities during the 1970s and early 1980s. Unable to cope with the influx, the Nigeria government passed legislation to deport nearly one million Ghanaians who had settled legally and illegal immigrants who had settled in Nigeria.

CHAPTER 4

1. See United States Department of State (2008) Bureau of African Affairs (http://www.State.gov) for additional background information regarding the civil war in Sierra Leone.

2. It is significant to point out that from the perspectives of the refugee women, economic and political factors converged to cause their displacement. The Danes, however, sought to distinguish among the refugees in terms of economic and political exigencies primarily to determine the types and forms of services to be provided to the refugees.

3. See Nolin's (2006) account of how refugee women create social spaces to anchor refugee transnational identities.

4. As a researcher, I felt this was an encounter my academic training had hardly prepared me for. I listened with eagerness as she chronicled her refugee experiences. I could see and feel the sadness in her eyes, her deep concerns for the failed nation of Sierra Leone that she calls home. At the same time, I sensed in her solemn demeanor a resilience that she can surmount the obstacles confronting her refugee status in her new country.

5. See, for example, Holtzman's (2000), and Koltyk's (1998) accounts of the formation of African diaspora communities in the American heartland.

6. See, Edward's (2007) account of how African refugee women continue to transform their lives by dealing with problems posed by their reentry into the affairs of their host societies and their social and cultural institutions.

CHAPTER 6

1. See, for example, Kevane's (2004) and Bay's (1982) accounts of how women in Africa shape their respective societies via work.

2. See, for example, Holtzman (2000), Gough (1971), and Kok (1992).

CHAPTER 7

1. See Fraser and Gordon (1994) and Leo Chavez (2007) accounts of how Black and Latino women's fertility are often represented as threats to America's social, political, and cultural identities.
2. For a discussion of the importance of old-age security and fertility behavior, see Willis (1973); Mueller (1976); Repetto (1976); Ben-Zion and Razin (1975).
3. Gloria referenced the psalmist King David to further support her pronatal stance that "Children are the heritage of the Lord. As arrows are in the hand of a mighty man, so are children of the youth. Happy is the man that hath his quiver full of them; they shall not be ashamed, but they shall speak with the enemies in the gate."
4. See also Fishbein's (1972) findings that attitudes toward specific fertility acts, including normative beliefs and motivation may all converge to explain fertility behavior.
5. For a comprehensive critique of fertility theories, see Namboodiri (1980).
6. See, for example, Bradley's (1995) account of the centrality of economic empowerment variables in fertility reduction behavior among African women.
7. For a complete discussion of American minority fertility rates, see Leo Chavez (2007).
8. See Dodoo and Takyi's (2006) account of income earnings among African immigrants in the United States.

CHAPTER 8

1. See Albrow and King (1990), Zlotnik (1991, 1995), Giddens (1990), Lubbers and Koorevaar (1999) for the internal and external conditions causing African migration to global centers of commerce and economic production.
2. See Adgepoju's (2002) discussion of these issues.
3. See Diamond (1998) for a detailed discussion of the attitudes of African Americans toward U.S. immigration policies.
4. For a detailed description of how Black African and Caribbean immigrants construct and manifest racial and ethnic identities, see Waters (1994), Gadsby (2006), Vickerman (1999), Arthur (2000), and Foner (1987).
5. See Ong, Cheng, and Evans (1992), and Chang (1992), for a discussion of the migration of skilled and highly educated immigrants to the United States.
6. See, for example, Gadsby's (2006) work on how Caribbean women writers use literature to depict the contents of Caribbean immigrant identities in transnational locales.

References

Adepoju, Aderanti. 2002. Fostering free movement of persons in West Africa: Achievements, constraints, and prospects for intraregional migration. *International Migration* 40 (2): 3–25.

———. 1991. South–North migration: The African experience. *International migration* 29: 205–21.

———. 2000. Issues and recent trends in international migration in sub–Saharan Africa. *Social Science Journal* 52: 383–89.

———. 1995. Emigration dynamics in sub–Saharan Africa. *International Migration Review* 33 (3/4): 315–68.

Afkhami, Mahnaz. 1994. *Women in exile*. Charlottesville: University Press of Virginia.

Agrawal, Anuja. 2006. *Migrant women and work*. New Delhi, India: Sage.

Aguilera, M., and D. Massey. 2003. Social capital and the wages of Mexican migrants: New hypotheses and tests. Social Forces, 82 (2):671–701.

Agyemang, Konadu, Baffour Takyi, and John Arthur, ed. 2006. *The new African diaspora in North America*. Lanham, Maryland: Lexington Books.

Albrow, Martin, and Elizabeth King, eds. 1990. *Globalization, knowledge, and society*. U.K.: Sage.

Amin, S. 1974. *Colonialism in West Africa*. New York: Monthly Review Press.

———. 1977. *Imperialism and unequal development*. New York: Monthly Review Press.

Apraku, Kofi. 1991. *African emigrés in the United States*. New York: Praeger.

Arthur, John. 2008. *The African diaspora in the United States and Europe. The Ghanaian experience*. UK: Ashgate.

———. 2000. *Invisible sojourners. African immigrant diaspora in the United States*. Westport, CT: Praeger.

———. 1991. Inter-regional migration in West Africa: Causes, consequences and policy implications. *African Studies Review*, 34: 65–87.

Arya, Sadhna and Roy Anupama, eds. 2006. When poor women migrate: Unraveling issues and concerns. In *Poverty, gender, and migration*. ed. Sadhna Arya and Roy Anupama, 19–48. New York: Sage.

———. 2006. *Poverty, gender, and migration. eds*. New Delhi, India: Sage.

Ayitey, G. 1992. *Africa Betrayed*. New York: St. Martin's Press.

Bagozzi, Richard, and Frances Van Loo. 1980. Decision making and fertility: A theory of exchange in the family. In *Demographic behavior: Interdisciplinary perspectives on decision making.* ed. Thomas Burch, 91–124. Boulder, CO: Westview.

Barot, Rohit, Harriet Bradley, and Steve Fenton. 1999. *Ethnicity, gender, and social change.* New York: St. Martin's Press.

Batterbury, S. 1998. The African Sahel: 25 years after the great drought. Assessing progress, setting a new agenda. *Geographical Journal,* 164: 361–62.

Bay, Edna, ed. 1982. *Women and work in Africa.* Boulder, CO: Westview.

Becker, Gary. 1974. A theory of social interaction. *Journal of Political Economy* 82: 1063–91.

Ben-Zion, Uri, and Assaf Razin. 1975. An intergenerational model of population growth. *American Economic Review* 65: 923–34.

Bradley, C. 1995. Women's empowerment and fertility decline in Western Kenya. In *Situating fertility.* ed. Susan Greehalgh, 157–78. Cambridge: Cambridge University Press.

Buechler, H., and J. Buechler. 1987. *Migrants in Europe: The rise of family, labor, and politics.* New York: Greenwood.

Caldwell, John. 1969a. *African rural-urban migration: The movement to Ghana's town.* New York: Columbia University Press.

———. 1969b. *African rural-urban migration.* Canberra: Australian National University Press.

———. 1978. A theory of fertility: From high plateau to destabilization. *Population and Development Review* 4 (4): 553–78.

Campani, Giovanna. 1995. Women migrants from marginal subjects to social actors. In *The Cambridge survey of world migration,* ed. Robin Cohen. Cambridge: Cambridge University Press.

Castles, S., and M. Miller. 1993. *The age of migration.* London: Macmillan.

Cerrutti, Marcela, and Douglas Massey. 2004. Trends in Mexican migration to the United States, 1965–1995. In *Crossing the border: Research from the Mexican migration project,* ed. Jorge Durand and Douglas Massey, 187–200. New York: Russell Sage Foundation.

Chang, S. 1992. Causes of brain drain and solutions: The Taiwan experience. *Studies in comparative international development* 27 (1): 27–43.

Chant, Sylvia. 1992. *Gender and migration in developing countries.* London: Belhaven Press.

Chavez, Leo. 2007. A glass half empty: Latina reproduction and public discourse. In *Women and migration in the U.S.-Mexico borderlands,* ed. Denise Segura and Patricia Zavella, 67–91. Durham, NC: Duke University Press.

Coale, Ansley. 1973. The demographic transition. In *International union for the scientific study of population,* 347–55. Liege, Belgium: International Population Conference.

Cohen, Robin. 1992. Migration and the new international division of labor. In *Ethnic minorities and industrial change in Europe and North America,* ed. Malcolm Cross. New York: Cambridge University Press.

Conway, Dennis, Adrian Bailey, and Mark Ellis. 2001. Gendered and racialized circulation-migration: Implications for the poverty and work experience of New York's Puerto Rican women. In *Migration, transnationalism, and race in a changing New York*, ed. Hector Cordero-Guzman, Robert Smith, and Ramon Grosfoguel, 146–63. Philadelphia: Temple University Press.

Cordero-Guzman, Hector, Robert Smith, and Ramon Grosfoguel, ed. 2001. *Migration, transnationalism, and race in a changing New York*. Philadelphia: Temple University Press.

Cornelius, Wayne. 1990. Mexican immigrants in California today. Keynote presentation given at conference on *California Immigrants in a World Perspective*. Immigration Research Program, University of California, Los Angeles (April 26–27).

Crush, Jonathan. 2000. Migrations past: An historical overview of cross-border movement in Southern Africa. In *On borders. Perspectives on international migration in Southern Africa*, ed. David McDonald, 12–24. New York: St Martin's.

Curran, Sara and Estela Rivero-Fuentes. 2003. Engendering migrant networks: The case of Mexican migrants. *Demography*, 40 (2): 187–200.

DaVanzo, J. 1981. Microeconomic approaches to studying migration decisions. In *Migration decision making: Multidisciplinary approaches to microlevel studies in developed and developing countries*, ed. Gordon DeJong and R. W. Gardner, 90–129. New York: Pergamon Press.

———. 1976. *Why families move: A model of the geographic mobility of married couples*. California: Rand Corporation.

De Jong, Gordon, and R. W. Gardner, eds. 1981. Introduction and overview. In *Migration decision making: Multidisciplinary approaches to micro level studies in developed and developing countries*, 1–12. New York: Pergamon.

De Jong, Gordon, Brenda Root, and R. G. Abad. 1986. Family reunification and Philippine migration to the United States: The immigrant's perspectives. *International Migration Review* 22 (3): 598–612.

———. 1985. Migration intentions and behavior: Decision making in a rural Philippine province. *Population and Environment* 8 (1/2): 41–62.

Diamond, Jeff. 1998. African American attitudes towards United States immigration policy. *International Migration Review* 32 (2): 451–70.

Docquier, Frederic and Abdeslam Marfouk. 2006. International migration by educational attainment, 1999–2000. In *International migration, remittances, and the brain drain*, ed. Caglar Ozden and Maurice Schiff, 151–99. New York: Palgrave Macmillan.

Dodoo, Nii-Amoo F. 1997. Assimilation differences among Africans in America. *Social Forces* 76 (2): 527–46.

———. 1991a. Minority immigrants in the United States: Earnings attributes and economic success. *Canadian Studies in Population* 18 (2): 42–55.

———. 1991b. Immigrant and native black workers' labor force participation in the U.S. *National Journal of Sociology* 5 (1): 3–17.

Dodoo, Nii-Amoo F. and Baffour Takyi. 2006. Africans in the diaspora. Black-white earning differences among America's Africans. In *The new African diaspora in North America*, ed. Konadu Konadu-Agyemang, Baffour Takyi, and John Arthur, 168–88. Lanham, Maryland: Lexington Books.

Dodson, Belinda. 2000. Women on the move: Gender and cross border migration to South Africa from Lesotho, Mozambique and Zimbabwe. In *Perspectives on international migration in Southern Africa*, ed. David McDonald, 119–50. Ontario: St. Martin's.

Eades, Jeremy. 1987. Anthropologists and migrants: Changing models of realities. In *Migrants, workers and the social order*, ed. Jeremy Eades, 1–16. London: Tavistock.

Easterlin, Richard. 1978. New directions for the economics of fertility. In *Major social issues: A multidisciplinary view*, ed. J. M. Yinger and Stephen Cutler. New York: Free Press.

Edward, Jane. 2007. *Sudanese women refugees*. New York: Palgrave Macmillan.

Falola, Toyin, and Niyi Afolabi. 2007. *The human cost of African migrations*. New York: Routledge.

Farley, Reynolds, and Walter Allen. 1987. *The color line and the quality of life in America*. New York: Sage.

Fawcett, J. T. 1985–86. *Migration psychology: New behavioral models. Population and environment* 8 (1/2): 5–14.

Fawcett, J. T. and F. Arnold. 1987. Explaining diversity: Asian and Pacific immigration systems. In *Pacific bridges: The new immigration from Asia and the Pacific Islands*, ed. J. T. Fawcet and B. V. Carino, 453–74. Staten Island, NY: Center for Migration Studies.

Fishbein, Martin. 1972. Towards an understanding of family planning behavior. *Journal of Applied Social Psychology* 2: 214–27.

Foner, Nancy. 1979. West Indians in New York City and London: A comparative analysis. *International Migration Review* 13 (2): 284–97.

———. 1983. *Jamaican migrants: A comparative analysis of the New York and London experience*. Occasional Paper No. 36. New York Research Program in Inter-American Affairs, New York University.

———. 1985. Sex roles and sensibilities: Jamaican women in New York and London. In *International migration: The female experience*, ed. C. Brettell and R. Simon. Totowa. Totowa, NJ: Rowman and Littlefield.

———. 1987. The Jamaicans: Race and ethnicity among migrants in New York City. In *New immigrants in New York*, ed. Nancy Foner, 131–58. New York: Columbia University Press.

———. 2001. What's new about transnationalism? New York immigrants today and at the turn of the century. In *Migration, transnationalism, and race in a changing New York*, ed. Hector Cordero-Guzman, Robert Smith, and Ramon Grosfoguel, 35–57. Philadelphia: Temple University Press.

Fraser, Nancy, and Linda Gordon. 1994. A genealogy of dependency: Tracking a keyword of the U. S. welfare state. *Signs* 19: 309–35.

Gadsby, Meredith. 2006. *Sucking salt. Caribbean women writers, migration and survival.* Columbia, MO: University of Missouri Press.

Gates, Henry, Jr., and Cornel West. 1996. *The future of the race.* New York: Vintage Books.

Giddens, Anthony. 1990. The consequences of modernity. Stanford, CA: Stanford University Press.

Glantz, O. 1978. Native sons and immigrants: Some beliefs and values of American born and West Indian blacks at Brooklyn College. *Ethnicity* 5:180–202.

Glazer, Nathan, and Patrick Moynihan. 1963. *Beyond the melting pot: The Negroes, Puerto Ricans, Jews, Italians and Irish of New York City.* Cambridge, MA: MIT Press.

Gordon, April. 1998. The new diaspora. African immigration to the United States. *Journal of Third World Studies* 15 (1): 79–103.

Gough, K. 1971. Nuer kinship: A re-examination. In *The translation of culture*, ed. T. O. Beidelman, 79–121. London: Tavistock.

Grosfoguel, Ramon, and Hector Cordero-Guzman. 1998. Social capital, contexts of reception, and transnationalism: Recent approaches to international migration. *Diaspora* 7 (3): 351–69.

Guglielmo, Jennifer. 2002. Italian women's proletarian feminism in the New York City garment trades, 1890s–1940s. In *Women, gender, and transnational lives*, ed. Donna Gabaccia and Franca Iacovetta, 247–327. Toronto: University of Toronto Press.

Harris, J. R., and M. P. Todaro. 1970. *Migration, unemployment and development: A two sector analysis.* American Economic Review, 60: 126–42.

Holtzman, Jon. 2000. *Nuer journeys. Nuer lives. Sudanese refugees in Minnesota.* Boston: Allyn and Bacon.

Kanaiaupuni, Shawn. 2000. Reframing the migration question: An analysis of men, women, and gender in Mexico. *Social Forces* 78 (4): 1311–47.

Kaufman, Robert. 1983. A structural decomposition of black-white earnings differentials. *American Journal of Sociology* 89: 585–611.

Kennes, W. 1999. African regional economic integration and the European Union. In *Regionalisation in Africa: Integration and disintegration*, ed. D. C. Bash. Cambridge: James Currey.

Kevane, Michael. 2004. *Women and development in Africa. How gender works.* Boulder, CO: Lynne Rienner.

Khapoya, Vincent. 1994. *The African experience.* Englewood Cliffs, NJ: Prentice Hall.

Kok, Peter. 1992. Adding fuel to the conflict: Oil, war, and peace in Sudan. In *Beyond conflict in the horn*, ed. M. Doornbos, L. Cliffe, Gaffer M. Abdel, and J. Markakis, 104–22. Hague, Netherlands: Institute of Social Studies.

Koltyk, Jo Ann. 1998. *New pioneers in the heartland.* Boston: Allyn and Bacon.

Lenoir, Gerald, and Nunu Kidane. n.d. African Americans and immigrants: Shall we hang together or hang separately? *The Black Scholar* 37 (1): 50–52.

Lichter, Daniel. 1989. Race, employment hardship, and inequality in the American nonmetropolitan south. *American Sociological Review* 54: 436–46.

Lubbers, R. F., and J. G. Koorevaar. 1999. *The dynamic of globalization.* Paper presented at the OECD Forum for the future (Conference on 21st century social dynamics: Towards the creative society), 6–12. Berlin.

Mabojunge, A. L. 1990. Systems approach to a theory of rural–urban migration. *Geographical Analysis* 2: 11–7.

McDonald, David. 2000. Labour migration to South Africa: The lifeblood for Southern Mozambique. In *On borders. Perspectives on international migration in Southern Africa*, ed. David McDonald, 46–70. New York: St. Martin's.

Mahler, Sarah. 2002. Suburban transnational migrants: Long Island's Salvadorans. In *Migration, transnationalism, and race in a changing New York*, ed. Hector Cordero-Guzman, Robert Smith, and Ramon Grosfoguel, 109–30. Philadelphia: Temple University Press.

Malkin, Victoria. 2004. We go to get ahead: Gender and status in two Mexican migrant communities. *Latin American Perspectives* 31 (5): 75–99.

Mora, Jorge, and Edward Taylor. 2006. Determinants of migration, destination, and sector choice: Disentangling individual, household, and community effects. In *International migration, remittances and the brain drain*, ed. Caglar Ozden and Maurice Schiff, 80–112. New York: Palgrave Macmillan.

Morrison, Andrew, Maurice Schiff, and Mirja Sjoblom, eds. 2008. *International migration of women.* Washington, DC: World Bank/Palgrave Macmillan.

Mueller, Eva. 1976. The economic value of children in peasant society. In *Population and development: The search for selective interventions*, ed. R. G. Ridker. Baltimore: Johns Hopkins University Press.

Namboodiri, Krishnan. 1980. A look at fertility model building from different perspectives. In *Demographic behavior: Interdisciplinary perspectives on decision making*, ed. Thomas Burch, 71–90. Boulder, CO: Westview.

Nolin, Catherine. 2006. *Transnational ruptures. Gender and forced migration.* Aldershot, England: Ashgate.

Ojo, O. B. 1999. Integration in ECOWAS: Successes and difficulties. In *Regionalisation in Africa: Integration and disintegration*, ed. D. C. Dash, 40–59. Cambridge: James Currey.

Ong, Paul, Lucie Cheng, and Leslie Evans. 1992. Migration of highly educated Asians and global dynamics. *Asian and Pacific Migration Journal*, 1 (3–4):543–67.

Ould-May, M. 1996. *Global restructuring and peripheral states: The carrot and the stick in Mauritania.* Lanham, Maryland: Rowman and Littlefield.

Oxfam. 1999. IMF: *Wrong diagnosis, wrong medicine.* Oxford: England, Oxfam.

Pessar, P. A. 1982. The role of households in international migration and the case of the U.S. bound migration from the Dominican Republic. *International Migration Review* 16 (2): 342–64.

Phizacklea, Annie. 1999. Gender and transnational migration. In *Ethnicity, gender and social change*, ed. Rohit Barot, Harriet Bradley, and Steve Fenton, 29–44. New York and London: Macmillan.

Portes, A., and R. Bach. 1985. *Latin journey: Cuban and Mexican immigrants in the United States.* Berkeley: University of California Press.

Reeder, Linder. 2002. When the men left Sutera: Sicilian women and mass migration, 1880–1920. In *Women, gender, and transnational lives*, ed. Donna Gabaccia and Franca Iacovetta, 45–75. Toronto: University of Toronto Press.

Repetto, Robert. 1976. Direct economic costs and value of children. In *Population and development: The search for selective interventions*, ed. R. G. Ridker. Baltimore: Johns Hopkins University Press.

Richter, Susan, and Edward Taylor. 2008. Gender and the determinants of international migration from rural Mexico over time. In *The international migration of women*, ed. Andrew Morrison, Maurice Schiff, and Mirja Sjoblom, 51–99. Washington, DC: World Bank/Palgrave Macmillan.

Rodney, Walter. 1982. How Europe underdeveloped Africa. Washington, DC: Howard University Press.

Schmink, M. 1984. Household economic strategies: A review and research agenda. *Latin American Research Review* 19 (3): 87–101.

Segura, Denise, and Patricia Zavella, eds. 2007. *Women and migration in the U.S.-Mexico borderlands.* Durham, NC: Duke University Press.

Sjaastad, Larry. 1962. The costs in addition to returns of human migration. *Journal of Political Economy* Volume 70 (5): 80–93.

Snyder, Margaret, and Mary Tadesse. 1995. *African women and development.* Johannesburg: Witwatersrand University Press.

Sowell, Thomas. 1981. *Markets and minorities.* New York: Basic Books.

Stark, Oded. 1991. *The migration of labor.* Cambridge, UK: Basil Blackwell.

Staudt, Kathleen. 1999. Seeds for self sufficiency? Policy contradictions at the U.S.–Mexico border. In *Gender and immigration*, ed. Gregory Kelson and Debra DeLaet, 21–37. New York: New York University Press.

Takougang, J. 1995. Black African immigrants to the United States. *Western Journal of Black Studies* 19 (1): 50–57.

Todaro, M., and J. Stilkind. 1981. City bias and rural neglect: The dilemma of urban development. New York: Population Council.

Uka, E. 1984. *ECOWAS and the economic integration of West Africa.* Ibadan, Nigeria.

United Nations. 2006. *Trends in total migrant stock: The 2005 revision* CD-ROM Documentation. POP/DB/MIG/Rev. 2005/Doc. New York: United Nations.

United States Department of State (Bureau of African Affairs). 2008. Washington, DC: http://www.state.gov.

Vecchio, Diane. 2002. Gender, domestic values, and working women in Milwaukee: Immigrant midwives and businesswomen. In *Women, gender, and transnational lives*, ed. Donna Gabaccia and Franca Iacovetta, 160–85. Toronto: University of Toronto Press.

Vickerman, Michael. 1999. Crosscurrents: West Indian immigrants and race. New York: Oxford University Press.

Wanyeki, Muthoni, ed. 2003. *Women and land in Africa*. South Africa: David Philip.

Waters, M. C. 1994. Ethnic and racial identities of second-generation black immigrants in New York City. *International Migration Review*, 28 (4): 795–826.

Watkins, Kevin. 1995. *The Oxfam poverty report*. Oxford, England: Oxfam.

Willis, Robert. 1973. A new approach to the economic theory of fertility behavior. *Journal of Political Economy*, 81: 514–64.

World Bank. 1990–2000. *World development reports*. New York: Oxford University Press.

Zachariah, K. C., and Julien Conde. 1981. *Demographic aspects of migration in West Africa*. Washington, DC: World Bank.

Zlotnik, H. 1991. Trends in South–North migration: The perspective from the North. *International Migration* 29 (2): 317–31.

———. 1995. The South-to-North migration of women. *International Migration Review* 29 (1): 229–54.

Index